Industrial
Journal

EUROPEAN ANNUAL REVIEW 1997

Industrial Relations Journal
EUROPEAN ANNUAL REVIEW
1997

Edited by

BRIAN TOWERS *and* MIKE TERRY

Copyright © Blackwell Publishers Ltd 1998

ISBN 0-631-21148-9

First Published 1998

Blackwell Publishers
108 Cowley Road, Oxford OX4, 1JF, UK

and

350 Main Street, Malden, MA 02148, USA

British Library Cataloguing in Publication Data
A CIP catalogue record for this book is available from the British Library

Library of Congress Cataloging-in-Publication Data
Data applied for

Printed in Great Britain by Page Bros, Norwich

Printed on acid free paper

I am very pleased to welcome this first edition of the Industrial Relations Journal's European Annual Review. It will undoubtedly make a valuable contribution to our understanding of key developments in European industrial relations both at this critical time and in the future. The Review will be of much value to both practitioners and scholars in Europe and elsewhere.

Padraig Flynn,
European Commissioner for Employment and Social Affairs

ACKNOWLEDGEMENTS

The editors wish to acknowledge and thank the following for refereeing and reading manuscripts and offering advice and assistance in the preparation of the Review.

Alain Airth
Colin Bourne
Jeff Bridgford
Lesley Dingle
Michael Dunn
Richard Hyman
Brian Kirtley
Eric Owen Smith
Janet Parker
John Philpott
Catherine Singh
John Thirkell
Peter Zawarde

Contents

Editorial

Mike Terry and Brian Towers

The *Industrial Relations Journal European Annual Review* is providing exactly what its title suggests, i.e expert presentations of, and comments on, the previous year's important developments in key aspects of industrial relations policy and practice in the European Union (EU) member states and at European level. Additionally, though inevitably in less detail, the Review will provide an annual, authoritative commentary on developments in the newly emerged, and emerging, states of Central and Eastern Europe. A number of these states are on course to become EU members within the next ten years; but even without membership the countries of this important and volatile region are strongly influenced by, and influence, developments within the EU itself. It is primarily a work of record, designed both to inform and, over the years, to constitute a source of data and ideas that may serve as a basis for more thoroughgoing and systematic comparative analyses. Chapters dealing with specific subjects are commissioned from recognised experts, (including political scientists and economists to contribute the wider contexts to industrial relations) each of whom will normally take on this task for three years, providing continuity of presentation and analyses, before handing over to another. Authors are asked to pay particular attention to the key events of the preceding calendar year (so for this first issue the formal reference period is 1997) locating them where necessary within wider analytical and historical contents. The aims are therefore modest but challenging: to produce a top-quality 'journal of record' presenting and explaining key events in the ever more complex world of European industrial relations. It is designed to supplement and complement the existing journals in the field, not to compete with them. It is filling a new market niche, not vying for business in an already well-stocked market.

There should be little need to justify such a 'journal of record' dealing with key events in labour relations, labour law, employment, social affairs and other related areas in the member states of the European Union and its Central and Eastern European neighbours. The task of merely of trying to keep up-to-date with a bewilderingly large set of events in several countries, much of which may

Mike Terry is Professor of Industrial Relations and Organisational Behaviour at the University of Warwick. Brian Towers is Professor of Industrial Relations at Nottingham Trent University and Emeritus Professor at the University of Strathclyde.

1

be relevant to teaching, to research, or to policy development, but which busy people simply do not have time to digest and absorb in the 'raw' state, would be justification enough. The *Review* is just one of a number of powerful tools designed to assist in this task. One other obvious example is the immensely valuable *European Industrial Relations Observatory* funded and managed by the European Foundation for the Improvement of Living and Working Conditions, whose regular published updates in *EIRObserver* and on-line (on the World-Wide Web at http://www.eiro.eurofound.ie/) are invaluable sources of information. We are particularly pleased and grateful to have established a strong working relationship with the *Observatory*, in particular through Mark Gilman who, together with Tina Weber, has used the *Observatory* database to produce the first of a series of annual 'Chronicles'. We are very grateful to the Foundation for their co-operation in this arrangement.

The Review's primary emphasis on the recording of events at national level as well as across the EU, is deliberate. Increasingly we all need to be aware of developments in the member states, for teaching purposes, as more students require knowledge of countries other than their own in which they might work, and for the development of comparative research analysis, a rapidly-developing and enriching area of research. But there are other reasons. First, innovations at national level often give us a foretaste of the implications of wider develop-ments—the innovative 'European Works Councils' pioneered by some large French and German multinationals well before the implementation of the Direc-tive provided fertile ground for preliminary research and anticipation of some of the practical problems encountered. Second, perhaps more important, the future direction of European industrial relations lies in the processes of reciprocal interac-tion between national systems and international innovations. Putting to one side the naïve and ill-founded argument that somehow the European Union is seeking to impose a uniform straitjacket of labour market regulation on all member states, we can see that the evolutionary trends, if any, towards a 'European' industrial relations, must come through directives and other supra-national initiatives being integrated into very different national models, and as national events stimulate new thinking at a European level. All the key actors will continue to operate within a framework structured by the familiar and understood patterns of national systems, despite the occasional drawbacks of such a perspective. The very diversity of European national systems will ensure that these processes will be uneven and full of surprises, and this because of the particular evolutionary processes associated with the development of human institutions such as those of industrial relations, irrespective of more formal concepts such as subsidiarity. The case for a journal such as this regularly to monitor such events is very strong.

But in addition to acting as a thorough record of events the *Review* will, as the data cumulate year-on-year, provide an authoritative basis for the testing of ideas and concepts concerning the direction of labour relations, broadly defined, mainly, though not exclusively, within the 'Europe' of the European Union. Quick reference to the *Review* will enable users to ask, for example, whether the emerging patterns support any of the broad portfolio terms sometimes applied to European developments such as 'convergence' (or its opposite), 'decentralisation', 'deregulation', 'flexibilisation' and the rest, all of which have become part of current language across the EU, applied as if their meanings are both self-evident and, more dangerously, the same in all member states and all processes. The *Review* also provides our authors with the unique opportunity to develop their ideas by returning to the same subject annually over a three year period; readers will follow a consistent and evolving set of ideas and data. So, it is likely, that after three years we will give our authors a rest and commission work from other experts, and we are keen to involve people from as many countries as possible.

The first such 'changeover' will also give us an opportunity to review the categories to which we have assigned the work. For reasons of convenience and familiarity we have adopted a structure that reflects long-standing and 'safe' institutional frameworks. Sensible though that might be as a starting point, we are sensitive to the argument that it may prove to be an essentially conservative approach, focusing attention on established institutions and practices, possibly of diminishing importance, and missing innovation and novelty. The erosion, if not the breakdown, of national systems of regulation; the major problems of representativeness confronting trade unions; the shifts of employment into 'non-traditional' areas and contractual forms; and the implications of the rapidly-increasing proportion of women in employment, just to take some of the most obvious examples, may not be accorded the significance they merit in our present approach. It will be necessary to critically evaluate the approach we have taken not only to check that it has provided good quality materials but that it has not contributed to the inadvertent omission of important trends.

While no doubt the editors of all new journals claim, always with justification, that the moment for such an initiative is particularly appropriate, in our case this really is true! European developments take on a new significance in the UK as we move, albeit still with some reservation, towards acceptance of the EU approach towards the development of what used to be called the 'Social Dimension' and new initiatives in other countries now require analysis not just on the basis of envy or distaste, according to political preference, but because they may come to affect our own way of doing things. As the UK comes to terms with the consequences of the extensive deregulation and dismantling of labour market institutions, with a new government that talks of restoring elements of fairness and security into employment and employment relations, practitioners and scholars in this country will be looking for ideas as to how to achieve this, through ideas and processes not previously tried here. The Trades Union Congress's formal abandoning of the 'single channel' of employee representation provides one clear example of this. More fundamentally, 12 of the 15 member states are now formally committed to entering a single currency, and it is inconceivable that the economies of the other three will not be significantly affected by this. The implications for national and international patterns of industrial relations, broadly defined, are only beginning to be thought through. We do not yet know what the responses will be in countries, such as our own, which have made use of currency devaluation on occasion to preserve competitiveness and, by implication, jobs, when that freedom may no longer exist. A single currency may expose more starkly than before performance and productivity differences, and lead to employer approaches to investment and to wage-bargaining that seek to exploit such coercive comparisons. These may in turn fuel initiatives in international union co-operation that have thus far been muted and sporadic, largely because of the continuing dominance of national institutions and priorities. The differences between sectors that operate in international markets and those that are primarily or exclusively national, may well become even more pronounced. But at this stage this is simply speculation. We need to be able to monitor and evaluate these fundamental changes on the basis of reliable and detailed data emerging from the experiences of the member states, and over the years the *Review* will provide this.

Finally the *Review* may also give a developing insight into the changing use of the *language* of European industrial relations. Richard Hyman has provided a compelling account of the importance of understanding how the different cultures and ideologies of industrial relations theory and practice across Europe may be reflected in the different languages deployed (Hyman, 1995). The language of this *Review*, English, uses the industrial relations language rooted in the practices and ideologies of (primarily) the British system, with for example a limited vocabulary related to 'rights', and a still slimmer one to ideas such as 'partnership' and consensus. Words like 'social partnership', 'concertation' and so on still sit uneasily in this lexicon, but they are increasingly used as the common currency of European discussion. We will be able to contribute to a continuing process of the development and evaluation of a language appropriate to the common (and divergent) experiences of the member states of the European Union, expressed in a single language, but often trying to express the ideas and perspectives of non-UK authors writing about non-UK experiences.

With that we welcome you to the first edition of the *Industrial Relations Journal European Annual Review* and hope that it will enrich your knowledge of important developments at present not as accessible or comprehensible to all of us as they should be.

REFERENCES

Hyman, R. (1995) 'Industrial Relations in Europe: Theory and Practice', *European Journal of Industrial Relations*, 1:1, 17–46.

The politics of Europe:
(un)employment ambivalence

Christopher Pierson, Anthony Forster and Erik Jones

Unemployment dominated the politics of the European Union in 1997. The Irish presidency closed 1996 with a 'declaration on employment'. The spring 1997 Dutch presidency brought employment into the revised Treaty on European Union. And the autumn 1997 Luxembourg presidency centred its agenda on the related problems of labour market flexibility and job creation. The situation was little different within the member states. From one December to the next, German Chancellor Helmut Kohl saw the jobless rolls climb from 11 to more than 12 per cent of the labour force. Meanwhile, in May, French president Jacques Chirac, having been elected on a platform to fight economic and social exclusion, witnessed the humiliation of his prime minister by an electorate determined to see government action for more jobs. The victory for French Socialist Lionel Jospin was short lived, however. By December, Jospin faced a jobless revolt of his own as unemployed workers occupied social welfare offices across the country.

Europe's unemployment problem dominated the politics of the Union in 1997 because it was at the same time unacceptable and intractable. National politicians could not afford to be seen to be doing nothing about the most important issue of the day, and neither could the institutions of Europe. Nevertheless, there was little for national politicians or European institutions to do. The heads of state and government had few illusions that European action could resolve the jobs crisis. The 1993 White Paper on *Growth, Competitiveness, Employment* (European Commission, 1993) is explicit in asserting that unemployment is properly a problem of micro-economic causes and local dimensions. Although it spreads across the continent, European unemployment is not one discrete challenge, but many separate and simultaneous ones. Therefore, large investment in continental infrastructure such as the proposed 'trans-European networks' can provide only temporary relief from joblessness. According to the 1994 *OECD Jobs Study* (OECD, 1994), macro-economic policies can do little more than facilitate (and are more likely to hinder) local efforts at institutional reform for job creation. From this per-

Christopher Pierson is Professor of Politics, and Anthony Forster and Erik Jones are Lecturers in Politics at the University of Nottingham.

spective, the European challenge is to coordinate national and even sub-national reform measures in a variety of different institutional contexts, while confronting an equally diverse political opposition to reform.

In this, our first annual review of EU politics, 1997 is a year of (un)employment ambivalence—dominated by a problem everyone would be seen to be tackling but for which few are willing to accept the burdens and which no-one expects to resolve. We develop this interpretation in five stages. The first provides an overview of Europe's unemployment crisis as well as some necessary background to explain how it emerged on the European agenda for 1997. The second section provides an overview of the year's events both within the member states and at the European level. The third section places unemployment in the context of other major policy developments by focusing in on the negotiations at the Amsterdam summit under the Dutch presidency and the jobs summit hosted in Luxembourg. The fourth section broadens the discussion to consider what Europe's obsession with unemployment may mean for the future of the 'European Model'. The fifth section presents our conclusions and projections for the future. If early signs are indicative, 1998 is likely to afford far less ambivalence with regard to (un)employment than its predecessor.

THE SOURCES OF (UN)EMPLOYMENT AMBIVALENCE

Unemployment has been a major issue in Europe since the early 1980s. Across the Union, roughly ten per cent of the labour force has been out of work at any given point in time in the last 16 years, with a low in 1981 of 7.2 per cent and a high in 1994 of 11.5 per cent. In human terms, the 11.5 per cent unemployment in 1994 represented more than 19 million workers without jobs—almost double the 1981 figure of 10.6 million (OECD, 1997, pp. A24 and A26). The waste of human capital is staggering, and larger than the raw data for unemployment would suggest. Over time, skills deteriorate, motivation declines, and huge sections of the labour force give up looking for work altogether. Some sign on to early retirement, others to worker disability, and still more simply disappear from the labour market. Thus while the average unemployment rate was 11.4 per cent in 1996, estimates for the total number of people out of work (whether or not claiming benefits) were significantly higher.

Despite the social importance of unemployment, its political importance has been relatively small—at least until recently. National electorates returned conservative governments throughout much of the 1980s, and despite (or perhaps because of) claims that the state could do nothing to resolve the jobs crisis. Social scientists began to despair that unemployment had lost salience as a political issue at either the national or European levels. To the question 'politics matters, but does unemployment?' the answer was a cautious 'no'.[1]

The political salience of unemployment began to rise in the 1990s for three reasons: the cyclical downturn in Europe's economic performance quickly erased the modest employment gains made during the previous upswing, governments began to tighten fiscal policy in anticipation of monetary union, and currency markets fell repeatedly into crisis (in 1992, 1993 and 1995). These three developments are closely related, and yet arguably it is the third (repeated currency crisis) that was the most important in changing public policy. The electorate might tolerate unemployment, and governments might ignore it, but the speculators and fund managers who move international capital markets could not believe this malign neglect of the economy would last forever. Something would have to give, and so the market makers bet that this something would be exchange rates. The result was a self-fulfilling prophecy such that the ebb and flow of enormous volumes of capital forced both politicians and electorates to wake up to the jobs crisis.[2]

In the mid-1990s, unemployment exploded onto the European scene largely as a result of the linkages between the jobs crisis and popular support for monetary integration. Put simply, the proliferation of policy papers on *Growth, Competitiveness, Employment* (1993) and *Social Europe* (1995) could not hide the fact that unemployment was increasing as national governments struggled to meet the convergence criteria to create a monetary union. In such a context, whether these two processes—unemployment and convergence—were causally related became less important than whether they were linked in public perceptions. The European Trade Unions Confederation (ETUC, 1996) made this point brutally clear in a January 1996 press release stating: 'There is a rising groundswell of opinion in European debate that without credible initiatives to support economic growth and especially employment creation the single currency is unlikely to be accepted by workers and public opinion, and its very feasibility may be thrown into question'. The logic of the position was accepted by European Commission President Jacques Santer, who noted in a speech before the European Parliament delivered only four days after the ETUC press release that: 'Fears of unemployment ... chip away at faith in the single currency. These fears are unjustified. But we know and you know that perceptions can make or break policies, even the best ones'.[3]

Despite the rapidly growing political importance of the unemployment problem, the difficulty of attributing or accepting responsibility was manifest. Both

---

[1] Visser and Wijnhoven (1990) pp. 71–96. Statistical correlations of national economic performance and support for European integration during the 1970s and 1980s reveal a strong negative relationship between inflation and support for Europe, but only a weak (statistically insignificant) negative relationship between unemployment and support for Europe. See Eichenberg and Dalton (1993).

[2] For a recent discussion of these exchange rate crises, see Sandholtz (1998), pp. 191–226.

[3] Citation taken from *European Report* 2104 (3 February 1996) II.

policymakers and academics had a difficult time imagining a 'third way' between the cosy welfare states of the 1960s and the much more aggressive market-based approach seen in the United States. At the same time, active labour market policies became confused in debates about welfare state reform, placing national electorates between the Scylla of rising unemployment and the Charybdis of increasing income inequalities. Neither outcome seemed palatable to the electorate, and so the tendency among politicians has been to replace innovative policies with force of will—too often without success. German Chancellor Helmut Kohl declared his intention at the start of 1996 to halve unemployment by the end of the decade. Nevertheless the jobless rolls continued to lengthen and Kohl retreated from his ambitious objective even before the year was out (Traynor, 1996).

What exactly should (and could) be done about unemployment was unclear. One thing that was clear, however, was that Germany would brook no weakening of the convergence criteria for creating a monetary union. Throughout 1996, the German Finance Minister, Theo Waigel, argued that would-be participants in Europe's single currency should strengthen—rather than lessen—their efforts at convergence by accepting a 'stability and growth pact'. This stand brought him into direct conflict with the popular and trade-union perception that convergence was an obstacle to job creation, and also into confrontation with representatives of other countries, notably France.

European politics is defined more in terms of compromise than in terms of conflict. The compromise between German emphasis on the convergence criteria for monetary union and other parties more concerned with unemployment emerged piecemeal during the late autumn of 1996, partly at a special summit held in November between the Irish presidency and the social partners (meaning representatives of industry and labour) and partly at the European summit held in Dublin the following December. The first part of the compromise was a 'confidence pact' suggesting that there is a third way between the traditional welfare state and the US-style free market, and that all parts of society share an interest in preserving the European social model. The Pact's introduction states explicitly that '[a]ll must be made to face to face their responsibilities—national, regional and local authorities, the social partners and the Community institutions. The European Union (even less the Commission) cannot solve the problem of unemployment alone. But the Union must define the general framework for the fight for jobs and launch a concerted drive to seek the commitment of one and all'.

The second part of the compromise was that the heads of state and government accepted both 'the principles and main elements of the Stability and Growth Pact for ensuring discipline in EMU' and that 'the fight against unemployment is ... a priority task of the Union'.[4] In simple terms, EMU would not hinder the fight

---

[4] These citations are taken from different sections of the *Dublin European Council, 13 and 14 December 1996: Presidency Conclusions*, Official Publications of the European Communities, DOC/96/8, December

against unemployment and neither would efforts at job creation set back the project to form an economic and monetary union. The challenge for 1997, therefore, was to define the 'third way' and to articulate how job creation could be pursued without hindering prospects for monetary union. The year of reluctant activity was begun.

A YEAR OF RELUCTANT ACTIVITY

Although the Gregorian calendar starts and ends at midnight on the 31st of December, the European calendar starts and ends with summit meetings. The conclusion of the Dublin Council summit on 14 December 1996, ushered in a new European year with the promise of security, solidarity and credibility. And the Luxembourg summit brought that year to a close with the reassurance that 'extending the European integration model to encompass the whole of the continent is a pledge of future stability and prosperity'.[5] The record of initiatives put forward in the interim is striking. Having accepted responsibility for employment, the European Commission generated a large body of analysis and policy recommendations to be adopted at all levels of Europe's multi-level governance.

Much of the activity built upon the confidence pact of November 1996. Already by June 1997, the Commission could report that a wide number of initiatives for job creation had been adopted at the national, regional and local levels—initiatives spearheaded by industry and labour as well as by national governments and European institutions (European Commission, 1997a). Of these, perhaps the most important was the 6 June agreement between the social partners on the need to involve both industry and labour in future discussions of part-time working, and specifically of the application of full-time benefits to part-time workers. But also important were the growing number of so-called 'territorial pacts' to create jobs through small business ventures and other market-oriented schemes and which geographically covered some 35 million people in high-unemployment areas by the end of the year.

On the analytic front, the Commission pointed out the important relationship between demographics and unemployment. The challenge is not only to adjust Europe's labour markets to re-absorb the large numbers of the unemployed, it is also to prepare for a radically different labour force structure—one involving a much lower ratio of people in work to those dependent upon social security networks or family care (European Commission, 1997b). In positing this analysis,

---

1996. The first citation is taken from the section on economic and monetary union and the second is from the section on employment.

[5] *Luxembourg European Council, 12 and 13 December 1997, Presidency Conclusions*, Office for Official Publications of the European Communities, 13 December 1997.

the Commission was in large part echoing concerns already expressed at the meeting of the Group of Eight (the old group of seven advanced industrial countries plus Russia) in Denver. However, the problem of ageing is more important in Europe than in the United States or elsewhere, and so the Commission's analysis was more pointed than the summit's conclusions. It is not enough for Europe to resolve the jobs crisis. The resolution must also be sustainable over the longer term.

The larger framework for Commission activity derived from the Dublin Declaration, and from the subsequent adoption of a title on employment in the Amsterdam Treaty, a development which may prove highly significant in the long term (see below). In its preliminary explanation of the unifying themes behind its approach to the jobs crisis, the Commission argued that Europe should focus on 'entrepreneurship, employability, adaptability, and equal opportunities' (European Commission, 1997c). The entrepreneurship reflects the belief that most jobs are created by small and medium enterprises. The employability and adaptability apply to the need to make efforts to train and retrain Europe's workforce. The equal opportunities emphasis derives from a recognition that women are and will increasingly constitute a vital segment of the workforce. Moreover, these broad principles changed little through successive negotiations with the other institutions, the member states, and the social partners during the autumn of 1997. By December, the Commission felt confident to put its guidelines forward as an expression of how Europe should confront the jobs crisis (European Commission, 1997d).

Despite the Commission's confidence—and the sheer volume of Commission activity—the results are more ambiguous than the diplomatic language of European Council Presidencies would suggest. Both the Union and the member states made progress in handling a long and complicated agenda—that included not only the jobs crisis, but also the institutional preparations for European enlargement and the further development of Union responsibilities for Common Foreign and Security Policy (CFSP) and for Justice and Home Affairs. Nevertheless, Europe's politicians ended the year no closer to a resolution either of the nature of the European social model or of the perceived compatibility between monetary union and job creation. If anything, the ambiguity surrounding the resolution of the jobs crisis deepened in the face of considerable European activity.

This point is most easily illustrated with reference to the divisions arising from Tony Blair's electoral victory in the United Kingdom and Lionel Jospin's in France. Both leaders come from the centre-left, and yet they are worlds apart in their understanding of state-society relations: Blair seems more focused on mitigating inequality without allowing the state to disrupt the functioning of the market, while Jospin holds a much more interventionist vision of the state. This dichotomy may derive from different circumstances. Blair was elected despite his Conservative predecessor's achievements in decreasing unemployment while

Jospin was elected in large part because his predecessor failed to resolve the jobs crisis. Nevertheless, the schism on the center-left is too widespread across countries to permit such an easy circumstantial interpretation. Italy, Germany, the Netherlands, and many of the smaller countries all reveal symptoms of a fundamental confusion over what should constitute the future of social democracy in Europe—and therefore over how best to resolve the problem of unemployment.

The growing ambiguity over the resolution of Europe's jobs crisis was also apparent at the European level—in relations between states as well as between groups within states. To illustrate this point, however, it is necessary to abstract from the analysis and recommendations made by the European Commission and to focus in on the negotiations taking place in the European Council. The negotiations of interest took place at Amsterdam in June, and in Luxembourg the following November.

FOCUS ON AMSTERDAM AND LUXEMBOURG

The Amsterdam Summit was the culmination of almost two years of continuous negotiations on how to adapt the institutions and responsibilities of the European Union to the challenges which it now faced. The international context had changed significantly since the last round of treaty reform in 1990 to 1991 which led to the Maastricht Treaty on European Union. Ten states had formally requested membership of the EU and the 15 member states had committed themselves to opening up accession negotiations once the Amsterdam Treaty had been signed. The enlargement issue therefore provided an important backdrop to the negotiations. Institutions created for six member states, and incrementally adapted to cope with 15, now faced the prospect of absorbing a further five to ten new member states—a prospect which held out the real possibility of institutional overload. There was also a crowded internal agenda.

Formally, the negotiations were convened to revise the Maastricht Treaty to improve the effectiveness of the mechanisms and institutions of the EU, revise the co-decision procedure (which gave the European Parliament a veto power over EU legislation), adjust the weighting of votes in the Council of Ministers and review the number of European Commissioners. Informally, the issues at stake were the balance between the governments of the member states and the supranational institutions of the EU; whether all governments should move towards closer integration at the same time and in the same way, or whether some form of diversity was permissible; the relative importance of small versus large states and the issue of effectiveness versus representation. The challenges facing the negotiators were therefore great, and indeed, the hard choices involved along with the prospect of having to ratify a new treaty so soon after the

Maastricht Treaty, steadily reduced the expectations of participants and diminished the prospect of radical change.

Instead, national governments focused on incremental change to the established agenda rather than a fundamental recasting of it. As one official noted, the objective 'was more of a 10,000 mile car service than a complete overhaul'. Hence key decisions were postponed and short-term concerns dominated the negotiations, particularly as other governments became frustrated with the increasingly Euro-sceptic British Conservative Government. The final treaty was thus far more modest than its predecessor, avoiding measures which might arouse public anxiety, and made few new commitments in terms of policy responsibilities. It was 'more of a mouse than a mountain' (*Economist*, 1997).

Nevertheless, there were some noteworthy outcomes, principally regarding the balance between intergovernmental and supranational institutions within the EU. The Maastricht Treaty had set up a three-pillared structure in which economic issues were handled by the supranational institutions of the EU (first pillar). Common foreign and security policy (CFSP) and justice and home affairs issues—the second and third pillars respectively—were dealt with inside the EU institutional framework but using intergovernmental procedures. So far as decision making procedures within these pillars was concerned, the balance between states and supranational actors now shifted somewhat towards majority voting and away from unanimity.

On first pillar issues, majority voting in the Council of Ministers was extended, in effect limiting the issues on which governments could exercise a national veto. On second and third pillar issues, where governments were most sensitive to the sacrifice of the national veto, various forms of abstention were introduced which permitted governments to opt out but at the same time prevented them from impeding the implementation of EU decisions. Although these opt outs were seen as an alternative to the introduction of majority voting in these pillars, they nevertheless represented an erosion of the principle of unanimity which had hitherto prevailed here.

On the question of the allocation of functions, however, an emerging consensus that the existing arrangements were not working well was not matched by a willingness to see second and third pillar functions fully transferred to the supranational institutions. The Amsterdam Treaty instead contained only a modest set of procedural changes. Regarding the second pillar, a High representative (the Council of Ministers Secretary General) was appointed to coordinate the activities of the Union and represent it in CFSP matters while a planning, analysis and forecasting unit was also created. Justice and Home Affairs, the third pillar, was a more contested area, in which some governments were willing to contemplate the transfer of key functions (allowed for in Article K.9 of the TEU) to the first (supranational) pillar but others were not.

In the event the treaty transferred policies on asylum, immigration and visas to the first pillar and provided that the Schengen frontier-free zone should gradually become part of the first pillar. However, reflecting the sensitivities involved, legislation on these issues was to remain subject to unanimous vote in the Council of Ministers and Denmark, the UK and Ireland won legally watertight guarantees allowing them to retain their own border controls indefinitely. This served to strengthen the principle of permanent opt outs and built on the EMU opt outs of Britain and Denmark enshrined in the Maastricht Treaty.

Respect for the concerns of the individual governments, as opposed to supranational institutions, therefore played a large role in determining the Amsterdam decisions on the allocation of functions between the Maastricht pillars. A similar outcome was seen on the other major issue addressed by the Treaty, the question of the pace and the nature of future integration. Since 1992 a key question inside the EU had been whether all states should agree to deepen integration at the same time and in the same way or whether some form of diversity might be permissible. A number of ideas were proposed in the run-up to the Amsterdam European Council. In 1994 the German Christian Democrats proposed a 'core Europe' which envisaged a small group of five or six states (France, Germany and the Benelux, and perhaps Spain) moving ahead on monetary union and defence. In December 1995 Chancellor Kohl and President Chirac proposed an *avant-garde* group of governments which would form a more closely integrated group and provide collective leadership for a more diverse and less coherent EU. The British Prime Minister proposed a more flexible framework of integration within an expanding EU.

The final agreement reflected this mix of ideas. Regarding issues already within the scope of EU competence, some limited flexibility was permitted, as we have already seen, and in particular, the British and Irish Governments were permitted a permanent opt out from EU border controls. In possible new areas of integration there was agreement that member states could move forward with enhanced integration, but a national interest clause was inserted which allowed governments which did not want the others to move forward to exercise a veto if they proposed to use the institutional structure of the EU to do so. Once again, therefore, the interests of individual states took precedence over supranational concerns.

In something of a contrast with this outcome, however, the Amsterdam Treaty also saw a significant strengthening of the role of the supranational European Parliament in the legislative process. Co-decision (which gave the EP greater ability to exercise a veto over legislative proposals and greater leverage power over the Council of Ministers), was extended to more areas than under the Maastricht Treaty and was henceforward the rule, with any other decision procedures the exception. A further step was to strengthen the role of the EP vis-à-vis the Commission. In particular the EP was given a greater say over the appointment of the Commission President. Since this meant greater prestige for the Commission President, an important by-product of this move was to increase the influence of the President both generally and within the college of Commissioners.

A number of issues were simply too difficult to resolve. Above all, decisions concerning the institutional and procedural changes to permit enlargement were postponed until the EU reached 20 member states. The balance between large states and small states, and in particular, the weighting of votes and the number of commissioners for each member state was also deeply problematic. The negotiators discussed the possibility of those countries with two commissioners losing one at the next enlargement, so long as Council votes were re-weighted to recognise the importance of the large member states, but ultimately this issue was left unresolved. The negotiators were aware that failure to agree on a treaty might have prevented the formal opening of accession talks. Thus while the partial compromise on Commission representation and voting weights was far from ideal, 'At least it isn't a disaster' commented one negotiator.

There was however one issue which had very nearly brought the negotiations to the brink of collapse, and this was the insistence of the new French Socialist government that ambitious employment measures be incorporated into the Treaty. This threatened to undermine the commitments to low inflation and control of public expenditure contained in the Maastricht Treaty itself and reaffirmed by the Stability and Growth Pact agreed in principle at the Dublin summit of December 1996. In the event, however, the French were forced to settle for an employment chapter which gave the EU a formal role in coordinating employment creation and encouraged cooperation among governments, set out guidelines to help create jobs and provided for limited spending on pilot projects.

This was sufficient to allow the French Socialist government—which had come to power on the promise of job creation—to claim a victory of sorts. Ultimately, however, it was the views of other governments, led by the Germans, to whom the French demands for job creation and spending on public works appeared to be a direct attack on the budgetary rigour enshrined in the Stability Pact and an indirect attempt to overturn the European Central Bank's commitment to monetary stability and replace it with responsibility for high employment, which prevailed. The German approach to this issue was straightforward. In the words of Finance Minister Waigel, 'there will be no money flowing from Germany for additional jobs-creation programs' (Buerkle, 1997a, p.1). For all the rhetoric of the Amsterdam employment chapter, the Maastricht convergence criteria for EMU were therefore left unchanged. Even French Finance Minister Dominique Strauss-Kahn had to admit defeat, noting that the results were 'a little timid' (Buerkle, 1997b, p.2).

Indeed between the agreement on the Amsterdam Treaty in June and the jobs summit held in Luxembourg in November, the background context was dominated by this perception that addressing the issue of jobs might endanger the single currency objective. The German and British governments took the lead in opposing any new spending on European-wide job creation programmes, and any potential infringement on national governments' powers, though they differed on alternative solutions. There were two other fears: first, the Luxembourg Prime Minister Jean-Claude Juncker expressed concern that as with other EU summits there might be a great deal of talk about the need for job creation (December 1993 in Brussels, December 1994 in Essen and December 1995 in Dublin) but no tangible action to accompany it. Second, there was a fear that any new strategy for addressing unemployment would lead to an unbridled race towards excessive deregulation and flexibility, led by the British government, and anathema to the continental members of the EU.

In the event, the solution to these concerns reached at the Luxembourg extra-ordinary 'Jobs Summit' of 20–21 November was twofold. First, agreement emerged that there was a 'third way' between the Anglo-Saxon model of deregu-lation, low unemployment and fewer welfare benefits, and the European model of job protection, high unemployment and generous welfare provision. This third way, a new European employment model, would balance social protection, com-petitiveness and welfare provision with sound finance. Second, the summiteers agreed to mimic the success of establishing the EMU convergence criteria, that is, the establishment of clear verifiable targets that could be routinely monitored with peer pressure brought to bear on member states that had not been following the plans laid down. The Commission put forward ambitious proposals to create a new culture of entrepreneurship and employability based on key elements: encouragement to entrepreneurship; improved employability; greater adaptability and promotion of equal opportunities. The proposals included the aspiration to raise the proportion of the working age population in employment from 60 per cent to 65 per cent within five years; reducing unemployment from 11 per cent to 7 per cent and creating 12 million new jobs within five years.

After two days of hard bargaining, a modest package of measures to deal with unemployment and job creation was therefore endorsed. According to agreed guidelines, all those under 25 years of age would in principle be offered new employment opportunities before being out of work for six months, while the same guarantee would apply to those over 25 within a year of being out of work. Other measures included raising the number of unemployed offered training from the EU average of 10 per cent to 20 per cent, and guidelines to simplify rules on small businesses, to develop more flexible markets and to reverse the trend of higher taxes and charges on labour. The European Investment Bank would raise ECU 10 billion and the EU would seek to find ECU 450 billion over three years to fund job creation. It was further agreed that national plans would be presented in Cardiff in June 1998.[6]

The key weakness of the jobs summit however was that notwithstanding the so-called 'third way', there remained a fundamental inability to define what

---

[6] For an edited version of the text see *Agence Europe*, 23 November 1997.

would be the future shape of the European model. The President-in-Office, Jean-Claude Juncker spoke for the majority of governments when he suggested that the jobs summit would provide the '... means to save the European model, to keep its nobleness' (*Agence Europe*, 12 September, 1997). How this nobleness would translate in institutional terms, however, remained unclear. A second weakness was the underlying confusion of the policy objectives. As the *Financial Times* noted for instance, the Commission's suggestion of lower taxation on labour could only follow a reduction in public spending of which welfare state expenditure was the most significant outgoing. Likewise, the summit agreed that there should be adaptable forms of labour, but at the same time, declared that 'those in non-standard work should be given greater security and occupational status' (*Financial Times*, 6 November, 1997). Finally, as was so clearly not the case with the single currency project, the member states had not committed themselves to a specific goal. Nor did the summit conclusions provide for binding and enforceable guidelines with effective sanctions and incentives for reform. Compromise may lie at the heart of European politics, but cannot substitute for coherent reform.

UNEMPLOYMENT, GLOBALISATION, AND THE COMING 'EUROPEAN WELFARE STATE'

Despite the persistent confusion over Europe's 'third way', the renewed focus upon the intractable problem of unemployment lends credibility to the possibility that a 'European welfare state' regime of a particular sort might eventually develop. This possibility is both new and paradoxical. It is new in the sense that, in general, the principal focus of European Union studies—reflecting experience within EU institutions themselves—has been upon the economics of single-market making and the constitutional issues raised by 'an ever closer union'. Social policy has been discussed largely as an adjunct of these processes and 'Social Europe', though much cited, is a peculiarly evasive concept (Hantrais, 1997). A 'social dimension' can be traced all the way back to the Treaty of Rome and has a declamatory history running through the 1961 Social Charter and the Social Action Programme to the 1989 Community Charter and the 'Social Chapter' of the Maastricht Treaty.

Nevertheless, there is a well-grounded suspicion that the most substantive stipulations of Social Europe are those that relate to market-making (especially the free movement of labour and its attendant welfare provisions). Where rights are identified, as in the *Community Charter of the Fundamental Social Rights of Workers*, they have been granted to workers not citizens, reflecting their orientation around labour market participation, and implementation is 'the responsibility of Member States, in accordance with national practices' (European Community, 1989). There has been no shortage of prospectors for something we could call the 'European Welfare State' but a near-universal agreement that, in anything like its classical nation-state guise, it simply does not exist.[7]

For some, social policy remains quintessentially within the domain of domestic nation-state activity (Streeck, 1995). Others, including Stephan Leibfried and Paul Pierson (1995), make the case for a much more significant role for the European Union in shaping the welfare regimes within its constituent states. They argue (Leibfried and Pierson, 1995, p. 47) that positive attempts by the European Commission to construct a substantial 'social dimension' at Union level have had a very limited impact: 'substantive policy enactments have ... been rare'. If, however, we focus not upon positive enactments but upon the extent to which EU institutions have constrained the social policy autonomy of constituent states or the ways in which enactments in other policy fields have had a social policy effect, the role of the European Union looks much more extensive. Thus, 'the last three decades, and especially the most recent one, have witnessed a gradual, incremental expansion of EU-produced regulations and, especially, court decisions that have seriously eroded the sovereignty of national welfare states' (Leibfried and Pierson, 1995, p. 51).

Hence, the prospect of a 'European Welfare State' is paradoxical in that it coincides with the decline of national welfare states as well as with increasing European constraints on national welfare-state activities. European Court of Justice determinations have had a significant policy-making impact in areas such as working hours, equal pay, pension rights and parental leave. Moves to ensure the integrity of a comprehensive single market have involved subjecting national state's social security provision and employment law to community-wide regulation, giving rights to non-citizens and to citizens living beyond the boundaries of their native nation-state. Numerous measures have been taken to limit the opportunities for 'social dumping', 'regime hopping' and various forms of 'regulatory arbitrage'. At the same time, the Community has always pursued social policies under some other name and, in this context, the role of the Structural and Social Funds is dwarfed by the salience of the Community's enduring 'big spender': the Common Agricultural Policy.

Among academics, interest in EU social policy is still largely a case of 'spillover' from more 'mainstream' concerns. Probably the most pressing 'spillover' social policy issue in recent times has been the project for European Monetary Union. The convergence criteria for entry to monetary union established under the Maastricht Treaty required participating governments to reduce their budget

---

[7] See S. Leibfried, 'Towards a European welfare state?' in C. Jones, *New Perspectives on the Welfare State in Europe*, pp. 133–156; S. Leibfried and P. Pierson, *European Social Policy: Between Fragmentation and Integration*, (Washington, DC, Brookings Institute, 1995); L. Cram, *Policy-making in the EU*, (London: Routledge, 1997).

deficits to 3 per cent of GDP by 1997. With constrained opportunities for increasing tax revenue, this placed great pressure upon public spending, thus upon social expenditure and, within this and for continental welfare states especially, upon public pension provision.

In 1997, however, the situation may be changing again. EU institutions have always been most prominent and effective in areas of market governance. In the traditional domain of welfare states—above all in the realm of social security and income maintenance—efforts by the Commission to take a more active role have been repeatedly thwarted (Ross, 1995). But, in fact, the general character of welfare state interventions is changing and this in ways that bring social policy and labour market policy into a still closer relationship and, at least potentially, transforms the relationship between national and supranational institutions.

The driving force behind this process of change is not simply heightened concern for unemployment, but rather more general concern for globalisation. At its simplest, the argument is that processes of globalisation (above all, the integration of financial and labour markets) are stripping national governments (and their regional surrogates in the Union) of discretion over domestic economic policy. Sometimes these problems of welfare state regimes in the EU are explained in terms of changes in the 'real' global economy. The transfer of jobs into cheaper labour markets (above all, in the Far East) is seen to generate long-term unemployment in European economies and thus to bring an irresistible pressure to bear on prevailing welfare arrangements. In recent times, still greater attention has been focused upon financial aspects of globalisation. In the contest for footloose international capital, governments (and the governing institutions of the EU) are seen increasingly to be obliged to deliver the most attractive conditions for international investors. Upon these accounts, this requires a lean (and inexpensive) welfare state plus a disciplined, skilled and cheap workforce. Newly-industrialised countries, with much more rudimentary welfare states and much lower wages, are seen to be at a considerable advantage in this competition for job-creating investment. If more developed states with more extensive welfare states are not able to compete by offering technically more proficient workers, they face the prospect of declining social protection and/or the creation of a permanent 'underclass' of unskilled unemployables.

Few serious commentators on social policy accept the globalisation story in its simplest form. Not all capital is, after all, perfectly mobile and investors are searching for something more than the lowest possible wages. At the same time, there remains a persistent diversity in states' tax and spending profiles which defy any straightforward account of convergence at the bottom. Nonetheless, there is a good deal of support for the view that states have been obliged to recast their social policies under the imperatives of global economic forces. Phil Cerny (1990, p. 179; 1995) is characteristic in arguing that we have witnessed a general move from 'the welfare state to the competition state' with 'a shift in the focal point of party and governmental politics from the general maximisation of welfare within a nation … to the promotion of enterprise, innovation and profitability in both private and public sectors'.

One of the most influential expressions of this tendency is Bob Jessop's account of a transition from the Keynesian Welfare State towards a new and *Schumpeterian Workfare State*. Under this new formation, the state's social policy interventions are directed towards the twin goals of sponsoring innovation and technological know-how amongst its 'own' players in an open international market economy (the element loosely identified with Schumpeter) whilst subliminating social protection ever more explicitly to the needs of 'competitiveness' and a transformed labour market (workfare in intent if not always in practice). In Jessop's words, 'it marks a clear break with the KWS [Keynesian Welfare State] as domestic full employment is de-prioritised in favour of international competitiveness and redistributive welfare rights take second place to a productivist re-ordering of social policy (Jessop, 1994, p. 24).

This change of orientation has a quite explicit consequence for the politics of the EU. 'Traditional' welfare state policy may still be principally in the hands of domestic governments and given the substantial institutional differences between these several welfare states (not just in terms of entitlement but also in terms of revenue-raising, the balance between public and private provision, the balance between cash and in-kind benefits) it may be likely to stay this way. But, in practice, domestic policy-makers have become ever more concerned about the ways in which welfare provisions interact with labour market policies, an area in which we have seen EU institutions develop a much greater competence. Though a huge swathe of welfare policy has comparatively little to do with labour markets (paying for existing pensions commitments, for example), increasingly welfare policy is becoming labour market policy. And, in contrast to the expectations of new right commentators in the 1970s and 1980s, the greater subservience to market pressures that this entails has not led to a straightforward withdrawal of the state. Indeed, we see in the differing policy stances of the Jospin and Blair governments and in the EU's own recommendations arising from the Luxembourg Jobs Summit an increasingly interventionist attitude amongst the public authorities.

These changes reflect a move away from a 'passive' welfare state, based upon income maintenance for those displaced by the market economy, to an 'active' welfare state designed to encourage labour market participation above all by increasing human capital and 'employability' (rather than, as more traditionally, through increasing overall demand). This requires a greater emphasis upon training, work-ready polyvalent skills and flexibility for labour; lowered social costs, ease of set-up and employment subsidies for employers. This is an initiative not just of national governments or of EU institutions but of a more general 'Washington Consensus', if we take this to refer to the views of those very senior policy-makers in international organisations such as the IMF, the World Bank and the OECD who 'advise' governments throughout the world on the best or (as it may seem) only means of securing the great desideratum of long-term economic growth. Of especial importance in this context are the following key priorities:

- *fiscal discipline*: government budget deficits should be small or preferably non-existent
- *tax reform*: tax regimes should be broadened and redesigned to reduce marginal rates and spur economic participation
- *public expenditure*: government spending should be concentrated on those areas which are economically productive (giving priority to 'investment' in health and education rather than 'redistribution' through social transfers)
- *deregulation*: governments should reduce regulation to promote economic activity (including the deregulation of labour markets and a reduction of social costs for employers).

Such a strategy clearly does not mean a straightforward 'withdrawal' of the state in the manner beloved of neo-liberals. States may certainly withdraw or at least reduce various forms of social protection. In employment-related areas, the intention is generally to make labour markets more 'flexible', while elsewhere the motivation is more straightforwardly to hold down costs. At the same time, states may actually increase their interventions in the welfare sphere to *impose* a 'competitiveness' agenda. As the character of welfare states change, we may see the growth of EU competence in social regimes which are now much more about inducing a particular form of market-making regime.

What this does not resolve, of course, is what such a new regime—the EU's 'third way'—might actually look like. As we have seen, the issue raised by globalisation is not really the 'withering away of the welfare state' but rather the further erosion of the 'social protection' model of welfare in favour of social policies which are more explicitly sublimated to the changing 'needs of the economy'. In renovating Europe's welfare states, senior figures in the EU have been anxious to avoid the suggestion that the European Model will have to be abandoned in favour of a leaner 'Anglo-Saxon' regime built around unabashed labour market deregulation. Indeed, EU pronouncements look to an enhanced regime of protection for just those workers (in part-time or atypical employment) whom the new employment order produces in growing numbers.

At the moment, it is quite unclear (one suspects as much to policy-makers as to commentators) just how this existing commitment to social protection is to be reconciled with the simultaneous and just as firm commitment to greater flexibility and entrepreneurialism. Having said this, it is important to register that global financial markets and the 'new' international division of labour do not simply 'dictate' policy to reluctant governments. Rather, they make policy choices harder and their consequences more uncertain.

CONCLUSION

The conclusion to this year of reluctant activity was already mentioned at the outset. If 1997 could be termed a year of (un)employment ambivalence, developments in 1998 are likely to be more pressing, and the member states more decisive. Already in the first three months of the year, negotiations for a further enlargement of the Union have begun and a decision on which member states are to participate in EMU is taking shape. Both of these developments will place pressure on European labour markets, and so arguably the heads of state and government will have to act.

How they will act in response to Europe's unemployment crisis is becoming more clear as well. The shift toward a market-based and more active welfare state has long been evident in member states such as the United Kingdom and Ireland—and the impact of these examples was strongly reinforced by the election of Tony Blair—but it appears to be taking root elsewhere as well, as in Belgium, the Netherlands and Germany. Of these three recent converts, the Dutch case provides the most thorough (and widely celebrated) example of how job creation can be achieved despite the pressure of globalisation and parallel to a major effort at consolidating and redefining the welfare state. The Germans, in particular, have taken note of the Dutch example. Once the electoral contest between German Chancellor Helmut Kohl and his centrist SPD opponent Gerhard Schroeder is completed—and no matter what the outcome—there is every reason to believe that Germany will follow in the footsteps of its smaller neighbour.

That said, having established the broad contours of Europe's third way is no guarantee that it will end the jobs crisis. Even the celebrated Dutch model can be considered only a questionable success (IMF, 1997). All we can suggest is that finally Europe's unemployment problem is receiving the political attention it warrants. And that attention has moved beyond optimistic declarations, and into more careful considerations of reform. For all the ambivalence of 1997, at least now there may be reason for hope.

REFERENCES

Buerkle, T. (1997a) 'Stakes are High as EU leaders Gather for Summit', *International Herald Tribune*, 16th June, 1997.

Buerkle, T. (1997b) 'EU Compromise Tilts Toward German View', *International Herald Tribune*, 17th June, 1997.

Cerny, P. (1990) *The Changing Architecture of Politics*, Sage, London.

Cerny, P. (1995) 'Globalization and the changing logic of collective action', *International Organization*, 49:4, 55–65.

European Commission (1993) *Growth, Competitiveness, Employment: The Challenges and Ways Forward into the 21st Century*, Office for Official Publications of the European Communities, Luxembourg.

European Commission (1997a) 'European Pact of Confidence for Employment', December, 1996.

European Commission (1997b) 'Demographic Report', DOC/97/5, 9 July 1997.

European Commission (1997c) 'Employment in Europe: Countdown to the Jobs Summit, 20–21 November 1997', IP/97/835, 1 October 1997.

European Commission (1997d) 'Commission Adopts Guideline for Member States Employment Policies for 1998', IP/97/1069, 3 December 1997.

European Community (1989) *Community Charter of the Fundamental Social Rights of Workers*, Office for Official Publications of the European Communities, Luxembourg.

Economist (1997) 'Mountains still to Climb', 21ˢᵗ June, 1997.

Eichenberg, R.C. and Dalton, R.J. (1993) 'Europeans and the European Community: The Dynamics of Public Support for European Integration', *International Organization* 47:4, 507–534.

ETUC (1996) 'Support Monetary Union with a Pact for Jobs', *Press Release*, 29ᵗʰ January.

Hantrais, L. (1995) *Social Policy in the European Union*, Macmillan, London.

IMF (1997) 'Kingdom of the Netherlands—Netherlands—Selected Issues', *IMF Staff Country Report* 97/69.

Jessop, B. (1994) 'The Schumpeterian Workfare State', in R. Burrows and B. Loader (eds), *Towards a Post-Fordist Welfare State*, Routledge, London.

Leibfried, S. and Pierson, P. (1995) *European Social Policy*, Brookings, Washingon DC.

OECD/Organization for Economic Cooperation and Development (1994) *The OECD Jobs Study: Evidence and Explanations*, Paris.

OECD/Organization for Economic Cooperation and Development (1997) *OECD Economic Outlook. No. 62*, Paris.

Ross, G. (1995) 'Assessing the Delors Era and Social Policy', in S. Leibfried and P. Pierson, *European Social Policy*, pp. 357–388.

Sandholtz, W. (1998) 'L'union monétaire: une route semée d'embûches sans espoir de retour', in Anne-Marie Le Gloannec (ed.) *Entre union et nations: L'État en Europe*, Presses de Sciences Po.

Streeck, W. (1995) 'From Market Making to State Building? Reflections on the Political Economy of European Social Policy', in S. Leibfried and P. Pierson, *European Social Policy*, pp. 389–431.

Traynor, I. (1996) 'Kohl Prescribes Germany Bitter Medicine on Jobs', *The Guardian*, 22 October 1996.

Visser, W. and Wijnhoven, R. (1990) 'Politics Do Matter, but Does Unemployment?' *European Journal of Political Research* 18, 71–96.

The European economy: regional disparities and social exclusion

David Sapsford, Steve Bradley and Jim Millington

Our aim in this paper is to provide a review of the performance of the European economy in 1997. In order to set the context for this we provide a brief overview of the economic performance of the major European economies over the period since 1990 set against the backcloth of the move towards the establishment of the Single European Market and the launch of a Single European Currency. As will become clear, the adjustments that have been required in order to meet the pre-conditions that were specified as necessary for the successful implementation of these two programmes (especially when taken together with the consequences of the German reunification process that began in 1990) have imposed significant stresses on a number of the major European economies during the 1990s.[1] The main criteria imposed under the Treaty of Maastricht (1992) for qualification for membership of the Single European Currency (referred to hereafter as simply the Euro) were cast in terms of macroeconomic aggregates which are briefly examined below. However as we shall see, it has nevertheless proved to be the case that the implementation by European governments of policies designed to satisfy these convergence criteria has exerted significant knock-on effects upon the European labour market and the industrial relations environment.

There are three recurring themes in this review. The first concerns the issue of *real* convergence in GDP per capita and unemployment rates, which is regarded as a necessary pre-condition for the attainment of nominal convergence of inflation rates, etc. To examine this we take a broader view of the European economy, looking back over the whole post-war period at a regional level. The second theme relates to the issue of labour market disadvantage at the individual and household level, which has received prominence in recent years in terms of the discussion of an 'underclass' or 'social exclusion'. The third and related theme concerns the issue of labour market 'flexibility' and the relationship which is seen in some circles as existing between such flexibility and economic per-

---

David Sapsford is Professor of Economics, Steve Bradley is Senior Lecturer in Economics and Jim Millington is Research Associate in Economics at the University of Lancaster.
[1] See Greenaway, Leybourne and Sapsford (1998) for a detailed statistical evaluation of the effects of European integration upon the growth performance of member states.

formance at the level of the individual member state.[2] The issue of labour market rigidity and its relationship to the unemployment rate is addressed. As we shall see, this relationship may not in reality be as straightforward and clear cut as at least some policy makers and commentators would appear to believe. Finally, we provide an assessment of the major policy challenges to be faced by the European economy as it approaches the new millennium.

THE EUROPEAN ECONOMY IN THE 1990S: AN OVERVIEW

Tables 1 to 3 provide a summary of data relating to a selection of macroeconomic aggregates for EU member countries over the recent past.

Unemployment in Europe

Parts (a) and (b) of Table 1 reports data on Standardised Unemployment Rates[3] for a number of member countries over the period following the major recession of the early 1980s. Part (a) provides a convenient summary of the period up to and including 1986. Data relating to 1995, 1996 and 1997 are set out in Part (c).[4] Part (b) provides standardised rates for two separate sub-periods, as well as a breakdown of the rate into its short-term and long-term components, where long-term is defined as a duration in excess of one year.[5]

Taking the period 1983–1996 as a whole we see that European unemployment rates displayed an enormous variation, ranging from an average value of 6.2 per cent in West Germany up to an average value of 19.7 per cent in Spain: a greater than threefold variation! The second striking feature to emerge from Table 1 is the fact that the variation in the long-term unemployment rate is considerably

---

[2] See, for example, Artis and Weaver (1994).

[3] Standardised Unemployment Rates for European Union member countries are compiled by the Statistical Office of the European Communities (Eurostat). The Standardised Unemployment Rates are based on definitions of the 13th Conference of Labour Statisticians (referred to as the *ILO guidelines*). According to these definitions the unemployed are persons of working age who, in the reference period, are without work, available for work and have taken specific steps to find work. Application of this definition produces estimates that are more comparable internationally than those based on national definitions. The Standardised Unemployment Rates reported in Table 1 are calculated as the number of unemployed persons, expressed as a percentage of the civilian labour force, where the latter is defined as the sum of the numbers in civil employment and the numbers that are unemployed. Note that comparable data are not available for Greece and are only partially available for Luxembourg.

[4] The Standardised Unemployment Rates reported in Part (c) for Germany are not comparable to those reported in Part (a) because, given the reunification process that began in 1990, they include the territories of the former East German State, whereas the figures in Part (a) refer to Western Germany only.

[5] See Dreze and Bean (1990) for a detailed econometric analysis of both the short and long-run determinants of European unemployment. Detailed econometric evidence relating to the UK experience is reported in Barrell (1994), while evidence relating to the EU as a whole is well summarised by Siebert (1997).

TABLE 1
Unemployment in Europe: Standardised Unemployment Rates

Part (a) Total Unemployment Rates in the EU, 1983–96

Belgium	9.7
Denmark	9.9
France	10.4
Germany*	6.2
Ireland	15.1
Italy	7.6
Luxembourg	n.a.
Netherlands	8.4
Portugal	6.4
Spain	19.7
UK	9.7

Part (b) Short and Long-Term Unemployment Rates in EU, 1983–88 and 1989–94

1983–88	Total	Short-term	Long-term
Belgium	11.3	3.3	8.0
Denmark	9.0	6.0	3.0
France	9.8	5.4	4.4
Germany*	6.8	3.7	3.1
Ireland	16.1	6.9	9.2
Italy	6.9	3.1	3.8
Luxembourg	n.a.	n.a.	n.a.
Netherlands	10.5	5.0	5.5
Portugal	7.6	3.5	4.2
Spain	19.6	8.3	11.3
UK	10.9	5.8	5.1

1989–94	Total	Short-term	Long-term
Belgium	8.1	2.9	5.1
Denmark	10.8	7.9	3.0
France	10.4	6.5	3.9
Germany*	5.4	3.2	2.2
Ireland	14.8	5.4	9.4
Italy	8.2	2.9	5.3
Luxembourg	n.a.	n.a.	n.a.
Netherlands	7.0	3.5	3.5
Portugal	5.0	3.0	2.0
Spain	18.9	9.1	9.7
UK	8.9	5.5	3.4

TABLE 1

Continued

Part (c) Total Unemployment Rates in 1995, 1996 and 1997

	1995	1996	1997
Belgium	9.9	9.8	9.5
Denmark	7.2	6.9	6.1
France	11.7	12.4	12.5
Germany*	8.2	8.9	9.7
Ireland	12.3	11.6	10.2
Italy	11.9	12.0	—
Luxembourg	2.9	3.3	3.7
Netherlands	6.9	6.3	—
Portugal	7.3	7.3	6.4
Spain	22.9	22.1	20.9
UK	8.8	8.2	7.1

Note: *The figures for Germany in Part (b) refer to Germany *inclusive* of the former Eastern Germany state, unlike those in Part (a) which refer to West Germany alone.
Source: *OECD Employment Outlook, UK.*

greater than that in the short-term rate. Given the body of evidence (e.g. Layard *et al.*, 1991) that suggests that long-term unemployment, as distinct from its short-term counterpart, has very little to do with holding down wage pressure and inflation one might follow Nickell (1997) by pointing out that while European economies all appear to require some short-term unemployment in order to meet stable inflation targets of the sort imposed under the terms of the Maastricht Treaty as a condition for joining the Single European Currency club, long-term unemployment might be seen as something of an optional extra.

Growth and Living Standards in the European Economy

Table 2 reports statistics on a number of measures which enable us to build up a picture of how the economies of Europe have performed over recent years in terms of delivering improvements in living standards to their populations. Part (a) of this table reports the latest OECD and Eurostat data on the annual percentage rate of growth of real Gross Domestic Product (GDP) for the existing 15 member states. These data, which have been constructed so as to be comparable across different member countries, reveal marked inter-member disparities in the rate of growth of the volume of GDP between 1995 and 1996. While the average growth rate thus measured was 1.6 per cent for the 15 current member states, the country specific rates varied from a low of 0.8 per cent for Italy through to the maximum value of 7 per cent that was achieved by the Irish Republic. Because of the possible presence of particular country-specific factors in any given year, a clearer picture of relative growth performance might be obtained by considering

TABLE 2
Part (a) Growth and Living Standards in the EU

The economy	EUR 15	Belgium	Denmark	Germany	Greece	Spain	France	Ireland
1994 Gross domestic product (GDP):								
at current prices (bn ECU)	6192.0	192.2	123.7	1724.8	80.3	407.1	1121.9	44.5
per inhabitant (1000 ECU)	16.7	19.0	23.8	21.2	7.7	10.4	19.5	12.5
1994 Gross value-added by sector (%):								
agriculture, forestry, fishing (')	2.2	1.7	3.7	1.0	13.7	3.7	2.5	7.5
industry (')	31.5	29.3	27.0	34.3	25.8	33.3	27.6	34.3
services (')	6.4	69.0	69.3	64.7	60.5	63.0	69.9	58.2
1988–93 Annual growth of GDP atmarket prices (constant prices) (%)	1.8	1.8	1.1	3.8	1.3	2.0	1.4	5.5
GDP in volume terms: Percentage growth between 1995 and 1996	1.6	1.3	1.9	1.1	2.2	2.1	1.3	7.0

	Italy	Luxem-bourg	Nether-lands	Austria	Portu-gal	Finland	Sweden	United Kingdom
1994 Gross domestic product (GDP):								
at current prices (bn ECU)	863.2	11.6	278.5	165.8	73.9	82.4	165.7	856.6
per inhabitant (1000 ECU)	14.8	28.8	18.1	20.7	7.5	16.2	18.9	14.7
1994 Gross value-added by sector (%):								
agriculture, forestry, fishing (')	2.9	1.5	3.6	2.4	5.1	5.2	2.8	1.6
industry (')	32.0	31.0	28.4	39.0	33.6	32.7	39.1	31.0
services (')	65.1	67.5	68.0	58.7	61.3	62.1	58.1	67.4
1988–93 Annual growth of GDP at market prices (constant prices) (%)	1.3	4.6	2.5	2.6	2.7	−1.5	−0.3	0.4
GDP in volume terms: Percentage growth between 1995 and 1996	0.8	2.4	2.7	1.1	2.6	2.5	1.7	2.4

Source: *Eurostat.*

TABLE 2

Part (b) Real Earnings Growth for Different Groups of Workers over the Past Five and Ten Years[a]

| | Compensation per employee (national accounts) | | Earnings of full-time workers[b] | | | | | |
| | | | Total | | Men | | Women | |
	Past 5 years	Past 10 years	Past 5 years	Past 10 years	Past 5 years	Past 10 years	Past 5 years	Past 10 years
Austria (1995)	5.5	17.9	8.0	—	7.0	—	8.5	—
Belgium (1994)	14.5	23.5	9.9	16.9	8.0	15.3	14.1	25.8
Denmark (1993)	5.3	9.6	0.1	5.3	0.0	—	2.7	—
Finland (1995)	4.9	22.7	4.6	21.5	4.8	21.9	5.4	22.1
France (1994)	5.8	10.2	2.6	7.2	2.1	6.7	4.4	10.0
Germany (1994)	4.1	14.1	9.9	21.0	7.6	19.7	15.7	26.1
Italy (1993)	10.3	20.1	0.8	10.4	3.1	12.4	2.5	12.6
Netherlands (1994)	3.9	7.3	3.3	9.3	2.7	8.4	7.7	17.1
Sweden (1994)	1.5	15.1	−2.3	9.3	−2.0	10.8	−0.2	10.0
United Kingdom (1996)	5.1	15.7	8.5	23.2	7.8	21.9	11.7	33.4

— Data not available.

[a]All nominal wage series have been deflated by each country's consumer price index. The latest year to which the data refer is shown in parenthesis. For the following countries, the data for earnings growth refer to a different period than indicated, but have been expressed in terms of a standard five-yearly or ten-yearly rate of change; for Italy, the past five years refer to the past six years; for Belgium and Finland, the past ten years refer to the past nine years; and for the Netherlands, the past ten years refer to the past eight years.
[b]The data for Austria also include part-time workers.
Source: OECD.

average performance over a run of years. Table 2 reports such information for the period 1988 through to 1993. Although the average annual growth rate across all members for the period 1988 to 1993 turned out to be 1.8 per cent per annum, the individual country growth rates ranged from a low of −1.5 per cent for Finland through to a high of 5.5 per cent for the Republic of Ireland. Excluding Finland, Sweden and Austria (on the grounds that they have only recently joined the Union) we see that in terms of this particular measure of growth performance it was the UK economy which grew most slowly amongst the 'older' members, achieving an average annual rate of growth of only 0.4 per cent over the period 1988 to 1993. Although useful, GDP growth rates do not tell the complete story when it comes to differentials in living standards. Accordingly, Table 2, Part (a) also reports some information relating to the *level* of GDP, expressed in current prices, per inhabitant. As may be seen, GDP per inhabitant in 1994 ranged from a low of 7.5 thousand ECU in Portugal to a high of 28.8 thousand in Luxembourg. Although, as we have already seen, the Republic of Ireland exhibited the highest rate of growth in GDP over the period 1988 to 1993, it was nevertheless still

TABLE 2
Part (c) A Measure of Workers' Perspectives on Job Security

	Percentage strongly agreeing that "my job is secure"		Change
	1989	*1996*	
Austria	53	37	−16
Belgium	—	28	
Denmark	—	56	
Finland	—	31	
France	—	21	
Germany	39	28	−11
Greece	—	34	
Ireland	23	34	−11
Italy	43	30	−13
Luxembourg	—	39	
Netherlands	25	40	+15
Portugal	—	25	
Spain	—	39	
Sweden	—	27	
United Kingdom	18	33	+15
United States	28	—	
Unweighted average	32	33	+1

Source: *OECD.*

the fourth poorest member country in 1994 in terms of GDP per inhabitant, which stood at only 12.5 thousand ECU, as compared to the Community average of 16.7 thousand.

Table 2 Part (a) also reports statistics on Gross Value Added, disaggregated by broad sectors. These data reveal especially marked variations between member states in value added in *agriculture, forestry and fishing*. Notice, in particular, that value added in this sector in 1994 ranged from a low of only 1 per cent in Germany, up to a high of 13.7 per cent in Greece, with the average across all 15 current member states being 2.2 per cent.[6]

Another dimension of living standards within the EU concerns the rates of real earnings growth achieved within different member states. Part (b) of Table 2 reports some recently available data relating to real earnings growth over the

---

[6] Analysis of the structure of aid in the form of income transfers from the rich regions of the Community to the poor regions, and their effectiveness (or otherwise), in removing regional disparities is beyond the scope of the present paper. However it is important that a distinction be drawn between aid to agricultural regions and to areas of industrial decline. The former still dominates EU regional policy expenditure: Denmark, for example, is a net recipient of EU funds, yet she has the second highest per capita income in part (a) of Table 2. Likewise one may ask why it is that the top regional aid status continues to be accorded in a blanket manner to East Germany when some western areas appear to have serious and persistent industrial problems?

past five and ten years in a sample ten member countries. These data again reveal major discrepancies in economic performance as between different member states. Considering the growth in real earnings achieved by full-time workers over the past five years we see that performance ranged from a low of -2.3 per cent for Sweden[7] through to a high of 9.9 per cent for Germany and Belgium.

One of the limitations of data such as those reported in Table 2 parts (a) and (b) is that they take no account of the 'non-pecuniary' factors associated with the achievement of a particular level or growth in measured living standards. Such 'non-pecuniary' factors are notoriously difficult to measure, not least because the nature and magnitude of such factors varies from one individual to another even when confronted with a given controlled situation. It is, however, possible to shed some, albeit limited, light on this question by the application of appropriately constructed survey procedures. One particular ingredient of the non-pecuniary dimension that has been studied recently concerns job insecurity. Part (c) of Table 2 reports some survey evidence that has recently become available. Although incomplete, this evidence would seem to suggest that the average degree of job insecurity across the 15 current member states does not appear to have changed appreciably between 1989 and 1996. However, this apparent constancy would appear to mask what, on more detailed analysis, might well turn out to be significant variations in feelings regarding job insecurity between different member states. In particular this evidence, such as it is, would appear to suggest that a marked worsening in workers' perspectives on job security occurred between 1989 and 1996 in Austria, Germany and Italy, while improvements of a roughly similar magnitude occurred over the same period in Ireland, the Netherlands and the United Kingdom.[8]

Monetary Union

The main criteria imposed under the Treaty of Maastricht (1992) for qualification for membership of the Single European Currency were cast in terms of straightforward macroeconomic aggregates relating to the size of the public deficit, debt ratios and inflation rates. More precisely, the main criteria set out in

---

[7] Of the 'older' member countries covered by this sample, the worst performer in terms of delivered growth in real earnings is Denmark, with a value of 0.1 per cent over the past five years. It is perhaps worth noting that the corresponding figures for the United States and Korea are -0.9 and $+43.5$ per cent respectively. Moving to the past ten years' measure the corresponding figures for the United States and Korea become -3.1 and $+116.3$ per cent respectively.

[8] Although comparable survey evidence is only available for the United States in 1989 it is relevant to notice that opinion polls there would seem to suggest the existence of widespread job insecurity in spite of low unemployment. Indeed, one recent study estimated the 'normal' level of employment insecurity in the US as being equal to 52%, which compares with an (unweighted) mean value across the whole of the OECD of 44%.

TABLE 3
Maastricht Convergence Criteria

Target	Deficit/GDP 1997 3%	DEBT/GDP 60%	CPI 2.7*
Austria	2.5	66.1	1.2[p]
Belgium	2.1	122.2	1.5
Denmark	0.7	64.1	2.0
Finland	0.9	55.8	1.2
France	3.0	58.0	1.2
Germany	2.7	61.3	1.5
Greece	4.0	108.7	5.4
Ireland	0.9	67[e]	1.2[e]
Italy	2.7	121.6	1.9
Luxembourg	1.7	6.7	1.4
Netherlands	1.7	70.4	1.9[p]
Portugal	2.5	62.0	1.9
Spain	2.6	68.3	1.9
Sweden	0.4	76.6	1.9
UK	1.9	53.4	1.9

Notes: e = estimated; p = provisional.
*Calculation based on average 1997 inflation data.

the Treaty are a public deficit of not more than 3 per cent of GDP; a public debt to GDP ratio of 60 per cent or less; an inflation rate of not more that 1.5 percentage points above the average of the three best inflation performers; long-term interest rates no more than 2 percentage points above the average rate prevailing in the three lowest inflation member countries, plus at least two years of exchange rate stability. While there does appear to be some room for debate in respect of whether the last of these criteria means ERM membership, it nonetheless will effectively require those countries, like the UK, that may seek to join the Euro at some later date to, in effect, shadow the Euro for at least two years prior to signing up.

On 27 February 1998 EU member countries formally filed statistical reports relating to their success, or otherwise, in meeting the Maastricht criteria. The evidence contained in these reports, which is summarised in Table 3, will be used as the basis for deciding which member countries will be permitted to join the single currency when it is launched on 1 January 1999.[9] Although the UK, along with Sweden and Denmark, has opted out of the first wave of entrants, Table 3 shows that it would have easily achieved the convergence criteria set out in the Maastricht Treaty as a prerequisite for membership of the single currency. Paradoxically, the UK appears to have met the criteria more comfortably than

[9] The roles of long-term interest and exchange rates, and the influence of short-term interest rates on these variables, are issues which space constraints prevent us from exploring in this particular review.

both Germany and France, arguably the strongest advocates of the single currency, at least in the initial attempts to get it off the ground. While Germany's deficit at 2.7 per cent of GDP meets the Maastricht limit, its ratio of debt to GDP at 61.3 per cent (and apparently rising) breaches the 60 per cent target.[10] Only the UK and Sweden remain outside of the ERM. As far as the UK is concerned this choice would appear to reflect its chosen policy of targeting the inflation rate and *not* the exchange rate; while it is arguable that by remaining outside of the ERM Sweden is retaining at least the scope for competitive devaluations, not withstanding the implicit assumption that she should shadow the Euro. These particular examples serve to highlight the importance of recognising that the direct constraints placed on fiscal policy by the Maastricht criteria are only a partial—if highly significant—explanation of monetary convergence. Moreover such considerations serve to highlight the policy dilemma of monetary *convergence* and regional *divergence*.

Italy's success in meeting two out of the three major targets has confounded many critics (especially its apparent achievement in reducing its deficit to GDP ratio to a level equal to Germany's), although its debt to GDP ratio at 121.6 per cent stands at more that twice the target level of 60 per cent. France appears to have just made it, announcing a deficit ratio of *exactly* 3 per cent, while Greece has accepted that it has fallen short of all of the main targets for January 1999 entry. Despite elements of what some commentators have seen as 'statistical fudging' the record of member countries in reducing deficits to the Maastricht target has been disappointing. Indeed only four countries (including the UK) have achieved the target. According to the small print of the Treaty, countries may still be able to join EMU if their debt to GDP ratio is approaching the 60 per cent target at a *significant pace*.

On 25 March 1998 the European Commission, effectively turning a blind eye to the spectacular failures of both Belgium and Italy to meet the Maastricht debt to GDP criterion, cleared the way for 11 countries to join the single currency when it is launched on 1 January 1999 by declaring that they had all met the entry conditions laid down in the Maastricht Treaty. These countries are as follows: France, Germany, the Netherlands, Belgium, Luxembourg, Ireland, Finland, Spain, Portugal, Italy and Austria. The EU summit held on 2 May 1998 subsequently endorsed these 11 countries as founding members of the single currency. Interestingly the business of the summit seemed to focus exclusively on the question of the nationality of the first President of the European Central Bank (into which the European Monetary Institute will metamorphose in the summer of 1998) to the apparent total exclusion of consideration of the funda-

---

[10] In an interview on 28 February the German Finance Minister argued Germany's failure to meet the public debt target should not be a problem, in that had it not been for reunification Germany's debt to GDP ratio would have been at a level equivalent to that achieved by France or the UK.

mental question of the extent to which all 11 founding member countries have *actually* achieved the degree of convergence stipulated in the Maastricht Treaty. It remains to be seen whether this bodes well or ill for the future of the shortly to be born Euro.

INTRA- AND INTER-REGIONAL DISPARITIES IN ECONOMICS PERFORMANCE IN THE EU

The previous section analysed the recent macro-economic performance of EU economies, and showed that *nominal* convergence of inflation rates and budget deficits, for instance, has occurred. In this section of the paper we focus upon the issue of *real* convergence, in terms of both GDP per capita and employment or unemployment rates. There are very wide disparities in GDP per capita and unemployment rates between the regions of the EU, and the reduction of those disparities is important for a number of reasons. First, the existence of regional disparities will threaten the attainment of nominal convergence (Collier, 1994). Second, wide disparities in GDP per capita and unemployment rates between the regions of the EU mean that there are substantial differences in the welfare of the people living in those regions, and should be reduced on equity grounds. Third, the existence of both intra-regional and inter-regional disparities threatens social cohesion within the EU. Fourth, if we can understand the causes of inter-regional unemployment disparities then it may shed some light on the reasons for the substantial national differences in unemployment rates between member states.

The existence of regional disparities in GDP per capita and unemployment raise several important questions:

(i)   Where are the high growth regions?
(ii) Will the poorest regions ever catch up with the richest regions?
(iii) Is there any evidence of convergence clubs within the EU?
(iv) What are the causes of the regional unemployment disparities?
(v)   What are the implications of further economic integration for regional disparities in GDP per capita and unemployment rates?

These questions are considered in turn together with the causes.

Where are the High Growth Regions?

National disparities in GDP per capita between southern and northern member states of the EU have been shown to be substantial. However, these national differences conceal even greater disparities between the regions of the EU. Furthermore, these disparities exist both within countries and between member countries, and reflect the uneven pattern of economic activity. Several high growth zones have been identified in the EU, such as the *La Dorsale* regions (London, Belgium, Frankfurt, Luxembourg and Rome in northern Italy), the *East–West core* regions (Paris, Luxembourg, Frankfurt and Berlin) and the *Arc Mediter-ranean* (Barcelona, Marseilles and Rome). These high growth zones compare with the peripheral regions which are to be found in southern Italy, Greece, southern Spain, Ireland and most of the UK, excluding the South East, East Anglia and the Midlands regions. This classification of regions into a core and periphery conceals the wide regional disparities that exist within EU member countries. Table 4 shows for each EU member state the extent of the regional disparities in GDP per capita in 1994.

Will the Poorest Regions ever Catch up with the Richest Regions?

The issue of convergence in growth rates has received considerable attention at the international level, and most of this research shows that there is very little evidence to support the view that the poorest countries are catching up with the rich. In the regional context, recent interest in the issue of convergence has been stimulated by the work of Barro and Sala-i-Martin (1991, 1992 and 1995). However, before we consider their findings it is worth reviewing some descriptive evidence on convergence.

TABLE 4
Regional Disparities in GDP Per Capita in the EU, 1994

Country	National average	Regional maximum	Regional minimum
Austria	112.6	159.5	72.0
Belgium	101.8	163.8	73.8
Denmark	129.4	131.7	118.2
Finland	116.0	148.0	93.8
France	116.2	178.5	79.3
Germany	113.2	212.9	55.8
Greece	37.8	49.6	25.6
Ireland	81.3	—	—
Italy	96.7	123.4	54.0
Luxembourg	121.9	—	—
Netherlands	104.3	150.8	70.3
Portugal	31.6	45.6	18.8
Spain	62.4	83.6	44.1
Sweden	144.0	173.4	119.3
UK	103.7	135.9	77.1

Notes: EU = 100. Regional maximum and minimum are calculated for NUTS2 level data using the EU's Nomenclature des Unites Territoriales Statistiques.
Source: *Taylor (1996).*

Table 5 shows how the coefficient of variation in GDP per capita has changed as the EU members have become more closely integrated. A fall in the coefficient of variation over time implies that convergence is taking place so that poor regions are catching up with the rich regions. In fact, in the 1950–1970 period there is clear evidence of convergence, corresponding with the early stages of economic integration in the EU. However, as integration deepened and membership of the EU widened the speed of convergence began to slow, so much so that by the early 1990s with the completion of the Single Market there was some slight evidence of divergence in GDP per capita.

However, the coefficient of variation is only indicative about convergence and should be treated with care because it is only descriptive and its value is sensitive to outliers. An alternative and more reliable way of testing for the presence of convergence in growth rates is to build an econometric model. Most of the recent work in this area has followed this approach, although there is some debate about the most appropriate specification of the model. For instance, economists such as Barro and Sala-i-Martin adopt a neo-classical, or supply-side, approach. In its most basic form the neo-classical model suggests that in the long run regional differences in growth rates will arise due to (i) variations in technical progress between regions; (ii) variations in the growth of the capital stock between regions; and (iii) variations in the growth of the labour force between regions. This approach can be extended to include a role for inter-regional factor migration, which acts as a supply-side adjustment mechanism, and inter-sectoral factor migration, where growth is stimulated by the movement of labour, for instance, from low productivity activities such as agriculture to high productivity activities like manufacturing. A prediction of the neo-classical growth model is that poor regions will eventually catch up with the rich regions, or converge.

TABLE 5
Convergence in the EU, 1950–92

Year	Coefficient of variation
1950	0.4568
1960	0.4212
1970	0.3671
1975	0.3181
1980	0.3231
1985	0.3235
1990	0.2991
1992	0.3005

Notes: Up to 1970 GVA is measured at factor cost and from 1975 onwards at market prices. The coefficient of variation is found by dividing the standard deviation of GVA by the mean of GVA. The data refer to 85 regions within the EU.
Source: *Armstrong (1995)*

The model that Barro and Sala-i-Martin actually estimate to test for the presence of convergence in the EU is summarised as follows:

$$\ln y_r^T/y_r^B = \alpha + \beta.\ln[y_r^B] + \text{other variables}$$

where y_r^B is the base year of (real) GDP for each region, r, and y_r^T is the value of (real) GDP for a subsequent year for each region, r. The 'other variables' included in their model act as proxies for the determinants of growth suggested by the neo-classical model. Their findings, which are summarised in Sala-i-Martin (1996) suggest that in Europe over the period 1950–1990 convergence in growth rates amongst 90 regions has occurred at a rate of 2% per annum. There were some slight variations in the pace of convergence. For instance, for the 11 UK regions the rate was higher at 3%, whereas for the 20 Italian regions it was lower at 1% and for the 17 Spanish regions 2.3%.[11] Evidence is also found to support the view that the distribution of income within each economy is converging. Sala-i-Martin (1996) therefore concludes that:

> the main lesson … is that there is convergence …across regions… The speed of convergence is extraordinarily similar across countries: about two per cent per year. (p. 1339)

The neo-classical model, which relies on market forces, is therefore vindicated, and the poor regions of the EU will catch up with their rich counterparts.

But, what are the implications of the estimates of the speed of convergence provided by Barro and Sala-i-Martin? Have their findings been accepted uncritically? The answer to the first question is that convergence is a painfully slow process with 75 per cent of the difference between the growth rates of the rich regions and the poor regions being eroded after 70 years. Policies may therefore be required to speed up the process. Armstrong (1995) criticises the Barro and Sala-i-Martin approach because they exclude some of the poorest EU member countries. He finds in favour of convergence over the period 1950–1992, but shows that the speed of convergence falls by half to 1 per cent per annum. Also, Armstrong admits the possibility that convergence could have been partly due to economic integration and EU regional policy. Dewhurst and Mutis-Gaitan (1996) find evidence of varying rates of convergence in growth rates over the period 1983–91 to a common equilibrium growth rate. In contrast, Cheshire and Carbonaro (1996) suggest that regions are inadequate as a unit of analysis, preferring instead to look at the growth performance of city regions, or functional urban regions. They correspond to concentrations of employment with an allowance for commuting, and are considered to be self-contained, local, economies. Their

---

[11] Barro and Sala-i-Martin have replicated their findings for the 48 US States (over the period 1880–1990), the ten Canadian provinces (1961–91) and the 47 Japanese prefectures (1955–90). In each case convergence occurs at about 2 per cent per annum.

analysis also considers a much larger number of influences on regional growth, including changes in tariffs, changes in transport costs, the presence of a coalfield in the area, industry mix, population and the number of R&D establishments in the locality. They find no evidence of either convergence or divergence. Country-specific studies have been more mixed in their findings. For instance, Chatterji and Dewhurst (1996) show for the counties of the UK that divergent growth has occurred, whereas Mas *et al.* (1996) analyse the 50 provinces of Spain over the period 1955–1991 and argue that convergence has occurred. The regression-based approaches to the analysis of convergence and divergence have recently been criticised because they cannot provide any insight into the evolution of the cross-section distribution of regions over time (Quah, 1996, 1997). The investigation of so-called distribution dynamics promises to be a fruitful area of research.

Is There any Evidence of Convergence Clubs within the EU?

A related issue to that of convergence in growth rates is that of the existence of convergence clubs. Can a north-south or centre-periphery be identified within the EU? Armstrong (1995) tests for the presence of convergence clubs and finds no support for the idea. On the contrary all regions in the EU were found to be converging on the growth rate of Ile de France—the lead region. For the UK, Chatterji and Dewhurst (1996) do find evidence in favour of a convergence club based on Greater London and including non-contiguous areas with a high growth rate, such as Cumbria, Cambridgeshire, Berkshire, Buckinghamshire, Hertford-shire, Surrey, Cheshire, Grampian and Lothian. Other county areas such as Cornwall, Merseyside, Dyfed were part of another club that had diverging growth rates and deteriorating economic performance.

Alternative explanations for the divergent economic performances of local economies have also been put forward. For instance, Bradley and Taylor (1996) examine the performance of 106 local education authorities in England over the period 1981–91 and suggest that high growth becomes self-perpetuating because of a process of cumulative causation. They show that there are links between the quality of schools, the socio-economic make-up and the employment per-formance of a local economy. Areas with high employment growth generate job opportunities for school leavers and stimulate the in-migration of 'high skill' workers. These groups—professional and managerial workers—provide extra resources to support their child's education which in turn leads to success in public examinations. The outcome is a better-educated cohort of school leavers which increase the competitiveness of local firms. As these firms grow and expand, circular and cumulative growth arises. Other localities experience the reverse and go into a cumulative decline.

What are the Causes of the Regional Unemployment Disparities?

Regional unemployment disparities in Europe are greater than the disparities in GDP per capita, which is in turn reflected in the national differences in unemployment rates discussed previously. For example in 1995 the unemployment rate in Italy averaged 14.3 per cent but regional unemployment disparities were extremely wide, ranging from 6.1 per cent to 25.9 per cent. In the UK the national rate was 8.8 per cent with regional rates ranging from 6.7 per cent to 13.0 per cent, and in high-unemployment Spain the national rate was 22.7 per cent but the regional rates ranged from 18.5 per cent to a massive 31.8 per cent. There are two important features of regional unemployment disparities in the EU. First, the dominating role of national macro economic fluctuations so that recessions, such as that in the early 1980s, tend to widen regional unemployment disparities whereas booms tend to lessen those disparities.[12] Second, the ranking of regions according to their unemployment experience has remained very stable over time, which suggests that regional unemployment disparities are persistent over long periods of time.

There have been numerous studies of the causes of unemployment at the macro-economic level (for reviews see Bean *et al.*, 1986; Blanchard and Summers, 1986; Layard *et al.*, 1991; Blackaby and Bladen-Hovell, 1992; Bean, 1994; OECD, 1994). This literature identifies five main determinants of national unemployment rates. First, negative shocks to demand should be met by a downward adjustment to real wages, but fail to do so because of real wage resistance (see Table 2(b) for national differences in earnings growth). Europe has less flexible labour markets in this respect, compared with say the US, and so unemployment is higher. The lack of flexibility is perhaps illustrated by the rise in wage inequality in the UK, and the slow down of productivity growth in some European countries such as Germany. The European economy has also been far less successful in generating new jobs compared with the USA. For example between 1970 and 1996 the European economy created 18 million new jobs (a 12 per cent increase) whereas the US economy created 47 million (a 58 per cent increase). Several causes of real wage resistance can be identified such as the power of trade unions, the institutional arrangements for wage bargaining, the duration of unemployment benefit payments and level of the replacement ratio. Second, mismatch between the demand for labour and the supply of labour, caused by changes in the pattern of demand in the product market which then feeds through to short run mismatch in the labour market, or because of occu-

---

[12] The last recession in the UK was unique because regional unemployment rates actually converged, so much so that at one point the unemployment rate in the South East actually exceeded that of Scotland. Taylor and Bradley (1994) show that the primary cause of the convergence in regional unemployment rates was the collapse of the housing market, which had a substantially greater impact in the south of England.

pational and geographical immobility of labour. Third, skill depletion due to the experience of long term unemployment, which may arise for a number of reasons, such as a widening skills gap between the employed and unemployed or unemployment duration being used by employers as a screening device. Fourth, capacity constraints, arising from the depletion of the capital stock through inadequate investment spending in the 1980s and 1990s, which reduces the ability of an economy to absorb the unemployed. Fifth, employment protection legislation in certain EU countries, such as Spain, raise firing costs and so employers are more reluctant to hire new workers (see OECD, 1994).

These factors can be expected to have a common effect across all regions within a country, and so it is necessary to consider other factors which may account for the wide and persistent regional unemployment disparities that exist in the EU. There may, for instance, be fluctuations in the demand for each region's output and, insofar as regions compete in different markets, this may generate differences in unemployment. A second explanation for regional unemployment disparities is concerned with variations in unit labour costs (the ratio of the real wage to labour productivity) which in turn affect the competitiveness of a region. Regions with high unit labour costs are likely to have higher unemployment rates. Differences in the industry mix between regions are a third possible explanation for regional unemployment disparities in the EU. For instance, regions with a large agricultural sector, such as southern Italy, are likely to be more sensitive to national and international competition, whereas regions with a traditional reliance on heavy manufacturing, such as parts of Germany and the UK, are more susceptible to the process of deindustrialisation.

The determinants of regional unemployment disparities in various EU member countries have been investigated by Taylor and Bradley (1997). Their analysis is conducted at the sub-regional, or NUTS2, over the period 1984–92. They find that the national unemployment rate has a large, positive and significant effect on regional unemployment rates, particularly in Italy and Germany. Unit labour costs also work in the expected direction for the UK, Germany, Italy, Spain and Austria, having a particularly strong impact in Italy, the UK and Austria. Simulations show that unit labour costs raise unemployment considerably in Stuttgart, Oberbayern, Basilicata, Calabria, Strathclyde and Dumfries, Merseyside and Northern Ireland. In contrast, Valle d'Aosta, Trentino-Alto Adige, Veneto, Bedfordshire, East Anglia, Berkshire, Buckinghamshire and Oxfordshire benefit from low unit labour costs which reduces their unemployment rates. One possible reason for the greater impact of regional disparities in unit labour costs in Italy is that labour productivity is substantially higher in northern Italy compared to the south, which undermines the competitiveness of the latter and therefore increases unemployment rates in southern Italian regions.

Freeman (1991) offers another complementary explanation for the apparent asymmetry in the observed relationships between local wages (and unit labour costs) and unemployment. His work allows for the effect upon wages of local differences in both aggregate demand and the institutional features of the labour market. An *inverse* relationship between local unemployment and wages is likely to be found in economies which are subject to localised demand shocks. Thus, a positive shock to local labour demand is likely to cause both higher wages and lower unemployment. On the other hand, differing levels of exogenous wage pressure (for example, as a result of spatial differences in union concentration) may result in a *positive* relationship as labour is increasingly priced out of work. In the former case, the incentive for labour in-migration is unambiguously increased and the resultant redistribution of labour supply will tend to reverse the initial changes in wages and unemployment. Thus, the more freely mobile is labour, the more ephemeral should be the observed inverse relationship. In the case of regional disparities in exogenous wage pressure however, the benefits of any higher wage are, to some extent, offset by a higher expected duration of future unemployment so the positive relationship may be sustained in the long-run. Given that a cursory study of the relationship between regional net migration rates and unemployment exhibited no obvious pattern, and given the substantial inertia observed in regional wage disparities within the EU, we may speculate tentatively that labour is far from freely mobile and/or that the high (mix-adjusted) wages of at least some EU regions, represent a compensation for high unemployment. (For discussions of the relationship between local wages and unemployment see Freeman (1991) and Blanchflower and Oswald (1995).)

In the case of Italian regions the reliance on agriculture tends to raise unemployment, whereas in Austria, Germany, Spain and the UK a larger public service sector widens regional unemployment disparities. Industry mix is therefore an important determinant of regional unemployment disparities within EU member countries. The combined effect of industry mix in the high unemployment regions of Schleswig-Holstein, Hannover and Braunschweig is to raise unemployment rates by 2.8, 2.2 and 1.4 percentage points, respectively. The magnitude of the effect in the high unemployment regions of Italy is even greater—Calabria (+7.1pp), Basilicata (+7.0pp) and Sicilia (+3.5pp).

What are the Implications of Further Economic Integration for Regional Disparities in GDP Per Capita and Unemployment Rates?

The wide and persistent disparities in GDP per capita and unemployment suggest an urgent need for a fundamental revision of EU regional policy. Objectively, recognition of this fact has grown over time as more countries have joined the EU and as the process of economic integration has progressed (Taylor, 1996). Subjectively, intra- and inter-nation state competition for limited EU regional funds, particularly in the event of further widening, creates seemingly intractable obstacles. Moreover, deepening in the form of EMU and the completion of the

Single Market will cause regional economic disparities to widen and so threaten social cohesion. There are two reasons for this. First, as larger markets are created firms are likely to merge to benefit from internal and external economies of scale, so creating greater regional specialisation. Overall the EU will benefit but there will be winners and losers at the regional level, with further decline likely in the low growth–high unemployment regions. Second, regions at the heart of the EU with Luxembourg at their centre are likely to act as a magnet for mobile factors of production and the increasing agglomeration of economic activity is likely to be detrimental to the poor, peripheral, regions. If one accepts this view then the outcome is likely to be cumulative and divergent growth unless significant regional policy interventions are implemented.[13] The implication is that there may be a need for countervailing powers to mitigate the worst effects of cumulative and diverging growth, perhaps via the Social Chapter.

The case for an EU-wide regional policy rests on the view that low-income members of the EU do not have the necessary resources to solve their own regional problems, and that stimulating growth in the peripheral areas will benefit all. This will occur because of a stimulus to output as demand increases, but also because the need for income transfers from rich regions to poor regions will fall. It could also be argued that regional policies are necessary to ensure that the benefits of integration are shared equally among the member states of the EU. For a discussion and evaluation of EU and member state regional policies see Armstrong et al. (1996), Taylor (1996), Bachter and Michie (1997) and Taylor and Wren (1997).

UNEMPLOYMENT, NON-EMPLOYMENT AND SOCIAL EXCLUSION

Regional disparities in economic performance are wide and if economic integration threatens to increase those disparities then it also threatens the labour market position of disadvantaged individuals and groups. Member states with a higher proportion of disadvantaged individuals are likely to require greater policy assistance if cohesion is to be achieved.

In recent years there has been increased debate about the emergence of a so-called underclass, a group of people who are socially excluded. The socially excluded are not simply the poor but are '…people who do not have the means, material and otherwise, to participate in social, economic, political and cultural life' (Tony Blair, quoted in The Economist, 6 December 1997, p. 31). The soci-

---

[13] It is worth recalling that Barro and Sala-i-Martin find a rate of convergence for the US states of approximately 2 per cent per annum over the period 1880–1990. These states have become more closely integrated over time and so their results imply that divergent growth is not the only possible outcome for the EU.

ally excluded are a broad and heterogeneous group including, for instance, discouraged workers who drop out of the labour market, the long-term unemployed, part-time workers and the long-term sick. Hutton (1995) refers to the UK as a 30–30–40 society. In this schema 30 per cent of the labour force are disadvantaged (e.g. unemployed or on a government scheme), a further 30 per cent are marginalised in the sense that they are not covered by employment protection legislation (e.g. part time, casual and temporary workers as well as the self-employed), and the remaining 40 per cent are advantaged. The socially excluded are likely to be drawn from the ranks of the disadvantaged and marginalised groups. Measuring the size of the excluded group is fraught with difficulties, but one approach is to focus on the non-employment rate rather than the unemployment rate.[14] The OECD also publishes data on the incidence of low pay for selected countries which may be a better guide. Alternatively, rather than treat the individual as the focus of attention, the household is taken as the unit of analysis which then gives rise to the idea of workless versus all-work households (Gregg and Wadsworth, 1996). In view of this the following questions arise:

(i)   How does the incidence of social exclusion vary between EU member states?
(ii) Who are the socially excluded? What is the geographical distribution of the excluded group?
(iii) What are the causes of social exclusion?

Each of these questions is considered in turn.

How Does the Incidence of Social Exclusion Vary Between EU Member States?

The OECD (1993) shows that non-employment rates for the 15–64 age group are greater for women compared with men. For instance, in the UK the non-employment rate for women averaged over the 1980s was approximately 40 per cent compared with just over 20 per cent for men. Unsurprisingly, non-employment rates are also higher for the poor members of the EU such as Spain, Italy Ireland and Portugal. Non-employment rates are also high in all member states for the young (15–24-year-olds) and the old (55–64-year-olds). Italy, France, Spain and Ireland have the highest youth non-employment rates, whereas Italy, the Netherlands and France have a higher incidence of non-employment for the old. Part of the explanation for these variations may be the fact that member states have different benefit regimes. An alternative approach is to focus upon

---

[14] There is widespread agreement that the use of the unemployment rate is inadequate for this task because of the many changes in its definition, differences in benefit entitlements, changes in the nature of work with the growth in atypical employment, such as part-time, casual and temporary work, and the fact that at any point in time a significant proportion of the workforce may be inactive.

the incidence of low pay and to examine how this varies between member states and different groups in the population. Table 6 shows the cumulative years of low paid full-time employment for workers over the period 1986–1991.

Full-time workers in the UK spent more time in low paid work during the 1986–91 period. However, there are variations within and between countries for different gender and age groups. Females and older workers spent longer periods of time in low paid employment, especially in Germany and the UK.

Gregg and Wadsworth (1996) extend the analysis of non-employment rates to look at the household, and find evidence of growing employment polarisation which raises implications for income inequality and benefit dependency. The polarisation has occurred because of the simultaneous growth in all-work and workless households, and the decline of mixed households. Table 7 documents the growth in employment polarisation for EU member states. In 1994 the proportion of workless households ranged from a low of 10.5 per cent in Luxembourg to 22.3 per cent in Ireland. Conversely, the proportion of all-work households ranges from 31.8 per cent in Spain to 62.1 per cent in the UK. There is no clear relationship between either the level or the change in the proportion of workless households and the economic performance of EU countries described earlier. Nevertheless, Table 7 does suggest that employment polarisation is a feature of almost all EU countries and gives some further insight into the problem of social exclusion or labour market disadvantage within the EU.

Who are the Socially Excluded? What is the Geographical Distribution of the Excluded Group?

Previous work has identified the type of individuals at greatest risk of social exclusion (see for example Green, 1997 and Fieldhouse, 1996). The risk of unem-

TABLE 6

Average Cumulative Years in Low Paid Employment for Workers Low Paid in 1986, Selected EU Countries (1986–1991)

	France	*Germany*	*Italy*	*UK*
Total	2.8	2.8	2.8	3.8
Sex				
Male	2.6	2.2	2.7	3.3
Female	3.1	3.4	2.9	4.0
Age				
Under 25	2.6	2.4	2.5	3.1
25–34	2.8	3.0	2.7	4.1
35–49	3.0	3.5	3.5	4.6
50–64	3.3	5.1	3.8	5.1

Note: Low pay is defined as below 0.65 median earnings of weekly/monthly earnings of all full-time workers.
Source: *OECD* (16 February 1998).

TABLE 7
Employment Polarisation in the EU, 1983–94

Country	Workless (percentage of households)			All-work (percentage of households)		
	1983	1994	Δ94–83	1983	1994	Δ94–83
Germany	15.0	15.5	0.5	52.5	58.9	6.4
France	12.5	16.5	4.0	56.9	55.7	0.8
Italy	13.2	17.2	4.0	39.4	40.0	0.6
Netherlands	20.6	17.2	−3.4	40.3	55.7	15.4
Belgium	16.4	19.6	3.2	41.8	51.6	9.8
Luxembourg	10.9	10.5	−0.4	41.8	50.5	8.7
UK	16.0	18.9	2.9	53.9	62.1	8.2
Ireland	17.2	22.3	5.1	35.5	40.9	5.4
Greece	16.0	17.6	1.6	37.7	43.5	5.8
Spain	19.4	20.1	0.7	26.2	31.8	4.6
Portugal	12.7	11.0	−1.7	49.0	56.4	7.4

Source: *Derived from Gregg and Wadsworth, Table 1.*

ployment and so social exclusion is highest for the semi-skilled and unskilled, the least qualified, youths, ethnic groups, the single, widowed and divorced. Although these findings refer to the UK, similar evidence exists for all EU member states. Green (1997) also argues that the risk of persistent unemployment/non-employment is associated with residence in areas of high unemployment, or areas suffering large job losses, especially in the manufacturing, mining and port-related industries. Living in remote, rural areas also raises the probability of social exclusion. Therefore, those individuals and households suffering from social exclusion do not always live in the peripheral regions of the UK. In fact, these findings suggest that there are localised pockets of excluded groups, perhaps in stigmatised overspill housing estates and inner city areas which exist in both rich and poor regions.

What are the Causes of Social Exclusion?

Four broad determinants of the increase in social exclusion can be identified. First, macro-economic factors to do with structural changes in the economy. Of particular importance are the process of deindustrialisation occurring in many advanced economies in the EU, and the associated changes in the occupational structure. The outcome for the UK, for instance, has been the decline in the number of manual, operative and semi-skilled jobs and the growth of professional and managerial jobs. These structural changes have increased the risk of individuals sliding into social exclusion, and this risk has probably increased in recent years. The accelerated decline of manufacturing employment from 1979 has been termed a 'Thatcher effect' and was associated with policies to promote labour market flexibility (Blanchflower and Freeman, 1994). As flexibility increased so too did the risk of exclusion. Second, there has been a rise in family dissolution and this may increase the likelihood of exclusion not only for the adults, but also for the children (see Emrisch and Francesconi (1996), Emrisch and Di Salvo (1997) and Jarvis and Jenkins (1997) for a discussion of the interaction between social processes and labour market performance). Third, some people are born into disadvantaged backgrounds and a cycle of deprivation is apparent from some groups in society. Young people from poor backgrounds whose parents are less educated tend to perform less well in public examinations, and leave school with few qualifications. This places them at risk of exclusion once in the labour market.

LABOUR MARKET FLEXIBILITY: THE WHOLE STORY?

In a recent White Paper the European Commission (1994) has suggested the need to move away from policies to reduce unemployment to policies designed to increase employment. Supply-side policies are recommended to increase the flexibility of the labour market, a view echoed in the recent OECD Jobs Study (1994). According to the latter, governments should set macro-economic policy to create a stable environment and use supply-side policies to stimulate the creation and diffusion of technological knowledge. Policies are also recommended to increase wage flexibility, such as reducing non-wage labour costs and the abolition of minimum wages. Functional flexibility is to be encouraged through policies to increase work-time flexibility through, for instance, part-time work and the use of fixed term contracts. Enhancing the skills of the workforce is also recommended and so too is the use of Active Labour Market Programmes (ALMP), such as government training schemes, as a means of reducing long-term unemployment. Such measures may also be beneficial for the growing numbers who are excluded. Reform of unemployment and social security systems, such as restricting the length of entitlement and/or reductions in the replacement ratio, are regarded as the best way of increasing the incentive for individuals and households to find work. Many member states within the EU are, or have, introduced these policies, following the experience of the UK. However, as the discussion above showed, increasing the flexibility of the labour market may come at the price of increased income inequality and social exclusion.

In fact, recent research has begun to question this conventional wisdom and has posed the question: Is flexibility enough to reduce the high and persistent rates of unemployment in the countries and regions of the EU? Nickell (1997) shows that there are certain labour market rigidities that may not increase the average level of unemployment in Europe. For example, strict employment protection and labour standards, generous benefits, as long as the job search activities of the unemployed are policed and the duration of entitlement is limited, and powerful unions, providing that wage bargaining is highly coordinated. What really matters is the *combination* of institutional arrangements and incentives rather than any single aspect of labour market rigidity. Furthermore, the road back to full employment, without stimulating inflationary pressures, is to be found, according to Layard (1997), in (i) limiting the duration of benefit payments; (ii) the use of ALMP to improve the job prospects of the long-term unemployed; (iii) coordinated wage bargaining to avoid 'leap-frogging' in pay settlements; and (iv) an increase in skill formation. To this we would add (v) an EU-wide regional policy which seeks to reduce the wide disparities in economic performance.

Policy Challenges

If one accepts the view that it is the combination of institutional arrangements and incentives that is important for economic and employment growth, then, in view of the fact that EU states are at different starting points, the major challenge for policy-makers would appear to be one of finding the optimal mix of labour market policies. A single EU-wide labour market strategy may be inappropriate. This approach does not, of course, deny the possibility of 'policy borrowing'. On the contrary, in terms of skill formation, for instance, policy-makers may learn a considerable amount from the German dual-apprenticeship model. Similarly, in terms of ALMP, much can be learned from the Swedish model. While policy makers could learn a lot from the ongoing debates in Germany and Sweden, it is important to recognise that these models still have to be adapted and moulded to fit the peculiar institutional arrangements in each member state. Furthermore, the move to further economic integration in the form of EMU may exaggerate the already considerable regional disparities in economic performance, and this must be avoided at all costs since it threatens the cohesion of the EU.

ACKNOWLEDGEMENTS

The authors are grateful to an anonymous referree and the Editors for helpful comments on an earlier version. Special thanks are also due to Janet Parker. Without her assistance this review would not have converged given the authors' geographical divergencies when the writing was nearing completion!

REFERENCES

Armstrong, H. (1995) 'Convergence Among the Regions of the European Union, 1950–90', *Papers in Regional Science*, 74, 143–152.

Armstrong, H., Taylor, J. and Williams, A. (1996) 'Regional Policy', in M.J. Artis and N. Lee (eds) *The Economics of the European Union: Policy and Analysis*, Oxford, University Press, Oxford.

Artis, M. and Weaver, N. (1994) 'The European Economy' in M. Artis and N. Lee (eds) *The Economics of the European Union*, Oxford University Press, Oxford, pp. 32–61.

Bachter, J. and Michie, R. (1997) 'The Interim Evaluation of EU Regional Development Programmes: Experiences from Objective 2 Regions', *Regional Studies*, 31, 849–858.

Barrell, R. (ed.) (1994) *The UK Labour Market: Comparative Aspects and Institutional Developments*, Cambridge University Press, Cambridge.

Barro, R.J. and Sala-Í-Martin, X. (1991) 'Convergence Across Regions and States', *Brookings Papers on Economic Activity*, 1, 107–158.

Barro, R.J. and Sala-Í-Martin, X. (1992) 'Convergence', *Journal of Political Economy*, April.

Barro, R.J. and Sala-Í-Martin, X. (1995) *Economic Growth*, McGraw Hill, Boston, MA.

Bean, C.R. (1994) 'European Unemployment: A Survey', *Journal of Economic Literature*, 32, 573–619.

Bean, C.R., Layard, R.G. and Nickell, S.J. (1986) 'The Rise of Unemployment: A Multi-Country Study', *Economica*, 53, S1–S22.

Blackaby, D.H. and Bladen-Hovell, R. (1992) 'Unemployment and Labour Market Flexibility in Western Europe: A Survey', Discussion Paper 92–04, Department of Economics, University College, Swansea.

Blanchard, O.J. and Summers, L.H. (1986) 'Hysteresis and the European Unemployment Problem', in *National Bureau of Economic Research Macro Economics Annual*, MIT Press, Cambridge (MA).

Blanchflower, D.G. and Freeman, R.B. (1994) Did the Thatcher Reforms Change British Labour Market performance?, in Barrell, R. (ed) *op cit*.

Blanchflower, D. and Oswald, A (1995) '*The Wage Curve*', MIT Press, Cambridge (MA).

Bradley, S. and Taylor, J. (1996) 'Human Capital Formation and Regional Economic Performance', *Regional Studies*, 30, 1–14.

Chatterji, M. and Dewhurst, J.H.LI. (1996) 'Convergence Clubs and Relative Economic Performance in Great Britain, 1977–1991', *Regional Studies*, 30, 31–40.

Collier, J. (1994) 'Regional Disparities, the Single Market and European Monetary Union', in Michie, J. and Grieve Smith, J. *Unemployment in Europe*, Academic Press, London, chapter 9.

Dewhurst, J.H.L and Mutas-Gaitan, H. (1996) 'Varying Speeds of Regional GDP Per Capita Convergence in the European Union, 1981–91', mimeo.

Dreze, J. and Bean, C. (1990) 'European Unemployment: Lessons from a Multicountry Econometric Study', in B. Holmlund and K.G. Lofgren (eds) *Unemployment and Wage Determination in Europe*, Blackwell, Oxford, pp. 3–33.

Emrisch, J. and Di Salvo (1997) 'The Economic Determinants of Young People's Household Formation', *Economica*, 64, 627–644.

Emrisch, J. and Francesconi, M. (1996) 'Partnership Formation and Dissolution in Great Britain', Working Paper No. 96–10, University of Essex, Research Centre on Micro-Social Change in Britain.

European Commission (1994) 'White Paper on Growth, Competitiveness, Employment', European Commission, Brussels.

Fieldhouse, E.A. (1996) 'Putting Unemployment in its Place: Using the Samples of Anonymised Records to Explore the Risk of Unemployment in Great Britain in 1991', *Regional Studies*, 30, 119–134.

Freeman R. (1991) 'Labour Market Tightness and the Mismatch between Demand and Supply of Less-Educated Young Men in the United States in the 1980s', in Schioppa (ed) '*Mismatch and Labour Mobility*', Cambridge University Press, Cambridge.

Green, A.E. (1997) 'Employment, Unemployment and Non-Employment', *Regional Studies*, 31, 505–520.

Greenaway, D., Leybourne, S. and Sapsford, D. (1998) 'Smooth Transitions and GDP growth in the European Union' (forthcoming).

Gregg, P. and Wadsworth, J. (1996) 'It Takes Two: Employment Polarisation in the OECD', Discussion Paper No. 304, CEPR, London School of Economics.

Hutton, W. (1995) 'The 30–30–40 Society', *Regional Studies*, 29, 719–722.

Jarvis, S. and Jenkins, S.P. (1997) 'Marital Splits and Income Changes: Evidence from Britain', Working Paper No. 97–4, University of Essex, Research Centre on Micro-Social Change in Britain.

Layard, R. (1997) 'The Road Back to Full Employment', Occasional Paper, CEPR, London School of Economics.

Layard, R., Nickell, S. and Jackman, R. (1991) *Unemployment: Macroeconomic Performance and the Labour Market*, Oxford University Press, Oxford.

Mas, M., Perez, F., Uriel, E. and Maudos, J. (1996) 'Growth and Convergence in the Spanish Provinces', mimeo.

Nickell, S. (1997) 'Unemployment and Labor Market Rigidities: Europe versus North America', *Journal of Economic Perspectives*, 11: 3, 55–74.

OECD (1994) 'The OECD Jobs Study: Evidence and Explanations', 2 Volumes, OECD, Paris.

Quah, D. (1996) 'Regional Convergence Clusters across Europe', *European Economic Review,* 40, 951–958.

Quah, D. (1997) 'Regional Cohesion from Local Isolated Actions I: Historical Outcomes', Occasional Paper No. 378, CEPR, London School of Economics.

Sala-Í-Martin, X. (1996) 'Regional Cohesion: Evidence and Theories of Regional Growth and Convergence', *European Economic Review*, 40, 1325–1352.

Siebert, W.S. (1997) 'Overview of European Labour Markets', in J. Addison and W.S. Siebert (eds) *Labour Markets in Europe: Issues of Harmonisation and Regulation*, Dryden Press, London, pp. 229–243.

Taylor, J. (1996) 'Regional Problems and Policies: A European Perspective', *Australasian Journal of Regional Studies*, 2, 103–131.

Taylor, J. and Bradley, S. (1994) 'Spatial Disparities in the Impact of the 1990–92 Recession: An Analysis of UK Counties', *Oxford Bulletin of Economics and Statistics*, 56, 367–382.

Taylor, J. and Bradley, S. (1997) 'Unemployment in Europe: A Comparative Analysis of Regional Disparities in Germany, Italy and the UK', *Kyklos*, 50, 221–245.

Taylor, J. and Wren, C. (1997) 'UK Regional Policy: An Evaluation', *Regional Studies*, 31, 835–848.

Industrial relations and social Europe: a review

Peter Cressey, Colin Gill and Michael Gold

Recent developments in international trade have led to the ever-closer integration of the European economies into a global economy dominated by large multinational companies. The emergence of the Single European Market can be seen as centrally important in this development as European businesses have sought to enhance their competitiveness in world markets. As technological innovations based on microelectronics and telecommunications have progressed, European firms have competed by moving away from standardised mass production to customised, quality 'high-tech' products which are aimed at niche markets.

Superimposed on these developments has been the inexorable rise in unemployment which abated only slightly throughout the European Union (EU) in 1997. By November 1997, unemployment in the EU as a whole stood at 10.7 per cent, with levels of 10.0 per cent in Germany, 12.6 per cent in France and 20.8 per cent in Spain, whilst in Sweden, which had historically prided itself on its low unemployment levels, it had reached 9.7 per cent (*European Trade Union Information Bulletin*, 1998). This has been one of the main factors responsible for a shift in the balance of power against labour over the past decade or so, both at the political level and within labour markets, although the effects of this shift have been uneven across different European countries. One consequence of this is that there has been a marked refocusing of European social policy away from seeking to extend workers' rights to concentrating on employment creation and 'employability'. However, as we see later, new forms of social agreement at European level have gradually taken root as the social partners, the European Trade Union Confederation (ETUC) and the Union of Employers in Europe (UNICE) and their public sector counterparts (CEEP), concluded accords on paternity leave and a framework agreement on the rights of part-time workers. Similarly, there have also been a number of accords between the social partners

Peter Cressey is Senior Lecturer in Sociology and Industrial Relations at the University of Bath; Colin Gill is Lecturer in Industrial Relations and a fellow of Wolfson College, University of Cambridge; and Michael Gold is Lecturer in European Business and Employee Relations at Royal Holloway College, University of London.

at nation state level (e.g. in Italy and Spain) where agreements have formed the basis for subsequent legislation.

Major political changes have also affected EU countries. The post-war consensus between management and labour continued to erode in 1997 and there were further reductions in government expenditure on social welfare. European countries had to face growing budget constraints, and an endemic fiscal crisis of the welfare state has severely limited their ability to offer concessions to trade unions in exchange for restraint in wage claims. Many governments in EU member states were forced to adapt to a tighter international monetary regime, particularly in preparation for the introduction of the single European currency in 1999. As a result, this led to an outbreak of industrial action and large-scale demonstrations in protest at government expenditure cuts, particularly in France and Germany. The economies of the European Union have become increasingly interdependent, which has severely restricted the ability of national governments to pursue economic policies independently of others by seeking to maintain full employment.

Trade unions in Europe had to adapt to a much more diverse constituency of groups and interests as a result of these economic and political changes. Apart from the shift of employment to the services sector and the increasing importance of the 'knowledge' or white-collar worker, they have had to accommodate themselves to: increasing rates of female participation within the workforce; transformations of the traditional family structure; the growing individualisation of lifestyles; and the expansion of 'atypical' work e.g. part-time, temporary, agency and seasonal work. This means that European trade unions have to appeal to an ever more heterogeneous population across a range of diverse interests.

Associated with the introduction of new technology has been the trend towards 'flexibility': flexibility in hours, flexibility in pay, flexibility in tasks and a move towards company-specific rather than industry-specific training. The recession in Europe in the early 1990s encouraged management to embark on a process of 'downsizing' in order to contain labour costs.

Linked with moves towards greater flexibility has been a trend towards a devolution of industrial relations issues to lower levels, often as a result of management using their enhanced bargaining power and exercising their prerogative to shift bargaining from national or industry-wide level down to the level of the enterprise. Whilst management have frequently taken the initiative towards decentralisation, major political and economic forces have also been at work, such as the growth of international competition coupled with the growing volatility of international markets.

The tendency towards decentralisation of industrial relations has been accompanied by organisational changes in companies such as the growth of 'business units' with their own profit centres and autonomy in conducting the management of employee relations. All this means that European unions find it difficult to bring their own organisational strength to bear.

It would be a mistake, however, to assume that the nature and extent of decentralisation has been uniform across Europe. Whilst it has been most pronounced in the UK, and generally less so in countries like France, Italy, Portugal and Spain, there have been few signs of change in collective bargaining structures or the introduction of 'human resource management' initiatives in certain others like Austria. Similarly, although there is some evidence that there has been increased devolution of industrial relations issues to workplace level in countries such as Germany and Denmark (both of which are renowned for their relatively high degree of centralisation of collective bargaining and extensive regulation of their labour markets), such changes have generally been accommodated within existing procedures.

TRADE UNIONS

Trade unions across Europe have not been immune from the general turbulence and restructuring that has been affecting industry and services. The long-run changes in the sectoral distribution of the labour force are continuing to undermine some of the key strongholds of traditional trade unionism and trade union organisation. Indeed as organisations they have been at the forefront of change and have had to confront fundamental issues in the process. In this review we look at the way in which some European unions have been dealing with the new context, in particular by examining trends in membership, the increasing wave of union mergers and the new strategies being adopted.

Membership

The long-term trend established since the mid-1980s towards a decline in trade union membership appears to be continuing. It is necessary to state at the outset that reliable and accurate comparative figures on union membership are hard to find. However, although there is a picture of general, and unmistakeable, decline in union membership, that picture reveals some wide variations in union density, as Table 1 illustrates.

TABLE 1
Three Clusters of Union Density

High		Medium		Low	
Sweden	91%	Italy	44%	Portugal	26%
Denmark	80%	Lux'bourg	43%	N'lands	26%
Finland	79%	Austria	41%	Greece	24%
Belgium	52%	UK	33%	Spain	19%
Ireland	49%	Germany	29%	France	9%

Source: *World Labour Report 1997–98* (1997) ILO

Across the EU, recent evidence points to distinct problems in different countries. In Greece, for example, a so-called 'crisis of representation' is described especially among the low paid, women and young workers (Soumeli and Ioakimoglou, EIRO). In Portugal there has been a drop of 40 per cent over the last decade and in France membership has hit an all-time low. One relevant question is whether such changes are pushing more national situations closer to the low cluster and away from the high and medium ones.

The German Federation of Trade Unions (DGB) has reported a sharp membership loss of 24 per cent or 2.8 million people since 1991. The high-water mark for union density in Germany was reached after reunification and a significant decline has been felt in the East. However, closer analysis shows that this is a partial picture, and recent losses and union reorganisation plans locate the problems across the whole of the German economy and not simply in one geographical part. The heaviest fall in membership has been in the leather industry (47 per cent) followed by textiles (43 per cent), wood and plastics (33 per cent) and mining and energy (28 per cent). The recession and job losses in Eastern Germany account for some of these but much of it is attributed to increased competition and the employers' restructuring of the 'value chain' with the consequent use of outsourcing strategies (Schulten, EIRO). Membership of IG Metall, the world's largest free trade union, has fallen by 27 per cent (960,000) over the period 1991–97, and, with the latest figure standing at 2.66 million, it appears that the boost to membership which resulted from unification has melted away. IG Metall blames the destruction of jobs during the last recession and 'jobless growth' for the poor job-creation performance in its organisational area. According to Zagelmeyer (EIRO), the loss of Eastern members is one reason, but a second is that recruiting women, young people and salaried employees has proved increasingly difficult for traditionally oriented unions. Third, changes in workforce composition result in a workforce with a lower propensity for union membership. Finally, structural shifts in employment from the industrial into the services sector pose challenges to IG Metall's organisation. Companies in the metalworking and electrical industries have been diversifying their production into new, growing industries or services such as telecommunications or information technology and, with this, the demarcations of recruitment grounds between IG Metall and other unions are eroding.

In the UK, the latest Labour Force Survey in 1997 shows a similar picture with a 20 per cent drop in membership in the 1990s (to 7.2 million). Density now stands at around 33 per cent and according to a TUC report (1997) is set to fall further, with a further estimated drop of 500,000 by the year 2001, other things being equal.

The Nordic countries stand out as the exceptions to these trends. In Sweden, the union density rate rose 2.1 percentage points from 1990 to reach 83 per cent in the first quarter of 1997, according to a report published in May 1997 by the blue-collar Swedish Trade Union Confederation (LO). The increase is particularly significant among women and employees in the private services sector, though the numbers of white-collar workers, who traditionally have been organised almost to the same degree as blue-collar workers, have fallen. Overall, however, the unions have regained the losses of the late 1980s. Analysis of the figures attributes this increase to a rise in union membership among women workers as a whole, now 85.7 per cent compared with 80.3 per cent for men, but there is little indication available as to why this increase is taking place amongst women. However, this means that Sweden has managed to retain the highest European rate of union density and, according to Ahlberg (EIRO), not all of this can be attributed to the role the unions play in the welfare system as it is increasingly unnecessary for people to join unions to become a member of the national insurance fund.

Union Responses

Union responses have tended to fall into three categories—mergers, new recruitment strategies and Europeanisation. The first option is clearest in Austria and Germany where already large industrial unions are amalgamating further. The Austrian union confederation (ÖGB) will have only three affiliates representing manufacturing, services and the public sector. The first moves were started in January 1998 when, of the existing 14 unions, the Union of Printing and Paper Workers and the Union of Posts and Telecommunication Employees signed a co-operation agreement.

In Germany, restructuring went further in 1998 with the creation of the new Mining, Chemicals and Energy Union (IG BCE) which has a combined membership of 1.1 million. Also significant is the decision of the Textile and Clothing Union and the Wood and Plastics Union to merge with IG Metall from June 1998. This will boost IG Metall numbers to over the three million mark again whilst leaving the new unions some autonomy as trade groups within the new set-up. Possibly the most significant move is the intention of six service and public sector unions to merge in the future—these unions have signed a co-operation and planning agreement as a first step. The end result will be a very slimmed-down DGB with 11 unions in membership in 1998 and fewer still by the year 2000.

There is also much restructuring taking place amongst unions affiliated to the British TUC, particularly in the finance and white-collar sectors. In the Netherlands, a Dutch 'super union' has been formed representing 500,000 members from the industrial, services, transport, agricultural and foodstuffs sectors. The new union is called the Allied Unions (Bondgenoten) and will be a dominating force in the Dutch Trade Union Federation (FNV).

An alternative response has been to seek to organise those key groups of workers and employees in 'difficult-to-organise' sectors in order to realise the membership growth experienced in Sweden. The British TUC has inaugurated a 'new unionism' project to attempt to do that and, together with the implementation of the statutory union recognition pledge by the Labour Government, they foresee a rebuilding of trade union membership.

Finally, some unions have considered organising at the European level and breaking with nationally dominant systems of representation. A first step in this direction has been taken by the British GMB and the German IG Chemie-Papier-Keramik which have signed a reciprocal membership agreement. Such a development, whilst affecting few workers as yet, does seem like a logical first move towards a full merger of unions on a European basis. Indeed, there are already initiatives by Austrian, Dutch, German and Swiss trade unions in the printing sector to form a pan-European alliance.

COLLECTIVE BARGAINING

The trend towards flexibility and deregulation has created strains across the very different industrial relations systems in Europe. It is most manifestly apparent in the collective bargaining structures where pressures for diversity and decentralisation have to be handled. The overall picture across European countries is of a spectrum with institutions fixing pay and conditions that range from the highly statutory and rigid at one end through to the highly voluntarist and decentralised at the other. We would expect much of the deregulatory strain to be felt in the more rigid structures and this, to some extent, appears to be the case.

German Model under Stress?

In Germany, where collective bargaining is based on statute, multi-employer bargaining has traditionally set binding agreements for all firms within the employers' association. However, the rise of company bargaining, 'site pacts' and flexibility agreements driven by specific sectoral and company demands for cost-cutting and adaptability is severely testing the limits of such standardised pay and conditions. A recent report by a German institute (IAB) has shown some gaps in the collective bargaining coverage: empirical research reveals that only 61 per cent of companies and 83 per cent of employees fall within the net. Such figures hide wide variations in sectors, with companies in the shipbuilding and aerospace industries covered 100 per cent but precision engineering covered only 40 per cent. When one adds to this the rapid increase in company-level negotiations, this has led many commentators to refer to the erosion of the sector-level bargaining system. In 1997 there were notable developments across many important sectors.

(i) Metalworking

The metalworking sector has seen a sharp decline in employment: between 1991 and 1996 numbers employed plummeted by 1.5 million to 3.5 million. According to a study by IG Metall, almost all works councillors and workplace union representatives surveyed have been confronted with a continuing process of employment reduction, and in many companies this has not yet come to an end. Against this background, a majority of works councillors have been ready to accept all kinds of social concessions in order to secure at least the jobs of the core workforce. As a result, many companies have concluded some form of 'company pact' in which the works council agrees to a further reduction of labour costs in exchange for the management's commitment to making no redundancies for economic reasons over a given period of time.

The social concessions made by works councils have included a wide range of cost-cutting measures, including:

(i)   a reduction in company 'payments above contract wages' (the additional payments over and above the rates set in the sector-level agreement paid by many companies)
(ii) a reduction in contractual wages
(iii) working time reductions without wage compensation, or extensions in unpaid working time.

In some cases, these company pacts actually undermine valid collective agreements. However, most works councillors surveyed said that they felt 'blackmailed' by the management either to agree on social concessions or to accept further redundancies (Schulten, EIRO).

(ii) Chemicals

Again, competition and job reductions are creating circumstances in which pay is being discussed at plant level in contravention of statutory regulation. In the sectoral agreement reached by IG Chemie and the employers' association (BAVC), a creative response was worked out. They agreed the insertion of a 're-opener clause' which provides for a 'wage corridor' where companies and works councils can vary collectively agreed rates by up to 10 per cent. The chemical union has had experience of re-opener clauses before but usually in relation to work reorganisation and working time issues. Here the union sanctioned the move because both they and the BAVC have retained final control over any company-level agreement and whether it becomes legally effective or not. In this way, employers and unions can overrule the parties at company level.

Part of the reason for this initiative was the threatened breakaway by employers in subsectors of the industry, particularly in rubber and tyres. They indicated that they would withdraw from the general agreement if cost/wage reductions were not reached. The opening clause procedure has, for the moment, held together the existing collective system, enabling those subsectors under most pressure some leeway to deal with it.

France

A recent review of French collective bargaining has revealed a growth in sectoral and company bargaining but no expansion at the intersectoral level. The annual rate of increase in new company agreements is slowing somewhat, down from 15 per cent in the early 1990s to 7 per cent in 1997. The key collective bargaining issue has been working time following the national tripartite conference on employment, pay and the reduction of working time held in October 1997 at which the Government announced a bill to introduce the 35-hour working week. In one sector there have been consequences following this agreement. The French Banking Association (AFB) made plans for an immediate termination of the banking sector's collective agreement. The agreement lays down specific rules on social protection, pay setting, job classification, working time and so on. In their subsequent negotiations the employers have been seeking a decentralisation of pay determination, a reform of the rigid grading structure and the introduction of a more performance-oriented perspective. The unions reacted by handing in notice of a national strike. The two parties have 23 months to renegotiate the collective agreement and, until then, the existing agreement continues to apply in its entirety.

It seems as if the working time issue may lead to a new challenge in relation to the appropriate level at which labour relations should be regulated.

Nordic Countries

The relatively centralised 'Nordic Model' developed further cracks over the course of 1997. In Sweden, a number of LO-affiliated blue-collar unions were happy to accept performance-related and merit pay and in a number of industries collective bargaining was developed to company-level. The Swedish employers (SAF) and some of the sectoral bodies had stated that they were unwilling to enter centralised national-level negotiations when the current agreement expires. However, the first sectoral agreement by the white-collar unions was concluded in late 1997. LO opened their 1998 bargaining round by tabling 'solidaristic' elements—more to the lowest paid and payment for the job rather than for performance. They are also asking for pay flexibility to be dealt with through earmarking 1.5 per cent for sectoral or company bargaining. One aspect that worries the unions is the ability of the system to regulate subcontracted, agency and temporary workers who, in moving from job to job, also enter situations where different collective agreements apply.

In Denmark, since the early 1980s, the Danish trade union confederation (LO) and the Danish employers' association (DA) have lost influence because collective bargaining has been increasingly 'decentralised' to industry level. This process accelerated during the early 1990s. The Danish public sector was not immune from this trend either. For example, from January 1998, Government institutions could experiment with new forms of decentralised pay bargaining. From April 1998, 56 per cent of all local government employees and 60 per cent of all regional government employees were covered by a new system of pay determination—a system consisting of a centrally determined basic salary and three decentralised negotiated allowances based on function, qualifications and results. It also means a movement towards more individualisation of pay for those employees in the public sector who are covered by the agreement (Gill *et al.*, 1998).

In Finland, perhaps one of the most centralised collective bargaining systems in the EU, the central organisations are also gradually moving towards a more decentralised bargaining model. Centralised bargaining began to give way to more localised bargaining about two years ago as a number of issues negotiable at local level began to increase. Earlier, employers in both small and large businesses had demanded a greater degree of flexibility but their demands were usually refused by the trade unions which were particularly worried about the lack of regulation of sub-contracting. However, the trade unions are now taking a more positive view of flexibility and local bargaining because of the high levels of unemployment and the positive feedback they have been getting from workplaces.

Ireland

At the end of 1996, the Government and the social partners in Ireland concluded the fourth three-year agreement since the Programme for National Recovery (PNR) was agreed in the context of an economic and fiscal crisis in Ireland in 1987. Known as the Partnership 2000 (P2000) agreement, it was backed, not just by the Government, but also by the main opposition parties. This indicates a high level of political consensus for such centralised agreements in Ireland at a time when tripartite deals elsewhere in Europe have become less popular than they once were. The relatively successful experience which Ireland has experienced in relation to social partnership is in contrast to the experience of other EU member states.

In exchange for a commitment by the Government on controlled public spending and the maintenance of a firm exchange rate policy coupled with a commitment to economic and social solidarity, the social partners agreed a co-ordinated three-year agreement on pay, including the possibility of minimum wage legislation, tax changes and a package of job creation and training measures all in a context of protecting overall competitiveness.

However, the P2000 agreement came under pressure during the year as the voluntary approach to union recognition was severely criticised by the unions. Many foreign firms locating in Ireland had non-union policies and the dispute at the avidly non-union airline Ryanair highlighted the limitations of the Irish social partnership arrangements: employers and unions have failed to reach a consensus on union recognition.

MAJOR STRIKES

Renault Dispute

The shock announcement by French motor manufacturer Renault, on 28 February 1997, of the closure of its plant at Vilvoorde in Belgium, led to an unprecedented public display of condemnation among the political establishment of the European Union (EU). The closure of the plant, in the Belgian Prime Minister's constituency near Brussels, with the loss of 3100 jobs, was announced without prior consultation with worker representatives. The move was justified by Renault as being part of a wider reorganisation aimed at making savings of over FRF 825 million per year. The closure of the only Renault production site in Belgium was likely to lead to a further 1000 redundancies among suppliers and subcontractors, jobs which, in the current economic climate in Belgium, were unlikely to be replaced in the near future. The announcement came as a particularly heavy blow to a workforce who had thought their jobs safe, having negotiated a major flexibility and investment package only four years previously. The plant is generally regarded as being highly productive and has consistently achieved high levels of quality. The predicament of the workers at Vilvoorde led to an unprecedented display of worker solidarity, not only among employees at other Renault production sites in Europe, but also among workers in other troubled European industries.

The closure decision generated unprecedented levels of sympathy action, not only among Renault workers from production sites across Europe, but also from car workers in Belgium fearful of a similar fate, as well as workers in other threatened industries. Much of this activity was organised by Renault's European Group Committee with the support of the European Metalworkers' Federation (EMF).

Thousands of car workers in Belgium, France and Spain staged protests on 7 March. Renault plants in the three countries were hit by co-ordinated one-hour stoppages, while workers at Volkswagen, Volvo, Opel and Ford plants in

Belgium staged sympathy actions. The Spanish trade unions had immediately come out in support of their Belgian counterparts and criticised the Spanish Government for its indiscriminate use of aid requests. According to Spanish trade union sources, 90 per cent of workers joined the one-hour stoppage. This figure was disputed by management, but it did admit that production was, in fact, halted.

Over 10,000 workers attended a demonstration outside Renault headquarters near Paris on 11 March. Renault workers had come from Belgium, France, Spain, Portugal and Slovenia. This unprecedented show of support could be seen as the first in a line of Euro-strikes which, it could be argued, are likely to result as job losses across European multiply (European Business, 1997).

The decision of Renault's management to close the factory at Vilvoorde was condemned by the European Commission, the European Parliament, the Belgian Government as well as by the unions. On 3 April, a Brussels industrial tribunal ruled that Renault had contravened the rules on information and consultation when it announced the closure of the plant. Under the terms of a judgement handed down on the following day by a French court in Nanterre, Renault was barred from pursuing 'even through subsidiaries, the closure procedure of the Vilvoorde plant until it has fulfilled its obligation to inform and consult its European Works Council'. The French court ruled that consultations were necessary as the decision concerned 'Renault's strategic orientation and was a major change in a European subsidiary that would have repercussions at European level'. The court stated that the company had failed in its duty to inform employees of the impending closure.

The ETUC called for measures to strengthen and amplify existing legislation (on European works councils, collective redundancies and rights in case of company transfers) and create forums for consultation about industrial policies in key sectors affected by EU economic integration and the globalisation of the economy.

On 10 April, a majority of Renault workers at Vilvoorde voted to return to work after a five-week stoppage. Of 3100 employees, 2721 took part in the ballot and 68.7 per cent backed a union recommendation to return to work. On 10 June 1997, Renault management announced the appointment of an independent expert who would 'evaluate, on an economic basis, the potential measures envisaged to compensate for the inefficiency involved in the structure of Renault's production facilities'. By appointing an independent expert, Renault's management was seeking a way out of the dispute.

The events surrounding the closure of the Belgian plant of Renault raise a multitude of questions which are set to occupy the minds of European policy-makers for a long time after the dust of history has settled on the people of Vilvoorde.

Most seriously, the ability of a multinational company to flaunt the letter and spirit of EU legislation in such disregard of the social implications of its actions highlights the persistent gap between the reality of economic and social Europe. In the run-up to Economic and Monetary Union, the Commission is aware that it can ill afford to ignore the impact of budgetary stringency and the location decisions of multinational companies on employment opportunities and social integration, if it is to engender further support for the European project.

The weakness of EU employee protection legislation and its apparent inability to prevent 'social dumping' must be a cause for concern and needs to be addressed in future legislative proposals on employee representation. Recent events may well influence Commission decision-makers in their drafting of legislation on national employee representative bodies to supplement European works councils (EWCs). A proposal in this area is imminent and could be accelerated by the events at Vilvoorde. However, it has to be questioned whether bodies which have the right only to consultation can be effective in preventing such decisions. If information and consultation rights cannot be enforced at the level of EWCs, it seems unlikely that this can be done at the national level, when multinational companies clearly have the ability to play different national interests off against one another.

On the other hand, progress in the area of European workplace organisation is unmistakable, and was displayed during the demonstrations and stoppages which have marked this dispute. This is particularly noteworthy as national interests have in the past overridden European-level solidarity at a time when competition for jobs is intensifying. Disputes over the move of the French Hoover plant to Scotland and the recent negotiations at Ford were marked by a distinct lack of cross-country solidarity.

French Lorry Drivers' Dispute

This was the fourth such strike suffered by France in 13 years—the others being in 1984, 1992 and 1996. The strikes have always been spectacular with road blockades either to stop traffic on major routes or to close access to fuel depots, warehouses and so on.

The French lorry drivers' strike took on a real European dimension. This was primarily owing to the reaction from the public and other countries of the European Union which was often marked by violence and failure to understand the reasons for the strike. Other reasons included the direct involvement of the European Commission and the remedies it suggested. The strike was rooted in French deregulation policies that have not allowed the haulage industry to become competitive with other countries. On the contrary, they have in fact led to excessive internal competition by squeezing prices and wages. In a situation where there are a large number of small companies, employers' associations are faced with questions of legitimacy. They signed two agreements in 1994 and 1996, neither of which they upheld. It remains to be seen whether the new agreement and

French Government measures designed at cleaning up the industry will work. The European Commission is anxious to see an end to ferocious competition by companies due to varying legislation between member states.

Protests by the Unemployed in France

The protest movement of the unemployed began in Marseilles on 4 December 1997, under the initiative of the CGT unemployed committee for the Bouches du Rhône *département*, set up in 1990 when more than 4000 employees were laid off from the naval dockyard at La Ciotat. This locally-based movement spread steadily to other regions of France. Its development was encouraged by the launch of a national appeal, prepared for several months by unemployed associations, housing groups and certain unions. Sit-ins at social security offices, and also welfare and family benefit centres, began in several French *départements*, sometimes jointly organised by the unemployed associations and CGT unemployed committees.

This protest movement, whilst sporadic and patchy nevertheless had the backing of the French public. In a poll published on 31 December 63 per cent of French people either 'supported' or 'sympathised with' the protests. In response to the protests, the French Government had to increase its expenditure for the unemployed and introduced a Bill into the French Parliament in March 1998 containing wide-ranging measures to combat social exclusion.

EUROPEAN LEVEL

The European Union has been going through a period of consolidation recently, attempting to implement existing commitments such as the 1995–97 Social Action Programme and other outstanding pieces of legislation. However, important developments have also occurred—indeed there have been both important substantive and procedural developments over the last year or so. The substantive area has been dominated by the concern over employment and employability first systematically articulated at the Essen Summit in December 1994, which has now culminated in the provisions of the Treaty of Amsterdam (discussed below). Procedurally the main development has come in the development of a 'negotiation track' within the social dialogue process. We focus first on this development and the results achieved so far.

Social Dialogue

In 1996 and 1997 the social dialogue began to bear fruit following the very first framework agreements between the social partners on parental rights and part-time work. This 'negotiation track' offers a real chance for European collective agreements to become a key mechanism for European social reform. This development represents a significant change from the previous format for the social dialogue set by the early Val Duchesse process in 1985. That specified peak organisation consultation (initially ETUC and UNICE) about macro issues facing the Community at that time. The results of these discussions were Joint Opinions that gave a broad steer to policy making but had little direct influence on regulatory mechanisms or their content. The creation of sectoral social dialogue was an attempt to deepen such discussions and extend participation but again with a consultative perspective on the process of social reform that could be quite indirect.

Attempts to give closer involvement to the social partners—now joined by the public sector representatives (CEEP)—became more pressing following the social policy agreement and social protocol of the Maastricht Treaty, especially on issues likely to be sensitive. Under Article 3 of the social policy agreement—now the social chapter—the Commission has the task of 'promoting the consultation of management and labour at Community level . . .' The Commission is required to consult on 'the possible direction of Community action' and later, if it considers such action advisable, on 'the content of the envisaged proposal'. These changes have helped to unblock a host of measures previously vetoed and led directly to the development of mechanisms to translate the Social Charter into concrete reality. The 'negotiation track' allows the social partners to negotiate a European-level framework agreement that is then enforced through a directive. If negotiations fail, then the 'consultation track' allows the views of the social partners to be taken into account by the Commission which then draws up its own directive.

Since then, six issues have been fed into this process. Only two have resulted in framework agreements that were then turned into directives through the 'negotiation track': parental leave (adopted by the Council in June 1996) and part-time work (adopted December 1997). Failure to agree by the social partners has blocked the other four. Two of these were subsequently adopted by the Council as directives: European works councils (September 1994) and the burden of proof in equal opportunities cases (December 1997). The Commission is still to decide—as we see below—on how to make progress on the remaining two, sexual harassment and information and consultation at national level.

Given the long-standing controversial nature of European employment and social policy, the procedural implications of the social dialogue process are path breaking, as the Commission acknowledges in the preamble to the directive on part-time work:

> These procedures allow the European level social partner organisations to conclude framework agreements and request their implementation by a Council decision. As with the previous Directive introduced via this procedure—the Directive on parental leave—the Commission proposal does not seek

to amend in any way the agreement. Therefore the proposed Directive itself is limited to merely presenting the text of the agreement.

The content of the first framework agreement was modest, offering unpaid leave to either parent. However, the second agreement, signed in June 1997, ensures that part-time workers throughout Europe are set to get a legal right to equal treatment with full-time workers as the result of the agreement reached between European employers and unions. These provisions have a particularly significant impact for part-time workers in the UK where part-time work has traditionally been barely regulated at all. However, it should be noted in this context that most EU-level labour market regulation is likely to have a disproportionate effect in the UK as a result of 18 years of free-market experimentation under successive Conservative governments (1979–1997).

Davignon and Provisions on Information and Consultation

The gathering consensus that a mechanism was emerging that could allow disparate views to be heard, provide agreed workable solutions and avoid top-down imposition of legislation has been dealt a blow in recent months. The cause of this has been dissension over the need for information and consultation rights at national level. UNICE backed by the Confederation of British Industry (CBI) and German, Portuguese and Greek employers' bodies have indicated their out-right opposition to such a directive and have refused to start negotiations with the unions on the issue (*The Guardian*, 17 March 1998). What is possibly more surprising is the support given to this coalition by the British Labour Government which is insisting that this is not a European matter but, under the principle of subsidiarity, the province of national law.

As with many of the items of European social policy, this issue has a long history, effectively first mooted in the early 1970s as the European Company Statute. This was intended to give a common framework for worker involvement in companies established at European rather than national level. Following years of deadlock, the Commission set up an expert group under the chairmanship of the former Vice-President of the European Commission, Etienne Davignon, to try and identify a possible solution which would meet everyone's concerns. The Davignon Group's report was presented to the European Commission on 14 May 1997. However the furore over the Vilvoorde closure somewhat overtook these deliberations and highlighted the gaps in existing consultative arrangements in current domestic and transnational companies. The social and employment affairs directorate of the Commission, DGV, thereupon launched the first stage of its consultation procedures with the European social partners on the possible direction of policy on information and consultation at national level.

In doing so, Social Affairs Commissioner Padraig Flynn stressed that existing Community and national legislation should take into account:

(i) The need to respect the fundamental social right of employees to be informed and consulted in advance on any decisions likely to affect them.

(ii) The effectiveness of the process of consultation of employees which would permit a suitable response to the processes of change arising from economic and technical trends.

(iii) The recognition that the improvement of the competitiveness of European firms through increased productivity is better achieved by a workforce which is more committed and more willing to accept new types of work organisation.

(iv) The fact that worker involvement enhances job security by ensuring that the process of change will be managed in such a way that it strikes a balance between employees' needs and interests and those of the firm.

(v) The need to ensure the development of effective consultation, generating a collaborative spirit.

(vi) The importance of preventing the risks and anticipating the problems involved in the management of change by introducing efficient systems of forward management of employment.

However, the second stage of consultation launched in November broke down. This stage had focused on the possible content of the policy. The trade unions favoured an EU initiative and the establishment of binding rules, whilst the employers did not accept the need for a European-level initiative at all. The Commission had suggested measures in three areas:

● Mechanisms that allow the early identification of negative social consequences of changes in work organisation.
● The establishment of permanent, structured mechanisms for informing/consulting workers.
● The introduction of effective sanctions to be applied in cases of violation of the workers' right to be informed and consulted.

It is now unlikely that a framework agreement can be reached in this area, and the wider consequences have been described as a 'serious setback for the social dialogue' by the President of the Commission, Jacques Santer (*The Guardian*, 17 March 1998). However, in a move reminiscent of a previous breakdown over European works councils, Commissioner Flynn has indicated that he will present the Commission with a proposal for a directive on national level consultation and information. However, it is yet to be seen whether the Commission will actually adopt the consultation track and implement a directive against the views of the opposing coalition that could include in its ranks the German Government (European and Industrial Relations International, March 1998). 1998 is therefore likely to prove a defining year in terms of the social dialogue and its development.

Treaty of Amsterdam

With unemployment approaching 20 million across the 15 member states of the EU, job creation was one of the main problems continuing to confront the social partners in 1997. The single most significant event in this respect was the conclusion of the new Treaty on European Union (the Treaty of Amsterdam) under the Dutch Presidency in June (Goetschy and Pochet, 1997). The Treaty incorporated the provisions of the agreement on social policy agreed at Maastricht into the main body of the text, by which means the UK 'signed the social chapter', and introduced a new clause (Article 6A) conferring competence on the Council to take action 'to combat discrimination based on sex, racial or ethnic origin, religion or belief, disability, age or sexual orientation'.

However, from the point of view of job creation, the most important innovation was the insertion of a new chapter on employment and explicit references to the EU's role in promoting the 'co-ordination between employment policies of the member states with a view to enhancing their effectiveness by developing a co-ordinated strategy for employment' (Article 3). On the one hand, competence is limited under the Treaty to promoting co-operation and support which leaves intact current responsibilities for active labour market policies with the member states. On the other hand, member states are now required to submit an annual report to the Commission and Council on the steps they have taken to meet the guidelines to be adopted every year by the Council on employment policy. These guidelines will be proposed by the Commission and, following consultations, will be adopted by the Council by qualified majority voting. The Council, in assessing implementation of its guidelines, may make recommendations to individual member states on the basis of which it will draw up—in collaboration with the Commission—an annual report on employment conditions across the EU.

These measures were followed up in November under the Luxembourg Presidency by the first-ever Council focused entirely on employment issues—the 'Jobs Summit'. It agreed to implement the terms of the new employment chapter without delay so that employment policies of member states could be co-ordinated from the start of 1998. The guidelines adopted by the Council fall under four main headings: improving employability; developing entrepreneurship; encouraging adaptability; and promoting equal opportunities.

(i) Employability

Member states are urged to offer some kind of employability measure (such as training, retraining or work experience) to all young unemployed people within six months of becoming unemployed and to all adult unemployed within 12 months. The social partners should be involved in negotiating relevant measures and particular attention should be paid to the interests of the long-term unemployed. Young people should be discouraged from leaving the school system early.

(ii) Entrepreneurship

Setting up and running business should be encouraged—amongst other means—by easing the administrative and tax burdens on small- and medium-sized businesses (SMEs) and by aiming to cut labour costs to promote expansion and job creation.

(iii) Adaptability

The key word under this heading is 'flexibility', with member states recommended to investigate the legal bases of employment contracts and to consider introducing new forms that combine job security with adaptability. All new regulations should be assessed for their impact on employment and the social partners are encouraged to negotiate—at all levels—on new forms of flexible work organisation.

(iv) Equal Opportunities

Higher participation rates of women in the labour market should be encouraged. To this end child care provision should be improved and full compliance sought with existing legislation and agreements on part-time work, parental leave and career breaks. The interests of people with disabilities who are either in work or seeking work must also be protected.

Although member states may request exemption from these measures, the intention of the Summit was to promote convergence of labour market and employment policies much like the economic convergence required under the Maastricht criteria for entry into economic and monetary union.

No extra spending is required by member states, but a new budget heading—the European employment initiative—worth 450 million ECU over three years will be introduced to finance job creation in SMEs. In addition, the European Investment Bank will make 10 billion ECU available for SMEs, new sectors and trans-European networks. The general reaction to the Jobs Summit from both politicians and social partners was favourable. The Council of Social and Labour Affairs Ministers, meeting in December, subsequently adopted a resolution requiring them to draw up their own national employment plans by 15 April 1998 which would then be examined at the Cardiff summit under the UK Presidency the following June. The first annual report on the employment situation across the EU will be submitted to the December 1998 summit under the Austrian Presidency in Vienna.

LABOUR MARKET POLICY IN THE EU COUNTRIES

An analysis of developments in labour market policy across the member states in 1997 reveals a battery of measures which already reflect those recommended at the Luxembourg Summit. The four headings outlined above comprise what might be called a 'menu of policies' from which member states have already been selecting in line with their own particular national circumstances. Ad hoc measures were introduced in a number of countries, though major jobs packages were unveiled in Belgium, Denmark, France, Germany, Ireland, Italy, Spain and the UK in attempts to deal with certain structural problems associated with their individual labour markets.

The German Government adopted a wide-ranging set of amendments to the Employment Promotion Act in March. Most of these came into force on 1 January 1998, and were intended, according to Norbert Blüm, the Labour Minister, to preserve around two million jobs a year. The amendments aim to improve placement and training services, encourage new SMEs and revise current employment creation schemes. The State will take over responsibility from the employer for the sickness payments of recruits who had been long-term unemployed, and—in a restrictive measure reflected also in Denmark and the UK (see below)—clamp down on the criteria which the unemployed may use to refuse job offers.

The following month, in April, Spanish employers and unions agreed a set of three major reforms together known as the 'April Accords'. They covered long-standing areas of difficulty—employment security, collective bargaining and gaps in sectoral regulation left over from the Franco regime.

Of these, the most significant from the point of view of job creation, was the area of employment security. The Spanish labour market has in recent years been characterised by high unemployment (currently around 22 per cent) and an exceptionally high incidence of various forms of insecure employment. The national statistics office (INEM) has reported that around 96 per cent of new contracts signed in 1996 were temporary and that 70 per cent of fixed-term contracts were for a period of less than three months. Employers had complained that this situation was the result of the high cost of severance payments in cases of dismissal. Employers and unions agreed to introduce a new 'permanent employment promotion contract' aimed in particular at the young and long-term unemployed. When the agreement was enacted in May, the Government introduced incentives to employers to adopt these new contracts: a reduction in employers' social security costs of between 40 per cent and 60 per cent depending on the individual for the first two years, rising to 70–90 per cent for the entire duration of the contract if the new recruit has disabilities. Of all new contracts signed in June 8.5 per cent were permanent ones, compared with only 4 per cent in June 1996, a development that indicated early success.

This theme—a trade-off involving reductions in social security contributions as an inducement to create jobs—was a common one in 1997, though set against different national contexts. In Belgium, the social partners failed to conclude a national intersectoral agreement at the start of 1997, which left the Government to announce its own job creation programme in the wake of unrest over the closures of the Renault plant at Vilvoorde and the closure of the Forges de Clabecq steel plant. The plan centred on reductions in social security contributions as an incentive for SMEs to recruit, encouragement to reduce working time and subsidies to promote the training of workers who had been long-term unemployed. In Italy too, the Government enacted in June the 'Treu package' which, as in Spain, reflected changes that had already been agreed by the social partners in September 1996. The wide-ranging package included measures to legalise the use of temporary work agencies, regulate the extension of fixed-term contracts, improve training provisions, promote environmental protection and stimulate the use of part-time work through reducing employers' social security contributions. Further reductions will apply if, for example, the part-timers are young or women returnees to the labour market.

Interventionist measures were also much in evidence in the Labour Government's first budget in the UK, following its election victory in May. The 'welfare to work' programme, to apply across the country by April 1998, grants financial incentives to companies to recruit young people who had been unemployed for at least six months though these rise if the young person had been unemployed for over two years. Under the 'New Deal', young people are to be given the choice of employment, training, work in the voluntary sector or the chance to join an environmental task force. A windfall levy on the privatised companies, principally utilities, was imposed to pay for the programme.

A little later in the year, the Danish Government enacted its own 'welfare to work' programme, which as in the UK, aimed to make finding work more attractive. Access by the unemployed to social benefits has been restricted and measures introduced to promote the employment prospects of the young, the disabled and those with mental health and drug problems by rapidly offering work within the initial stages of unemployment. Then, in December, the Government's 1998 Finance Bill cracked down harder on the unemployed themselves: they are now required to accept a job outside their area of expertise within six rather than 12 months and they may be required to commute for up to four hours a day rather than three.

The incoming Irish Government—a Fianna Fail/Progressive Democrat coalition—elected in June quickly set out its social and employment policy programme that included commitment to the existing intersectoral pay agreement, Partnership 2000, a national hourly minimum wage and pledges to create 25,000 jobs targeted at the long-term unemployed and to improve training.

The new French Government, meanwhile, also elected in June, likewise moved quickly to fulfil its commitments on job creation. Its main pledge had been to create 700,000 jobs for young people, half in the private and half in the public sector. Those in the private sector were to be negotiated by the social partners in the context of a tripartite national conference on wages, employment and working time which duly took place in October. There, the Government announced that it would reduce the statutory working week to 35 hours by 1 January 2000 which, linked with modest pay rises, would give employers the framework within which to negotiate the creation of jobs. As encouragement, and in line with moves noted above in countries like Belgium, Italy and Spain, employers will receive social security subsidies on a mounting scale according to the level of reduction in working time, the number of new employees recruited and the kind of employee recruited (with more for young people). The subsidies will last for a five-year period.

In the public sector, the French Government passed legislation in September to create 350,000 jobs to meet 'emerging needs' not currently met. These include posts as school co-ordinators, housing agents, transport officers, justice mediators and environmental officers (judging from experience in Italy and the UK, the environment is clearly a growth area for employment creation across Europe). Local authorities, schools, hospitals, the non-profit making sector and other such agencies may apply to the Government for funding to recruit unemployed people between the ages of 18 and 26. They will be paid at the level of the statutory national minimum wage (SMIC), with the Government paying 80 per cent, including social security contributions. So far Ministries, the postal service, the State-owned railways and the utilities are participating, though it is not clear what will happen to these jobs once their five-year duration has elapsed.

SOCIAL SECURITY AND PENSIONS

Most EU member states were committed to joining the first wave of member-ship of European monetary union, and were therefore concerned to ensure that they met the Maastricht economic convergence criteria covering the rate of inflation, long-term interest rates, public sector debt and the budget deficit, within the context of a stable currency. As we have seen earlier in this article, the pressures required to meet these criteria resulted in a variety of disputes across member states as governments reined in ever harder on public spending.

For this reason, and as a result too of concerns about ageing populations and high rates of unemployment, most countries across the EU introduced over 1997 measures to reform social security and pensions arrangements.

In Italy, pensions reforms in the autumn temporarily forced the resignation of the Prime Minister, Romano Prodi, when the Party *Refondazione Comunista* (Reconstructed Communist Party—RC) refused to support the original proposals. In an extraordinary trade-off, RC subsequently agreed but only after Mr Prodi had agreed to introduce a 35-hour week by the year 2001 for all companies with over 15 employees. The package of measures, as agreed with the unions in November, includes increasing the number of years' contributions required to qualify for a full pension, raising the retirement age in stages and harmonising private and public pensions provisions.

The Italian reforms were based on a tripartite agreement concluded in 1995 (the 'Dini reforms') which no doubt explains their eventual acceptability to the unions. In the same way, when the Spanish Government enacted pensions reforms in July 1997, they too were based on an agreement reached in October 1996 by the social partners. These reforms increase contributions levels, lengthen the number of years required to qualify for the full State pension and reduce the appeal of early retirement, amongst much else. In the autumn, the Austrian Government also announced a range of reforms to the State pension system which included similar measures and came into force on 1 January 1998. At the end of the year, the Swedish Government, in consultation with other political parties, proposed a new method for calculating the State pension and diverting some of its financing from the public into the private sector.

Other countries too introduced a range of measures to control social security and pensions expenditure. Over the year the Dutch debated the use of tax windfalls to help finance State pensions, the UK restricted early retirement for teachers, and workers on the Barcelona Metro took strike action to oppose reductions in their pension entitlements. The social partners in Finland managed to agree on arrangements to safeguard the social security system against possible turbulence caused by entry into EMU but in Germany opposition from the Social Democrats in Parliament forced the Government to raise VAT rather than increase statutory pensions contributions. In Greece, a critical OECD report published in June recommended raising the retirement age and tightening pension eligibility requirements to save the country's social security system from collapse.

A striking feature of this overview of social security and pensions in 1997 is the large measure of consensus that has been achieved over the need for reform. Countries which have not been traditionally noted for social consultation—such as Greece and Spain—have managed to gain support for controversial programmes through the judicious use of social dialogue between employers, unions and government. They have then based legislation on the agreements between the social partners. Matters that once would have sparked industrial and political conflict are increasingly being seen as matters for technical resolution. This point should not be taken too far, since in both Italy and Germany political parties in parliament prevented their respective governments from exercising a free hand. Nevertheless, the apparent inevitability of European monetary union has led the social partners to accept a common foundation of discourse that fosters greater opportunities for consensus building than before. It is also noticeable that in certain other countries—such as Denmark and the UK —governments are introducing greater elements of compulsion to deal with unemployment and the reform of social security.

FURTHER DEVELOPMENTS

New Legislation

Much of the new labour legislation enacted across Europe in 1997 tended to support employers in their quest for flexibility in one form or another. In Finland, legislation taking effect from January 1998 tightened up on certain areas of employee participation, such as consultation periods over proposed redundancies. In Sweden, unions protested against amendments to the Security of Employment Act that, amongst other measures, allowed easier recruitment by companies following redundancies. In the Netherlands, the Government prepared a Bill to raise the threshold for works councils from 35 to 50 employees. However, in Denmark, the Health and Safety Act passed in May widens the role of employers and unions in setting appropriate standards at work and increases penalties on companies that flout the law (to the anger of the employers, who withdrew from the consultative forum).

One legislative theme that dominated the year in particular was the crackdown on immigrant and illegal labour. New legislation which came into force in the UK in January 1997 made it a criminal offence for an employer to recruit someone who does not have permission to live and work in the country. In March, France passed a law to combat work carried out in the informal sector of the economy but also—as in the UK—to increase penalties against employers found to be using workers without a work permit. In July, the Greek Government tightened up on the registration, residence and work requirements of immigrants, in an attempt to control those entering illegally from neighbouring countries. And Austria enacted legislation to restrict entry of non-EU nationals into the country from January 1998 and to tighten renewal of residency permits of certain of those unwilling to work.

Two innovations were the commitments by new governments in both Ireland and the UK to introduce a national minimum pay system, an instrument unknown in either country till then.

Working Time

At intersectoral level, reductions in working time in 1997 were often linked to job creation. This link was clearly established in France where an official report on the operation of the 1996 Robien law claimed that up to 900,000 jobs had been created or preserved through reductions in working time and accompanying cuts in employer social security contributions. The new Government announced that it would reduce the statutory working week to 35 hours by the year 2000, whilst a similar move was also declared in Italy—though in that case it was the result of a compromise between coalition partners in parliament. In Greece, by contrast, the tripartite confidence pact concluded in November ruled out any mention of the 35-hour week as a subject too contentious for inclusion at that stage. As a result, the General Confederation of Greek Labour (GSEE) was split internally and only narrowly agreed to sign the pact at all.

The terms of the working time directive were implemented in a number of countries, most notably in Austria where following years of negotiations on working time the social partners at last concluded an agreement in February which was then enacted the next month. The new law brings Austria into line with the directive but also improves flexibility by, for example, encouraging annualised hours systems.

In the Netherlands, the social partners negotiated a framework agreement to promote part-time work, whilst the Swiss union confederation (SGB) called for a referendum on the introduction of the 36-hour week in an attempt to create jobs. Developments elsewhere took place at sectoral and company level. Greek employers and unions in the retail sector agreed longer shop opening hours in March, whilst in Spain the savings bank, Caja de Madrid, decided to extend its opening hours, reinforcing a trend in that sector. In September negotiators in the metalworking sector in northern Germany reached a settlement on part-time work for older employees thereby averting a serious dispute.

Over the summer the Swedish National Board of Statistics sounded a note of warning when it revealed that labour force participation rates in 1996 were lower than at any point over the previous 20 years but that the total number of hours worked had not fallen in proportion. The conclusion was that workers were merely working yet longer hours and that—in Sweden at least—reducing working time would fail to create many jobs.

Equal Opportunities

The Dutch Presidency officially declared 1997 European Year Against Racism at The Hague in January. Information and communications events designed to highlight best practice in the fight against racism and xenophobia were held throughout the year backed by a budget of some 4.7 million ECU. One of the first acts of the newly elected Labour Government in the UK was to agree to the creation of a new EU centre to monitor racism and xenophobia to be based in Vienna, a move that had been vetoed by the outgoing Conservative régime. Later on in the year, the Swedish Government announced that it would draft legislation to amend existing race discrimination and sexual harassment laws which it subsequently submitted to the social partners for consultation.

During the course of the year, both Austria and Belgium adopted legislation to ensure gender equality in night work. In the case of Austria, the legislation allows collective agreements to overrule the statutory ban on women's night work, but further amendments are still required to bring the country's regulations on this issue into line with EU equality legislation. In the spring, some 650,000 Austrians (around 10 per cent of the electorate) signed a petition demanding improved rights for women at work, especially in relation to equal pay, social security coverage and child care provision. Around the same time, the Commission's first annual report on equal opportunities for women and men across the EU revealed increasing diversification in the position of women related to characteristics including age, skills and children. In addition, employment segregation continued, female unemployment had risen in relation to that of male workers and women's pay remains substantially less. Social dialogue between EU-level employers and unions on a possible agreement on sexual harassment broke down over the summer, though the Commission announced its intention to make progress on this issue in 1998. However, as we have seen, the Council of Labour and Social Affairs Ministers, at its meeting in December, adopted the directive on part-time work—the result of an agreement between the EU social partners in June—and the directive on the burden of proof in sex discrimination cases (which had been first proposed back in 1988).

The European Court of Justice, in a judgement issued in November, ruled that positive action that supports women over men for promotion is allowable provided that objective criteria are used to assess the candidates and that the male candidate will be promoted where the criteria are in his favour.

PROSPECTS: RETHINKING REGULATION

Globalisation in general and the Single European Market in particular have created pressures requiring a rethinking at all levels—intersectoral, sectoral and company—of notions of adaptability, flexibility and regulation. These pressures have themselves built up in the context of major long-term trends affecting European labour markets, including the growth of the services sector, increasing female participation rates and burgeoning forms of so-called 'atypical' work. It is hardly surprising, therefore, that preparations for European Monetary Union continued to intensify the debate about the development of new models of employee relations practice at all these levels during the course of 1997.

Signs began to emerge last year of more coherent responses to these pressures. The unions were still for the most part haemorrhaging membership and so continued with their recruitment drives and merger policies, notably in Austria and

Germany. However, in 1997 it became clear that they were preparing steps beyond merely national mergers by also planning cross-border alliances and other forms of EU-level partnership. There was also a major co-ordinated international protest against the closure of the Renault Vilvoorde plant in Belgium, which could herald further such action in the future.

One of the most significant moves towards this process of 'rethinking regulation' was the consolidation of the social dialogue process at EU level. The Council of Social and Labour Ministers adopted a directive on part-time work based on an intersectoral agreement concluded by employers and unions at EU level. EU sector-level social dialogue continued to develop and the number of European works councils soared throughout the year. Crucially, the newly elected Labour Government in the UK 'signed the social chapter' that made the social dialogue a genuinely pan-EU process. According to the UK Trades Union Congress this brought an extra 300 multinational companies world-wide within the scope of the European works councils directive, a global total of 1480.

These trends reveal the emergence—gradual but nevertheless distinct—of an EU model of employee relations based on agreement at intersectoral, sectoral and company levels and reinforced, at the intersectoral level, by legislation in the form of directives whether or not agreement can be reached. Europe has therefore not turned its back on regulation in favour of laissez faire flexibility. It is true that there was a period of uncertainty—especially during the 1991–97 phase between Maastricht and the defeat of the Conservative Government in the UK—but now Europe is beginning to rethink regulation. It is embracing new patterns of work, but acknowledging that flexibility must not lead to a free-for-all. On the contrary, workers must be protected from the excesses of adaptability and efficiency (for which many read 'exploitation') through the regulation of working time, parental leave and European works councils, amongst other areas. This is often linked to a greater awareness of the needs to integrate working and family life.

In 1997, this process went even further. For the first time, the EU adopted an explicit role in employment creation through the provisions of the Treaty of Amsterdam. These provisions provide for EU-wide parameters for the assessment of job creation measures on which member states must now report annually. To this extent EU social policy has refocused: from the rights of workers it now embraces the interests of non-workers—the unemployed whose numbers stood at 10.7 per cent of the labour force towards the end of the year.

This rethinking at EU level to a large extent reflects similar developments within member states. Action was taken in 1997 in most countries to rectify perceived rigidities in labour markets, but in many cases they involved consultations between the social partners and a measure of negotiated re-regulation but along different fault-lines: the growth of company pacts in Germany, the confidence pact in Greece, Partnership 2000 in Ireland, the 'Treu package' in Italy, the April Accords in Spain and the proposed national minimum wage in the UK, amongst many other examples, are all attempts within their respective national frameworks to bring a degree of security back into labour markets that, subject to pressure and turbulence, looked increasingly insecure. Explicit recognition of the problems of the unemployed in this context must be an advance for the development of 'social Europe' but the effects of EMU on employment levels remain to be seen.

ACKNOWLEDGEMENTS

The authors are indebted to The European Foundation for the use of material from its European Industrial Relations Observatory as well as the *European Industrial Relations Review*.

REFERENCES

Employment in Europe 1997 (1997), Unit A.1 DGV European Commission (Luxembourg: Office for Official Publications of the EC).
European and Industrial Relations International, Monthly Journal EIRI Associates, Dublin.
European Business, (1997), March 12, London.
EIRObserver (1997), January to December, Nos. 1–6.
European Industrial Relations Observatory, Dublin: European Foundation.
European Industrial Relations Review (1997), January to December, Nos. 276–287.
European Trade Union Information Bulletin, (1998) 1, MBO Education and Training Ltd. Huddersfield.
European Works Councils Bulletin (1998), January/February, No.13.
Gill, C., Knudsen, H. and Lind, J (1998), 'Are there cracks in the Danish Model of industrial relations?', *Industrial Relations Journal*, 29, 1, 30–42.
Goetschy, J. and Pochet, P (1997), 'The Treaty of Amsterdam: a new approach to employment and social affairs?', *Transfer*, 3, 3, 607–620.
World Labour Report 1997–98 (1997) International Labour Office, Geneva.

The new social dialogue: procedural structuring, first results and perspectives

Berndt Keller and Bernd Sörries

In the recent literature, the term 'social dialogue' has been used in a rather encompassing sense to include all forms of concertation between employees, employers and governments (ILO, 1997). Furthermore, tripartism at the national as well as the supranational level has been labelled under this heading.

In contrast to this rather confusing terminology, we define social dialogue as the relationship between management and labour, hereafter called the social partners, and with the Commission. These dialogues, which have their legal base in the revised Treaty on the European Union, can occur at both the interprofessional and sectoral European level. The focus of our analysis will be the interprofessional European level only, because the first European framework agreements have been signed here; signatory parties have been the European peak associations, i.e. UNICE (Union of Industrial and Employers' Confederation of Europe) for private industry and CEEP (European Centre of Enterprises with Public Participation) for public enterprises on the employers' side, and ETUC (European Trade Union Confederation) on the employees' side. In contrast to these results, there have been no framework agreements at the sectoral or regional level, although this alternative is of relevance in major member states and has not been excluded by legal provisions. Agreements at the level of multinational enterprises, which might be concluded between management and European Works Councils, will also be excluded because of their different legal base in the Directive on the 'Establishment of a European Works Council or a procedure in Community-scale undertakings and Community-scale groups of undertakings for the purposes of informing and consulting employees' (Marginson and Sisson, 1996; 1998).

After outlining a brief recent history of social dialogue, we will describe and explain the basic legal provisions of the new social dialogue and the emerging structure of procedural regulation (communications of the Commission) including

Berndt Keller is Professor of Labour Market Policy and Bernd Sörries is a doctoral student at the University of Konstanz.

their protracted, but widely neglected implementation problems. The main, empirical part of our paper will be devoted to the first, partly successfully completed, partly failed attempts of the European social partners to make use of their new opportunities (European Works Councils, burden of proof, parental leave, and part-time work). Finally, we will discuss likely perspectives and forthcoming problems (such as the implications of European Monetary Union and the employment chapter of the Amsterdam Treaty).

RECENT HISTORY OF THE SOCIAL DIALOGUE

Throughout the late 1970s and early 1980s social integration was only of secondary importance (Addison and Siebert, 1994). After these years of stalemate, the Commission, headed by Jacques Delors, sought to widen the so-far narrow scope of European social policy, which was regarded as a necessity to gain the support of workers and their representatives for the ongoing economic integration. The general idea was to strengthen the so-called social dimension of the internal market, which was to be completed by the end of 1992.

The Commission took the initiative and launched a new form of purely voluntary co-operation between the European institutions and the European social partners. The undisputed aim of the new strategy was, first, to bring the social partners back in, and, second, to promote a European version of collective bargaining. The social partners, having strict rights and obligations at the national level, were supposed to fulfil the same functions at the European level.

The history of the social dialogue can be traced back at least to the mid 1980s (Carley, 1993). The results of this old version of the social dialogue were a series of joint opinions (like introduction of new technologies, adaptability of labour markets, vocational training) which were not binding for the signatory parties (EIRR, 1997a). Although this form of dialogue fostered the mutual understanding of employers and employees, it was unable to meet the high expectations, especially of the Commission and European trade unions. The crucial factor was that the employers' associations considered this dialogue as sufficient and appropriate for European social policy making and were not willing to enter a new, more demanding phase of social dialogue with the negotiation of collective agreements as the main focus (Rhodes, 1991).

After more than one decade, this traditional, purely voluntary dialogue reveals a mixed outcome. On the one hand, the social partners could make a positive contribution to European social policy issues and they helped to stimulate and orient Community developments on questions of employment, macro-economic policies or training. On the other, the overall results were considered to be disappointing because of their non-binding nature.

In 1993, the member states of the European Community paved the way for the new social dialogue by ratifying the Social Protocol with its Agreement on Social Policy annexed to the Treaty on European Union. The member states wished to continue along the path laid down in the 1989 Social Charter and its accompanying Social Action Programme (Lange, 1993). As a result, the lagging behind of the social dimension was supposed to come to an end. However, this integrative impetus could not gain unanimous support from all member states: due to the opt-out of the UK, this part of the so-called Maastricht Treaty covered only 11 member states. As a consequence, a debate on the so-called variable geometry of European social policy was raised (Streeck, 1994). External observers argued that two forms of European integration, one for all member states, the other leaving out the UK, would lead to an incoherent process of social integration and would end in a Europe á la carte (Bercusson, 1994). This controversy, which had always been of doubtful practical importance, lost its significance when the new British government, elected in 1997, agreed 'to opt back in' and sign the Social Protocol. In the meantime, the new members who joined the European Union in 1994 (Austria, Finland, and Sweden) were covered by its provisions from the very beginning.

Finally, at the Amsterdam summit in mid-1997, the provisions of the Social Protocol were confirmed by all members and incorporated into European law as the revised social chapter (Article 117–119). Furthermore, an employment chapter was added to the Treaty. Both provisions might increase the EU authority to enter a new phase of social integration.

PROVISIONS OF THE SOCIAL PROTOCOL AND THE AGREEMENT ON SOCIAL POLICY

The Agreement on Social Policy can be traced back to a proposal submitted by the social partners within the tripartite framework of the old social dialogue, which took place at Val Duchesse. Their proposal was included, without major changes, under the heading of the Social Protocol in the Treaty on European Union (Buda, 1995).

Provisions of the Social Protocol seek to increase the impact employees and employers' associations, called the social partners, have on European social policy. Within the renewed, so-called principle of subsidiarity (van Kersbergen and Verbeek, 1994), private regulations by the social partners are given priority over initiatives put forward by the Commission and the member states. New rights and obligations are granted to the social partners, who are expected to be much closer to social policy issues than other, public authorities. Their importance at the national level is supposed to be replicated at the European one. Furthermore, the legitimacy of European social policy (Jachtenfuchs, 1995), a crucial problem from the start, can be improved by more and larger private participation in policy making. Finally, the provisions of the Protocol provide the EU with greater authority to address the social challenges emerging with the internal market project.

Throughout the 1980s, progress in European social policy was rather limited because of decision making rules that required unanimity in the vast majority of cases (Article 100). The Social Protocol tried to put an end to this stalemate by broadening the capacity of the European Union.

Legislation based on Article 2, section 1 requires qualified majority voting instead of unanimity in the Council to become European law. This legal base establishes the Community's legal power in particular for the improvement of the working environment. This includes the protection of workers' health and safety, working conditions, the information and consultation of workers, equality between men and women with regard to labour market opportunities and treatment at work, and the integration of persons excluded from the labour market.

Legislation based on Article 2, section 3 requires unanimity. It refers to social security, social protection of workers, protection of workers when their employment contract is terminated, representation and collective defence of the interest of workers and employers. This includes codetermination, conditions of employment for third country nationals legally residing in Community territory and financial contributions for promotion of employment and job creation, without prejudice to the provisions relating to the Social Fund.

Last but not least, it has to be stressed that, according to Article 2, section 6, regulations on strikes and lock-outs cannot be founded on the basis of the Agreement.

The Agreement officially recognises the social partners and provides a mandatory instead of a purely voluntary process for their consultation (see Figure 1). When formulating proposals in the social policy field, the Commission must consult the social partners twice: first, prior to submitting any drafts for legislation, on the possible direction of Community action; second, and more specifically, on the content of the envisaged proposal.

At stage two of the consultation process, the social partners should forward to the Commission an opinion or a recommendation on its proposal. They may also decide to inform the Commission that they wish to reach a European level agreement on the issue; thus, they have the ability to substitute the Commission's proposal by starting 'bargaining in the shadow of the law' (Bercusson, 1992). If the social partners manage to conclude an agreement, their negotiated compromise could be adopted by the Council and, thus, become the base for European social policy making. The Commission postpones its own initiative for the period of negotiation and withdraws it if an agreement is reached. Time frames, i.e. six weeks for the first and nine months for the second phase, are indicated to avoid conscious delays of the negotiation process; longer periods can be mutually agreed upon. As a consequence of this legal innovation with its extended and broadened form of participation, the social partners have obtained a status similar

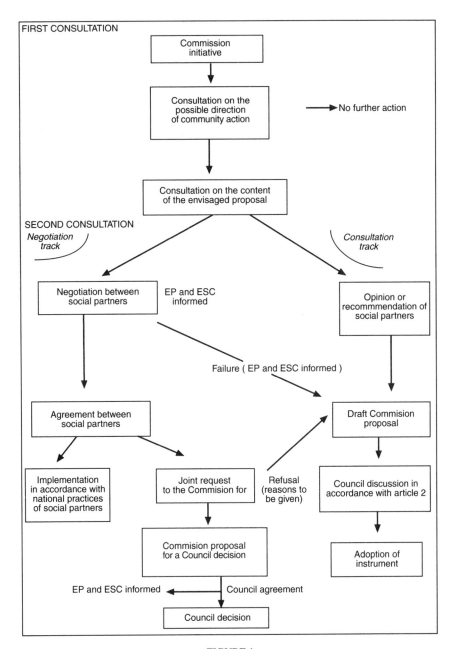

FIGURE 1
Operational chart showing the implementation of the Agreement on Social Policy (Com (93) 600)

to legislators. Thus, the Social Protocol has introduced a more formalised structure in comparison with the previous, more pluralist form of interest intermediation (Rhodes, 1995).

To summarise, the first part of the Social Protocol structures the phase of policy formulation and decision-making by defining procedural prerequisites. Of equal importance is the implementation of European wide agreements at the national level. The European Union in general and the Commission in particular, have no competencies and/or institutions of their own (Majone, 1997) and, thus, depend on procedures and institutions at the level of the member states. Furthermore, legal conditions and/or contractual circumstances of industrial relations differ significantly. Therefore, in its second part, the Protocol provides two alternatives for implementing framework agreements concluded on social policy matters mentioned in Article 2:

(i)   The social partners can implement them 'in accordance with the procedures and practices specific to management and labour and the member states' (Article 4, section 2).
(ii) The signatories to an agreement can 'jointly request a Council decision on a proposal by the Commission' (Article 4, section 2).

Both alternatives, which are considered to be equivalents, are not clearly specified. Therefore this focal issue had to be addressed by the Commission in more detail later. The first framework agreements served as test cases for the stepwise development of implementation procedures. Before the agreements, it was definitely not clear which instruments (according to Article 189) could possibly be used to transfer framework agreements into European law. The Social Protocol itself does not exclude any possible instrument of legislation (directive, decision among others).

DEVELOPMENT OF PROCEDURES

The above-mentioned general provisions of the Social Protocol are characterised by a significant lack of detailed regulation. Therefore, the Commission has tried to develop, at least to some extent, a more coherent frame of reference by structuring the process of political decision-making. Basically, it followed the policy cycle by addressing problems of recognition and participation first. Questions of implementation were neither tackled in detail, nor solved well in advance but left to the first framework agreements concluded by the social partners. These attempts at procedural regulation have consisted of different communications.

The First Communication

In the first, 1993 'Communication concerning the application of the Agreement on Social Policy' (COM (93) 600 final), the Commission institutionalised a two-step procedure of consultation, already described above, in more detail. In this communication, the Commission also followed suggestions made by the Val Duchesse social partners and defined which criteria organisations seeking to be acknowledged as social partners, at both the intersectoral and the sectoral level, have to fulfil.

(i) They have to be cross-industry or relate to specific categories and be organised at the European level.

(ii) They have to consist of organisations which are themselves an integral and recognised part of member state social partner structures.

(iii) They have to have the capacity to negotiate agreements, be representative of all the member states, and have adequate structures to ensure their effective participation.

However, this very first attempt to define the frame of reference leaves major problems unsolved.

First, these criteria for recognition, formulated by the Val Duchesse social partners and applied by the Commission, remain vague and some of the decisions taken in the first round of recognition could be considered as arbitrary (cf. COM (93) 600 final, Annex, for a complete list). As a consequence, the Commissions' first response to the new provisions restricted the emergence of a sustainable procedural regulation. Associations of both sides, which belong to the interprofessional as well as to the sectoral level, but had not been officially recognised as social partners in this first round have kept exerting political pressure for their recognition (EIRR, 1995a). The achievement of this status is of crucial importance because it would make them part of the policy network, grant official rights of participation in the consultation process, and ensure financial support. Otherwise, they will have to struggle for survival (Keller and Henneberger, 1997).

Second, despite some clarification in the process of recognition, different problems of voluntary framework agreements still remain unresolved. We know from our experience that the conclusion of national agreements creates one problem, their application constitutes another. Implementation of European framework agreements is even more difficult because an additional level has to be bridged. As mentioned above, two alternative modes, collective bargaining by national social partners and European as well as national legislation, are provided by the Social Protocol.

If the first alternative of private initiative was chosen, a coherent implementation would be extremely unlikely, due to major legal and institutional differences between national industrial relations systems (Locke, Kochan and Piore,

1995; Ferner and Hyman, 1998). Another crucial factor is that agreements voluntarily implemented have to ensure a coverage of 100 per cent of the work force. An implicit prerequisite would either be a very high level of centralisation of the national bargaining system and of the participating associations/confederations on both sides, or alternatively, close, strict co-ordination of sectoral bargaining.

A very high coverage rate would be a necessary precondition; however, we know from recent comparative studies that coverage rates differ very much across West European countries. Rates are rather high in some countries (like in Belgium, Finland, or Sweden), but comparatively low in some others (like the Netherlands, Portugal, and Spain at about 60 per cent) (Traxler, 1996a). Otherwise, a generally binding declaration (introducing the so-called 'erga omnes principle', *Allgemeinverbindlichkeitserklaerung*) would be necessary to extend the content of collective agreements to non-members of the signatory parties; however, this legal instrument does not exist in all EU member states (for example Italy or Denmark). For these different reasons, it is plausible to assume that this voluntaristic form of implementation will only be used in a small minority of cases—if at all. Furthermore, this procedure of 'législation négociée' does not exist in all member states.

The second mode of implementation is thus more important for future outcomes. In this case, different problems have to be solved before regulation at the national level can come into force.

First, would the Commission, in ensuring the validity and legality of the agreement (representative status of the contracting parties, their mandate, the 'legality' of each clause in the collective agreement in relation to Community law, and the special provisions regarding small and medium-sized undertakings set out in Article 2, section 2), have the legally provided right not only to comment on the content of the compromise reached by autonomous social partners, but also to change it? Thus, the balance of power could be shifted either towards the Commission or the social partners.

Second, could the Council make amendments, thus having the definite and final say? If this were the case, the influence of the Council would be the same as in all other processes of decision-making under the old provisions of the Treaty. If this were not the case, the power of the social partners would be significantly increased in comparison with all former options. Some national governments doubt if this increase in power should be accepted.

Third, the Commission argues that the Council should not enjoy substantial rights of change and threatens to withdraw its proposal if the Council tried to change the agreement of the social partners. A possible but unlikely scenario of conflicting interests could be the following: if the Council refused to agree, the framework agreement would be null and void. In that case, the Commission could possibly relaunch its own initiative and start once again the legislative process provided for in the Protocol, probably at the second stage of consultation of the social partners. Another political option could be that the Council would not be allowed to change the content of an agreement, but can decide on the appropriate instrument of implementation. All in all, the jockeying for positions is quite obvious.

Fourth, the choice of legal instruments to be taken by the Council is uncertain. The legal quality of the 'décision' (in French) in the meaning of Article 4 refers to Article 189 of the Treaty, but is not definitely determined. If the Council chose the specific instrument of the Directive as the appropriate means, member states would have to implement it without major opportunities to water down its content. In other cases, i.e. recommendation, their freedom to react to European regulation would be less restricted. In any case, the process of implementation at the national level constitutes additional difficulties which include lobbying by the national social partners. As we know from the experience with the implementation of the European Works Council Directive, supranational regulation defines only a broad frame of reference, which has to be specified by national 'customs and practices'. A relatively coherent transfer from the European to the national level is rather unlikely—if not impossible due to the rather different legal and institutional circumstances of industrial relations systems.

To sum up, this first communication aimed to establish some requirements for the application of the Social Protocol to get the new social dialogue started. Thereby, the Commission pursued a twofold strategy. First, it sought to ease the application, and, second, it wanted to avoid unintended consequences by itself defining the frame of reference.

The Second Communication

In its second, 1996 'Communication on the development of the social dialogue at Community level' (COM (96) 448 final), the Commission tried to cope with the problems described above. It raised a large number of questions about new participants of the social dialogue at the intersectoral and sectoral levels, criteria for representativity of organisations, about possible reforms, improvements of efficiency, better co-ordination of sectoral dialogues, procedural change, future of different committees, and the Councils' ability to change submitted drafts. It did, however, not answer these questions itself or solve the emerging problems. As far as the content of the future social dialogues is concerned, the Commission suggests that questions and policies of 'creating and securing employment' should become the first priority instead of a certain heterogeneity of topics.

The basic strategy was to ask a whole set of general questions that should be answered by the social partners—and not by the Commission itself. One could characterise this Communication more or less as a 'Green Book' because it only defines the preliminary agenda for future developments without going into details. Basically, it is supposed to stimulate debate among all actors, not solve outstanding problems. Reactions of national governments and social partners have been numerous and controversial (European Commission, 1997). It will be up to the publicly announced, but delayed third Communication to answer these questions and, therefore, to continue, and maybe finalise the process of procedural structuring.

SUMMARY OF FIRST RESULTS

So far there have been very few initiatives stemming from the Agreement on Social Policy.

European Works Councils

The question of the establishment of interest representation in multinational companies had been on the political agenda for more than two decades. Despite different proposals, the problem had remained unsolved because of the requirement of unanimity in the Council (Blanpain and Windey, 1994). In 1993, the very first attempt to make use of the new procedure failed before it had really started. The Commission proposed its renewed draft of the Directive on the 'Establishment of a European Works Council or a procedure in Community-scale undertakings and Community-scale groups of undertakings for the purposes of informing and consulting employees' and initiated the consultation process. Within the second stage of consultation, the social partners did not reach an agreement. The crucial factors behind the failure were not clear and each side blamed the other (EIRR, 1994). Some members of the ETUC questioned why the ETUC should negotiate at all if it could realistically assume that the Commission would pass its proposal regardless. It was also questioned whether UNICE would deviate from its status quo oriented strategy. Others argued that, on encountering the failure of negotiations, the first opportunity to test the new regulatory framework would be given away. UNICE intended to negotiate to avoid legislation, to control the process of policy formulation, and submitted a proposal to the ETUC despite internal problems of interest aggregation.

Thus, the social partners have not been able to conclude an agreement on this controversial, highly politicised issue of European industrial relations. Following this major failure of the new procedure, the Commission emphasised the political credibility of its proposal. It continued the process by first drafting and then passing legislation in 1994, which had to be implemented at the national level by late 1996 (Hall et al., 1995).

Burden of Proof

In 1995, the Commission proposed to deal once again with the old issue of the reversal of the 'burden of proof in sex discrimination cases', which had failed to achieve unanimous approval in the late 1980s. The social partners launched the first and second stage of consultation in early 1996, but 'have not informed the Commission of their wish to initiate the process' (COM (96) 340 final). They showed little enthusiasm to negotiate an agreement because the content would affect court procedures outside the scope of the social partners. Therefore, the initiative remained with the Commission. In mid-1996 it adopted, based on Article 2, section 1 of the Agreement, a draft Directive which was sent to the European Parliament and the Economic and Social Council for their opinions before being considered by the Council.

The aim of this Directive is to ensure that measures taken by the member states in the application of the principle of equal treatment in order to enable all persons, who consider themselves wronged by failure to apply to them the principle of equal treatment, to pursue their claims by judicial process after possible recourse to other competent authorities, are made more effective (Article 1 of the Draft Directive).

Parental Leave

Quite some years after the Protocol was passed, the social partners finally succeeded in reaching agreement on the issue of parental leave. This problem had been of some priority for the Commission since 1983/84, but a regulation which required a unanimous decision had been blocked within the Council by the veto of the UK. The last attempt had failed in the autumn of 1994, under the German presidency, for exactly this reason. Afterwards, the Commission came under political pressure from some member states and launched a new initiative on the base of the Agreement on Social Policy.

In 1995, the Commission suggested a proposal 'on reconciliation of family and professional life', which contained not only parental leave, but also family leave and educational leave issues. Thus, the Commission built a package of different proposals, which could not have been adopted otherwise. After the first consultation round, the social partners agreed to negotiate on the question of parental leave; ETUC, UNICE and CEEP asked the Commission to suspend its own initiative. After the second round of consultation, the negotiations started in July, and resulted in a 'framework agreement on parental leave' in November 1995. The proposal of the negotiating committee was accepted by all three confederations, and then was transferred by the Commission into a Directive, finally adopted by the Council.

The main content of the agreement is:

(i)   The establishment of minimum requirements for granting a right to parental leave in three countries where it formerly did not exist (Ireland, Belgium, Luxembourg).
(ii) Parental leave, not to be confused with maternity leave, would last at least three months, providing for the care of children up to eight years old.
(iii) The framework agreement constitutes an individual right for men and women independent of the others' occupational status and should in principle not be granted on a transferable basis.
(iv) Time off from work has to be granted on grounds of *force majeur*.

These minimum standards of regulation have to be implemented within three years at the national level. The social partners (Hornung-Draus, 1996; Lapeyre, 1996) and the Commission both consider the agreement to be a major success of the new procedure and stress its openness for national-specific implementation and its 'flexibility'.

External assessments are mixed. On the one hand, some independent, more euro-pessimist scholars argue that its content does not belong to the core parts of European social policy (Keller and Sörries, 1997). They maintain that, in contrast to the failed attempt on EWCs, the agreement does not create a zero-sum game; also, the majority of member states already have more far-reaching national rights, which will remain untouched by the agreement (EIRR, 1995b). It might well be that the social partners needed at least one successfully completed experiment. They had to prove, one way or the other, their ability and willingness to fulfil the high expectations of the Commission as well as of the member states referring to the opportunity structure provided by the Protocol. The legitimacy of the social partners was at stake before and during the Intergovernmental Conference that was started in March 1995.

On the other hand, euro-optimists argue more in favour of the agreement and emphasise that it could invigorate the relationship between the social partners (BDA, 1996) and be the first step towards euro-corporatism (Falkner, 1996). In this view, the agreement was also supposed to set a positive sign for the Intergovernmental Conference and the re-negotiation of the Treaty to be completed by mid-1997.

Part-time Work

The first consultation round on another set of formal negotiations, referring to an initiative on 'flexibility in working time and security for employees ('atypical work')', was started in September 1995. It finally became the second successfully concluded framework agreement, reconciling, one way or the other, employers' demands for more flexibility and part-time employees' desires for more equality with full-time employees at the workplace. The main content is 'to provide for the removal of discrimination against part-time workers and to improve the quality of part-time work' (clause 1). Thus, the principle of non-discrimination in relation to full-time workers is supposed to be codified. However, the agreement allows differential treatment 'on objective grounds' specified in three broad opening clauses: social security issues are explicitly excluded from the agreement; the member states are allowed to exclude 'casual workers' from the provisions of the agreement; and the member states may 'make access to particular conditions of employment subject to conditions such as a period of service, time worked or earnings qualification'.

The social partners as well as the Commission both assessed the agreement as a further major success in deepening the social dimension and in increasing employment. Critics (such as the European Parliament) emphasised its limitation to regular, permanent part-time work; the broad opening clauses as well as the widespread use of indefinite provisions will be open to nation-specific interpretation. Furthermore, it is unlikely that the agreement will have any major impact because of already existing, statutory provisions or collective agreements on part-time work in the majority of member states (EIRR, 1997b; EIRO, 1997). Within the ETUC, the agreement was not unanimously accepted; some national bodies, like the German Trade Union Federation, did not agree because of the unsatisfactory outcome (Kreimer-de Fries, 1997). Due to the high degree of 'negotiated flexibility' of the agreement, UNICE was, in contrast to other occasions, not faced with internal problems of interest intermediation.

Euro-pessimist, outside observers stress another problem: within the second phase of consultation, the social partners decided to negotiate, but to restrict the scope to part-time issues only. The question of atypical or non-standard employment had been part of the original proposal, but was excluded in the beginning of negotiations due to the fact that UNICE's mandate had been restricted to part-time issues only. It is now only mentioned in the preamble of the agreement under the heading 'of the intention of the parties to consider the need for similar agreements relating to other forms of flexible work'. Despite this non-binding declaration of intent there is no doubt that the remaining issues, being of increasing importance in all member states (Delsen, 1995), will be extremely difficult matters to negotiate and settle.

SUMMARY AND SOME PRELIMINARY CONCLUSIONS

Since 1993, after the initial years of the existence of the new social dialogue, it is at least surprising, and for euro-optimists even disappointing, that its opportunities have been used in only a few cases. The applications of the new provisions have not been able to give a significant impact on European social integration.

Despite opportunities for private peak associations having been broadened by the Social Protocol, the Commission still has to be considered as the prime mover within this arena of European policy making. Our evidence supports the argument that employers and employees associations differ widely in willingness and readiness to have an impact on European regulation. ETUC is basically interested in more and stricter regulation of market forces; from this perspective, the social dialogue can serve as a helpful instrument towards integration. UNICE's primary interest is to participate in the mandatory consultation stages to control the outcomes of the decision-making process, instead of being subjected to external, and therefore uncontrollable regulations. UNICE tends to enter the voluntary bargaining process only if the Commission's proposal to formulate binding legislation is considered to be a credible threat—and not because of a fundamental change of attitude (Jensen *et al.*, 1997a). UNICE's policy formulation is inspired by the principle of subsidiarity and by the employers' demand for more flexible labour markets instead of additional European regulation.

Our overview of the first attempts to apply the Social Protocol provisions reveals an ambivalent result.

1. So far, only two agreements have been concluded, i.e. on parental leave and part-time work. In both cases, the conclusion of the agreements was more important than their content. They were supposed to show that the social partners were willing and able to meet their new responsibilities, which they had introduced and demanded themselves. In our analysis, however, procedural issues were considered to be more important than substantive ones. Improvements of social standards will occur only in a small minority of countries.

2. The mere conclusion of the first two agreements has been claimed as a major success, not only by European actors, but also by some external observers (Dolvik, 1997). This assessment underestimates the problems of implementation at the national level. Framework agreements are not achievements in themselves, but only means to the end of improved social standards. The process of their implementation leaves ample room for strategic manoeuvring by governments and lobbying activities by national social partners. On the one hand, a high degree of internal flexibility is necessary to adapt European regulation to widely different national industrial relations systems. On the other, the substance of framework agreements can be watered down to a significant degree.

3. The first attempt at negotiating on the controversial issue of EWCs failed completely, during the second round of consultation. The Commission had to take over by initiating the legislative route instead of the Protocol procedure provided for in Article 4. This breakdown of negotiation supports the hypothesis that only non-conflictual issues are appropriate for self-regulation by the social partners and that successful applications of the new provisions still need a very active role of the Commission to solve the other cases. So far, key industrial relations issues (like employment) have not been addressed. This pattern has been underlined by the fact that the Agreement on Social Policy does not cover the regulation of wages and industrial conflict (Keller & Sörries 1997).

4. The social partners will not in any possible case participate actively in the process—and not make use of their increased and improved opportunities to conclude agreements, as the example of the 'burden of proof in sex discrimination' demonstrates. In general, this case shows that not all possible social policy issues initiated by the Commission are considered by the social partners as appropriate for negotiation and agreement.

So far the achievements of the dialogue cannot be treated as a basis for a more substantial process of negotiation between management and labour heading towards a European Industrial Relations system. It always takes two to tango.... Independent, voluntarily concluded agreements of the social partners have always been legally possible—but, for exactly the same reason, did not take place and will not be likely in the foreseeable future either. One could reasonably argue that, within the context of the Social Protocol, the enlargement of majority decisions has been more important than the inclusion of the social partners.

Last but not least, the shortcomings of the new social dialogue have to be linked to the Commissions' policies. It has not introduced any new initiatives, but instead relaunched old, so far unsolved issues, the majority of which date back to the Social Action Programme of 1989. The present Commission seems unwilling to initiate any new proposals in the field of social policy in general and industrial relations, in particular; it is rather obvious that it gives priority to consolidating the integration reached so far and implementing already existing regulation.

THE AMBIVALENT RELATIONSHIP BETWEEN SOCIAL DIALOGUES

In this article, we have focused on the interprofessional level—and its limited success. For theoretical as well as practical reasons, the same legal rules and established procedures could be applied at the decentralised level. One could argue that these sectoral versions of social dialogue could constitute necessary components for a forthcoming European system of collective bargaining (Jensen *et al.*, 1997b), because of the bargaining structure in the majority of member states.

Furthermore, scholars have argued:

> At this level, the problems of organising capacity are not yet so great as at the macro level, where they have become almost unmanageable; equally, at the meso level the fragmentation of interests is not yet so pronounced as at the micro level, where the risk is that trade unions may see their power position eroded (Traxler, 1996b: 296).

Thus, better and more appropriate, i.e. more flexible and tailor-made agreements could possibly be concluded. At least for the time being, the development of sectoral social dialogue has been constrained, first, by the non-existence of employers associations in the vast majority of sectors, second, by the organisational weakness of industry committees, the possible corporate actors on the union side (Keller and Sörries, 1998), and third, the reluctance of the Commission to move towards more encompassing sectoral integration.

The relationship between both forms, the interprofessional and the sectoral dialogue, is of an ambivalent nature and has been clarified neither in the Social Protocol nor in the 'Commission Communication concerning the Development of the Social Dialogue at Community level' (COM (96) 448 final). This could result in two different scenarios. First, the interprofessional dialogue will deal with general topics, while the sectoral ones will address more specific issues. The former should define frames of reference, the latter generate topics. The sectoral dialogue could possibly specify framework agreements adopted at the interprofessional level (Flynn, 1997), but such a relationship would require a fairly sophisticated internal division of labour within and between corporate actors, which does not presently exist and will be difficult to obtain. Second, the social partners at the sectoral level might favour an independent approach in defining and solving their own issues.

In the long run, some sectoral social partners would tend, because of organisational self-interests and economic reasons, to increase their influence and power towards the actors at the interprofessional level. This development would be caused by their national members, who are not willing to shift power to the peak associations. This trend would lead to an increase in the autonomy of the sectoral level.

As we know from recent research in other fields of integration, different kinds of European regulation have major impacts at the national levels (Windhoff-Héritier *et al.* 1996). In our particular case, we have to distinguish between at least two types of national systems of industrial relations. In so-called 'monistic' systems (like in the UK), all collective bargaining issues are basically addressed at the micro/enterprise level. So-called 'dual' systems (like in Germany or Austria) are characterised by collective bargaining at the meso/sectoral, and not at the enterprise level; in these countries, formally independent forms of interest representation have been in existence at both levels.

Due to these fundamental differences both types would be differently affected by sectoral social dialogues. Within monistic systems, corporate actors would not be interested in promoting and establishing sectoral dialogues because all interests are primarily focused on the lower level. In contrast, for dual systems sectoral dialogues would be more important. Two kinds of relationships could be thought of. In one case, if both sides had common interests (like restructuring of their sector), national associations and their supranational counterparts could develop new forms of co-operation at the European level. This alternative, however, is rather unlikely to become a general trend due to the above-mentioned weaknesses of sectoral organisations, especially on the employers' side. In the other case of opposing interests and, therefore, non-co-operation, paths of development would be determined by national interests. As a consequence, the establishment of a European bargaining structure would be seriously constrained.

In all of the above options, framework agreements can only be reached if both sides agree. Consensual topics constitute a necessary prerequisite for a new social dialogue, but could be difficult to identify. Thus, the content of framework agreements signed under the Agreement on Social Policy will be rather limited in number and very narrow in scope.

> The limited results in the intersectoral social dialogue, the rare initiatives undertaken in the sectoral dialogue risk making the European social dialogue a legal and institutional success without practical results (Villeneuve, 1997: 106).

The same hypothesis can also be formulated in a more general manner. Because social policy is highly fragmented within and between member states, any European regulation will only be possible in non-conflictual issues with common interests and shared goals (like health and safety) (Eichener, 1996; Konstanty and Zwingmann, 1996), or have to take place at the lowest common denominator. Therefore, a new instrument like the Social Protocol faces the same problem as all other attempts to cope with this diversity. Further achievements will basically be reached at the national level which could only be supported by European policy formulation within the social dialogue. The nation state remains of major importance despite the ongoing Europeanisation.

Last but not least, our empirical data indicate that social dialogue should definitely not be confused with collective bargaining. For that reason, a misinterpretation frequently made by external observers in general (Jacobi, 1995) and trade unionists in particular (Buschak and Kallenbach, 1994) should be avoided. Because of its consensual character, trilateral social dialogue should not be confused with bilateral free collective bargaining, including the threat to strike or even actual strike action. In contrast to the vast majority of member states and trade union confederations, employers associations have only very limited, if any, interests in European social policy regulation; they are more interested in non-binding recommendations and consultation only. This minimalist approach is mirrored in their political and organisational weakness, only to mention two undeniable variables for European collective bargaining. Within an overtly optimistic scenario, the provisions of social dialogue could constitute a predecessor of bargaining autonomy. However, without the European commitment of national actors, the new institutional provisions of the social dialogue do not enable European actors to move towards a more formalised and independent collective bargaining system. This scenario is enforced by the economic integration with its prevailing capacity of deregulation.

PERSPECTIVES

Are there any perspectives for the social dialogue at all? One possible future contribution towards social integration could take place within the implementation of the employment chapter that the member states finally agreed in the Amsterdam Treaty. Later on, the employment council stated its endorsement of an employment strategy comprising

> the continuation and development of a co-ordinated macro-economic policy, underpinned by an efficient internal market; and the harnessing of all Community policies in support of employment, in order to help unleash the potential for dynamism and enterprise to be found in Europe's economy (EIRR, 1997b).

One obvious problem is the fact that the EU budget is too small and too inflexible to pursue active labour market policies.

Concrete steps to be taken in the future have not been defined yet. One option could be to create a mechanism like in the case of the establishment of the European Monetary Union. The Commission and the member states would set up 'convergence criteria' concerning certain goals for the development of employment,

> improving employability, developing entrepreneurship, encouraging adaptability in business and their employees to enable the labour market to react to economic changes, and strengthening equal opportunities policy (Presidency Conclusions, 1997).

but leave the implementation of these guidelines to the member states which have to take appropriate measures. This mechanism could only come into force if an annual report on evaluation would be carried out by the Commission. Incentives for the member states not only to agree formally but to co-operate in the long run could be provided by connecting their employment performance to the amount of EU subsidies (like social funds).

As in other areas, the Commission itself would be unable to implement these policies due to the lack of instruments and institutions: it needs the support and willingness of national governments and their labour market institutions. According to the principle of subsidiarity and most recent political declarations, the social partners should be actively involved in the formulation of guidelines on employment policies. They are much more familiar with social challenges, demands at the level of the enterprise and individual needs. In response, the social partners themselves declared publicly 'to play their full role in the European employment process and ask to be fully consulted by the Employment and Labour Market Committee' (ETUC, UNICE and CEEP, 1997). If the European social partners were *de facto* willing and able to fulfil this new function, it would force them to co-ordinate employment policies of their national members. As already mentioned, the social dialogue is likely to focus on employment issues. Within its framework, the social partners would have to submit detailed proposals on the content of employment guidelines to the Commission. For that reason, the member states should incorporate social partners at all levels in their employment activities to assure a coherent European strategy to combat unemployment.

Another possible development of the social dialogue can be linked to the likely consequences of the introduction of the European Monetary Union. After the transfer of national monetary policies to the European level, and the likelihood of a rather similar development of fiscal policy despite its continued formal independence, one could assume that the remaining economic policies would also undergo major changes. This development most likely means that collective bargaining will also be Europeanised one way or the other. Within an optimistic scenario, more co-ordination could possibly be achieved within the framework of the only existing institution, the social dialogue. However, different problems analysed in this article indicate that this scenario for the interprofessional dialogue will be rather unlikely in the foreseeable future.

A related scenario would refer not to the macro, but to the sectoral level. In that case, shocks caused by the European Monetary Union would not affect national economies as a whole but only specific sectors (wage-intensive sectors like construction, textiles, among others). The appropriate response as far as social dialogues are concerned would have to be given at the sectoral level. As a possible result, sectoral shocks could be considered as push factors towards the development of sectoral dialogues. For the time being, however, the social partners have not built up institutions to address these challenges.

Considering the current political weakness of the social dialogue, a different trajectory of 'Europeanisation' could consist of more and improved co-operation between national unions, including information about or even co-ordination of national collective bargaining. The trade unions especially could be forced to set up such network relationships among themselves (Ebbinghaus and Visser, 1996). In this scenario, they would be more independent of the weak European employers' associations than in others. They would address their co-ordinated demands to their national and not to their European counterparts. As a consequence, collective bargaining at the national level would continue to dominate. 'The influence of national systems on the shaping of social Europe will probably be greater than expected, at least in the short run, given the slowing-down of the Maastricht policies…' (Treu, 1996: 185). Therefore, in this kind of scenario, unions would assess as their first priority to prevent a further development of the social dialogue. In that case, the social dialogue would not be given considerable additional impetus by the social partners at either the national or European level.

ACKNOWLEDGEMENTS

The authors are grateful for the financial support of the Hans Böckler Stiftung.

REFERENCES

Addison, J.T. and Siebert, W.S. (1994) 'Recent developments in social policy in the new European Union', *Industrial and Labor Relations Review* 48, 1, 5–27.

BDA (1996): Geschäftsbericht 1996, Köln.

Bercusson, B. (1992) 'Maastricht: A fundamental change in European labour law', *Industrial Relations Journal* 24, 4, 257–272.

Bercusson, B. (1994) 'The dynamic of European labour law after Maastricht', *Industrial Law Journal* 23, 1, 1–31.

Blanpain, R. and Windey, P. (1994) *European Works Councils. Information and consultation of employees in multinational enterprises in Europe*, Leuven, Peeters.

Buda, D. (1995) 'Auf dem Weg zu europäischen Arbeitsbeziehungen? Zur Perspektive des Sozialen Dialogs in der Europäischen Union', in Mesch, M. (Hg.), *Sozialpartnerschaft und Arbeitsbeziehungen in Europa*, Wien: Manz Verlag, pp. 289–333.

Buschak, W. and Kallenbach, V. (1994) 'Europäischer Gewerkschaftsbund EGB', in Lecher, W. and Platzer, H.-W. (Hg.), *Europäische Union – Europäische Arbeitsbeziehungen? Nationale Voraussetzungen und internationaler Rahmen*, Köln, Bund-Verlag, pp. 201–213.

Carley, M. (1993) 'Social dialogue', in Gold, M. (ed.), *The social dimension. Employment policy in the European community*, Chatham: Macmillan, pp. 105–134.

Delsen, L. (1995) *Atypical employment: an International perspective. Causes, consequences and policy*, Groningen, Woltersgroep Groningen.

Dolvik, J.E. (1997) 'Redrawing boundaries of solidarity? ETUC, social dialogue and the Europeanisation of trade unions in the 1990s', ARENA Report No. 5/97, Oslo, Arena/FAFO.

Ebbinghaus, B. and Visser, J. (1996) 'European labor and transnational solidarity: Challenges, pathways, and barriers', MZES Working Paper AB I/No. 11, Mannheim, MZES.

Eichener, V. (1996), 'Die Rückwirkungen der europäischen Integration auf nationale Politikmuster', in Jachtenfuchs, M. and Kohler-Koch, B. (Hg.), *Europäische Integration*, Opladen, Leske + Budrich, pp. 249–280.

ETUC, UNICE and CEEP (1997) *Social partners' contribution to the employment summit*, 13 November 1997, Brussels: ETUC, UNICE, CEEP.

European Commission (1997) *The future of the social dialogue. Synthesis of the social partners' contribution* (Brussels: European Commission).

European Industrial Relations Observatory (1997) 'Social partners reach framework agreement on part-time work', *EIRO*, 3, 2–3.

European Industrial Relations Review (1994) 'Social partners. Information and consultation talks fail', *EIRR*, 243, 3–4.

European Industrial Relations Review (1995a) 'UEAPME now closer to full EU acceptance?', *EIRR*, 259, 3–4.

European Industrial Relations Review (1995b) 'Parental leave in Europe', *EIRR*, 262, 14–18.

European Industrial Relations Review (1997a) 'Commission sets out options for the future of the social dialogue', *IERR*, 267, 24–29.

European Industrial Relations Review (1997b) 'Employment Council outlines jobs strategy', *EIRR*, 287, 2.

Falkner, G. (1996) 'The Maastricht Protocol on Social Policy: Theory and Practice', *Journal of European Social Policy*, 6, 1, 1–16.

Ferner, A. and Hyman, R. (eds.) (1998) 'Changing industrial relations in Europe', 2nd edn, Oxford, Blackwell.

Flynn, P. (1997) 'European forum on the future of the social dialogue. Closing address'. The Hague, 29 April 1997.

Hall, M. *et al.* (1995) *European Works Councils. Planning for the directive*, London-University of Warwick, Eclipse Group.

Hornung-Draus, R. (1996) 'Abkommen zum Elternurlaub verabschiedet', *Der Arbeitgeber*, 48, 3, 62–63.

ILO (1997) *World Labour Report 1997–98. Industrial relations, democracy and social stability*, Geneva, ILO.

Jachtenfuchs, M. (1995) 'Theoretical perspectives on European governance', *European Law Journal* 1, 2, 115–133.

Jacobi, O. (1995) 'Der soziale Dialog in der Europäischen Union', in Mesch, M. (Hg.), *Sozialpartnerschaft und Arbeitsbeziehungen in Europa*, Wien, Manz Verlag, pp. 257–287.

Jensen, C.S. *et al.* (1997a) 'The voice of European business and industry – The case of UNICE. A study of an employer organisation on the European labour market', in Flood, P. et al. (eds.), *The European Union and the Employment Relationship, Fifth IIRA European Industrial Relations Congress*, Held in Dublin, Ireland, 26–29 August 1997, Dublin, Oak Tree Press, pp. 37–54.

Jensen, C.S. *et al.* (1997b) *Phases and dynamics in the development of EU Industrial Relations regulations*, Ms., Copenhagen, FAOS.

Keller, B. and Henneberger, F. (1997) 'Prospects for social dialogue in the public sector – European confederations, sectoral federations and forms of interest intermediation', *Transfer. European Review of Labour and Research* 3, 1, 119–146.

Keller, B. and Sörries, B. (1997) 'The new social dialogue: New concepts, first results and future perspectives', in Flood, P. et al. (eds.), *The European Union and the Employment Relationship*. Fifth IIRA European Industrial Relations Congress, Held in Dublin, Ireland, 26–29 August 1997, Dublin, Oak Tree Press, pp. 17–36.

Keller, B. and Sörries, B. (1998) 'The sectoral social dialogue and European social policy – less facts, more fantasy', *European Journal of Industrial Relations*, 4, forthcoming.

Konstanty, R. and Zwingmann, B. (1996) 'Arbeitsschutzreform – bleibt Deutschland Schlußlicht in Europa?', *WSI-Mitteilungen* 49, 2, 56–70.

Kreimer-de Fries, J. (1997) 'EU-Teilzeitvereinbarung – kein gutes Omen für die Zukunft der europäischen Verhandlungsebenen', *Arbeit und Recht*, 45, 8, 314–317.

Lange, P. (1993) 'Maastricht and the Social Protocol: Why did they do it?' *Politics and Society* 21, 1, 5–36.

Lapeyre, J. (1996) 'First round of European negotiations – the parental leave agreement', in ETUI - Gabaglio, E. and Hoffmann, R. (eds.), *European Trade Union Yearbook 1995*, Brussels, ETUI, pp. 121–127.

Locke, R.Kochan, T. and Piore, M. (eds.) (1995) *Employment relations in a changing world economy*, Cambridge-London, MIT-Press.

Majone, G. (1997) 'The agency model: The growth of regulation and regulatory institutions in the European Union', *Eipascope/European Institute of Public Administration* 3/1997, 9–14.

Marginson, P. and Sisson, K. (1996) 'Multination companies and the future of collective bargaining: A review of the research issues', *European Journal of Industrial Relations* 2, 2, 173–197.

Marginson, P. and Sisson, K. (1998) 'European collective bargaining: a virtual prospect?', *Journal of Common Market Studies*, 36, (forthcoming).

Presidency conclusions (1997), 'Extraordinary European Council meeting on employment', Luxembourg, 20 and 21 November 1997, Brussels, European Commission.

Rhodes, M. (1991) 'The social dimension of the Single European Market: National versus transnational regulation', *European Journal of Political Research* 19, 2&3, 245–280.

Rhodes, M. (1995) 'A Regulatory Conundrum: Industrial Relations and the Social Dimension', in Leibfried, S. and Pierson, P. (eds.), *European Social Policy: between fragmentation and integration*, Washington: Brookings, pp. 78–122.

Streeck, W. (1994) 'European social policy after Maastricht: The "social dialogue" and "subsidiarity"', *Economic and Industrial Democracy* 15, 2, 151–177.

Traxler, F. (1996a) 'Collective bargaining and industrial change – A case of disorganisation? A comparative analysis of eighteen OECD countries', *European Sociological Review* 12, 3, 271–287.

Traxler, F. (1996b) 'European trade union policy and collective bargaining – mechanisms and levels of labour market regulation in comparison', *Transfer. European Review of Labour and Research* 2, 2, 287–297.

Treu, T. (1996) 'European Collective Bargaining Levels and the Competences of Social Partners', in Davies, P. et al., *European Community Labour Law. Principles and Perspectives*. Liber Amicorum Lord Wedderburn of Charlton, Oxford, Clarendon Press, pp. 169–187.

Van Kersbergen, K. and Verbeek, B. (1994) 'The politics of subsidiarity in the European Union', *Journal of Common Market Studies* 32, 2, 215–236.

Villeneuve, R. (1997) 'The role of the public services in building European citizenship', *Transfer. European Review of Labour and Research* 3, 1, 98–118.

Windhoff-Héritier, A. et al. (1996) *'Ringing the changes in Europe. Regulatory competition and the transformation of the state: Britain, France, Germany'*, Berlin, de Gryter.

Employers and employer organisations

Franz Traxler

While employer organisations are the collective voice of employers in industrial relations, any employer as such represents a collective entity. As a collective entity, individual employers are more powerful than individual employees and—in the case of large firms—are often superior to their own association as well. Hence employers do have a choice between collective and individual action when it comes to pursuing their interest in industrial relations. This makes the relationship between employer organisations and their potential members more delicate than in the case of other interest associations.

In the course of transforming individual member interests into collective goals, employer organisations—as any other association—have to deal with three organisational issues. First, they have to demarcate their representational domain in terms of membership and tasks. Second, they must be able to recruit members. Third, they have to make their members comply with associational goals and collective decisions. Olson (1965) has analysed the collective-action problem of associations as a problem of member recruitment. However, closer consideration shows that the two other organisational issues raise similar collective-action problems which are, nevertheless, independent of one another (Traxler, 1993). When dealing with these issues, associations face the logics of membership and of influence (e.g. Traxler and Schmitter, 1995). While the logic of membership represents the association's need to retain its legitimacy in relation to its constituency, the logic of influence follows the strategic requirements for effective interest politics. These logics put conflicting demands to an association's structure with regard to any of the three organisational issues. For instance, narrowing down the domain may help an association to recruit members; at the same time this may constrain its ability to exert influence. The following analysis is confined to the representational domains with regard to the national and supranational level of employer organisation in Europe.

Comparative analysis of Europe concentrates on the *differences* across nation states. Hence, there is a risk of overseeing the remarkable commonality of (West)

Franz Traxler is Professor of Industrial Sociology at the University of Vienna.

European industrial relations in comparison with overseas. Leaving aside the exceptional case of Britain, the collective (i.e. associational) option has remained the standard means of European employers to advance their interests in industrial relations. Most importantly, multi-employer settlements concluded by employer organisations on behalf of business cover far more employees than single-employer bargaining (Traxler, 1996). This contrasts with the non-European area, where employers have increasingly shifted to the individual choice. In the United States, employer organisations have never existed. In Canada, they are important only in certain sectors and regions. Japanese employer associations are normally not engaged in collective bargaining but confine their activities to co-ordination tasks vis-á-vis their member firms.

THE DEMARCATION OF DOMAIN: THE PROBLEMS AND GENERAL PATTERNS

Associations have to specify their domain in terms of tasks and membership. In doing so, they differentiate between interests which are either irrelevant or relevant to their activities. Business as such has interests not only in labour markets but also in other markets which will be designated here as product markets for brevity. Business associations may specialise in representing either product-market interests (i.e. pure trade associations) or labour-market interests (i.e. pure employer organisations); or they may combine both interests (i.e. mixed associations).

As regards pure trade associations and pure employer organisations, cross-national evidence shows that trade associations significantly outnumber employer organisations (Traxler, 1993). This means that the domain of trade associations is far narrower than that of employer organisations. This is plausible because the product-market interests of a certain business group must be often pursued in relation to other business groups (e.g. suppliers, retailers). Hence, trade associations tend to demarcate their domain along the lines of intra-class cleavages which mainly result from competing product-market interests. Such cleavages are of minor importance in the case of labour-market interests since the latter have to be advanced in relation to a non-business group: that is, labour.

This analysis is limited to pure and mixed employer organisations. Important criteria for their domain demarcation by membership are sectoral affiliations and firm size, reflecting corresponding segmentations of the labour market. For the above reasons, domain demarcation has to mediate between the conflicting logics of membership and influence. Attracting members becomes easier the more closely the domain is suited to a certain group of employers. In contrast to this logic of membership, the strategic imperative for employers is to control as many segments of the labour market as are covered by concerted union activities. Otherwise, there is a risk of becoming played off against one another. Cross-national analysis of 20 OECD countries for 1970–1990 reveals that a country's number of national peak associations of employers is highly correlated with the number of union confederations ($r = 0.66$; $p = 0.00$)[1]. This indicates that the logic of influence prevails in domain demarcation. Moreover, employer organisations echo organised labour, as the history of organised industrial relations demonstrates. Employers normally began to associate no earlier than in response to a labour movement that had learned to co-ordinate its politics at multi-employer level. Since employers have a feasible individual option, they rely on associations only to the extent to which mere union strength and/or a legal framework conducive to unionisation and multi-employer bargaining make collective action necessary. Under favourable conditions, employers may refrain from forming any association, as found in the United States. While the option of independent, individual action certainly weakens the position of employer organisations in relation to their members, rather the opposite is true in relation to labour. Employers are less interested in collective agreements in general and multi-employer settlements in particular than labour is. As rational choice theory shows, the actor less interested in an agreement is more powerful in bargaining (Elster, 1989). This is why recent debates among employers of the German metal industry about dissolving their association, Gesamtmetall, could work as a threat to the unions.

THE NATIONAL LEVEL

This section's unit of analysis is the national peak associations of employers. They claim to represent and co-ordinate the general (i.e. interindustry) interests of employers. As a consequence, they are normally associations of associations which are not subordinate members of another employer organisation. Table 1 presents basic information on the national systems of peak employer organisations in Europe. Given the complexity of employer organisation and the high degree of domain differentiation, this overview includes only associations which cover at least one complete two-digit ISIC sector.

Three borderline cases are worth mentioning. The first one concerns Austria, where the VÖI represents employer interests in addition to the WKÖ. Leaving aside its notable public-relations activities, the VÖI does so mainly via joint leadership positions with the WKÖ. Most importantly, the VÖI has not engaged in collective bargaining which is almost exclusively conducted under the umbrella of the WKÖ. Hence, Table 1 includes only the WKÖ. Another borderline case is the CBI whose industrial relations activities are very limited (Grant

---

[1]Cross-national data on employer organisation for which no other reference is given are from the project on 'Internationalisation, Labor Relations and Competitiveness' (ILC) directed by the author.

TABLE 1

The National Systems of Peak Employer Associations in Europe in 1990

	Number of Associations[1]	Specification of formal domain by:		
		Task[2]	Private sector	Other criteria
European Union				
France (F)	3	2	Yes	Yes
Germany (D)	1	1	Yes	No
Italy (I)	10	n.a.	Yes	Yes
Spain (E)	1	1	Yes	No
United Kingdom (UK)	(1)	0	Yes	No
Austria (A)	1	0	Yes	No
Belgium (B)	1	1	Yes	No
Denmark (DK)	1	1	Yes	No
Finland (FIN)	2	0	Yes	Yes
Ireland (IRL)	1	1	No	No
Netherlands (NL)	4	0	Yes	Yes
Portugal (P)	1	0	Yes	No
Sweden (S)	1	1	Yes	No
Non-EU Countries				
Norway (N)	1	0	Yes	No
Switzerland (CH)	2	1	Yes	Yes

[1] Peak associations with nation-wide domain which includes the private sector and at least one complete two-digit ISIC sector.
[2] Number of pure employer associations.
n.a. = not available. Data source: ILC project.

and Marsh, 1977). Hence, the CBI is put in parentheses here. It is included, since it is the only British association which comes close to the format of a peak employer organisation. Third, one may report the existence of two Spanish associations instead of one. While the CEOE is the predominant organisation, there is also the CEYPME which organises small and medium-sized enterprises. The CEYPME is not recorded here, because it is a semi-autonomous organisation of the CEOE (Lucio, 1992, p. 496).

There is a rather high degree of associational concentration in terms of the number of associations established. With the exception of Italy, France and the Netherlands, no country records more than two associations. Italy is very fragmented because there are several associations specialised in representation of co-operatives and the handicraft sector. The Netherlands were the only country in 1990 which had employer organisations differentiated by religion. Countries with more than one peak organisation generally miss a mutually exclusive demarcation of domains: the smaller association(s) represent certain subgroups covered by the larger organisation as well. As a rule, these subgroups are the craft sector and/or, small and medium-sized enterprises (SMEs). Finland is an exception in that the smaller association, PT (formerly LTK), is tailored to the service sector. In practice, representation of the service sector is split. Those companies and sectoral employer organisations whose operations are linked to manufacturing are members of the larger organisation, STK. The Finnish case underscores that employer associations may informally arrive at rather complementary domains, even when their formal domains overlap. Regardless of this, rivalry for members and representational tasks has not completely disappeared. Special interest associations of the craft sector and SMEs tend to be more militant than their more general counterparts. In connection with the fact that associational separation in the private sector most frequently involves craft production and SMEs, this militancy also underscores that the most pronounced segmentation of employers' labour-market interests is between this sector and large firms. Hence, it is most difficult for employer organisations to reconcile the interests of these two labour-market segments. A recent example is Ireland, where a group of SMEs broke away and established its own association, ISME, when the country's principal trade association and employer organisation amalgamated (see below). So far, however, the ISME has failed to acquire the status of a social partner equipped with a negotiating licence.

Apart from Ireland, national peak employer organisations confine their domain to the private sector. There is thus a clear organisational divide between the private and the public sector.

Concerning domain demarcation by tasks in 1990, countries where pure employer organisations existed slightly outnumbered those where only mixed associations were established. Meanwhile, however, amalgamations of the principal business associations took place in Denmark and Ireland. In 1991, DI, the Danish trade association, became a branch organisation of the employer peak association, DA. In Ireland, the FIE and the CII merged into the IBEC in 1993. In the mid-1980s Portugal's CIP transformed itself from a pure to a mixed employer organisation. Norway's peak employer organisation, NAF, combined with its trade counterpart, NHO, to form a mixed confederation. Several amalgamations of trade associations and employer organisations at the sectoral level occurred in Sweden. In 1998, the regional trade association and employer organisation of Bavaria formed a common association which some observers see as a first step towards an amalgamation of their national peak associations, BDI and BDA. Hence, there is a tendency of a gradual erosion of domain specialisation by tasks. In line with the thesis of a growing disorganisation of industrial relations (Lash and Urry, 1987), one might interpret this as a withdrawal of employer organisation from industrial relations in general and multi-employer bargaining in particular. Closer consideration does not confirm such conjectures. Both Ireland and Norway have seen a renaissance of centralised bargaining in the 1980s (Traxler,

1995). In Denmark, DA has retained control over a more decentralised bargaining system (Due *et al.*, 1995). The real reason for organising labour- and product-market interests under one umbrella is presented in the IBEC's 'prospectus' for the merger of CII and FIE. Accordingly, economic and social agendas have become interdependent at national and EU levels. Furthermore, amalgamations help to economise on resources (e.g. avoiding duplication of efforts in external representation). The latter argument also explains amalgamations between mixed associations in the Netherlands. In the 1990s, the two general confederations, VNO and NCW, merged, as did the two associations of SMEs, KNOV and NCOV. In Germany, proponents of an amalgamation of BDI and BDA aim to overcome by means of such amalgamations these associations' growing conflict over the country's social order. In open rivalry with the BDA, the general secretary of its trade counterpart, BDI, publicly encouraged employers to disregard multi-employer settlements (Der Spiegel, 1997).

Table 1 may suggest more coherence in the association of employers than is actually established. This is because only national peak associations are at issue here. In many countries sector-specific associations exist which are not affiliated to any peak association and thus amount to associational fragmentation. Such separate organisation often holds true for agriculture. Other examples of non-affiliated associations include banking in Denmark, Sweden and Norway. The construction industry stays outside in Ireland. Even in Austria, where more than 90 per cent of all collective agreements are concluded under the umbrella of the WKÖ, there are a few separate sectoral organisations.

Table 2 reports the main activities of the peak organisations from Table 1, as far as information is available. Almost all associations represent labour-market interests vis-à-vis government and parliament, do so on corporatist boards, conduct general consultation with union confederations and co-ordinate bargaining of their affiliates. The vast majority participates in the formulation of public programmes on occupational training, active labour-market policy, regional and industrial policy. Direct involvement in collective bargaining is rare. Less than 20 per cent negotiate and sign collective wage agreements and less than 40 per cent do so with regard to non-wage issues. This means that collective bargaining in the narrow sense is left to lower-level affiliates of the peak associations.

Interestingly, the scope of activities performed by pure employer organisations does not much differ from that of mixed associations. Seventy per cent of all pure employer organisations and 82 per cent of all mixed associations are involved in the formulation of industrial policy. Even 40 per cent of pure employer organisations participate in the formulation of programmes on research and development and 30 per cent do so with regard to quality control and product standardisation, which are regarded as key functions of trade associations. The corresponding figures for mixed associations are 91 per cent and 64 per cent respectively. These data also underscore the interdependence of labour- and product-market interests.

TABLE 2
Activities Performed by Employer Peak Associations in Europe[1]

Activities	Employer organisations
Influences national government or parliamentary bodies with regard to labour market issues	95.0
Represents members' labour market interests on national corporatist institutions	95.0
Conducts general consultations with union confederations	95.0
Negotiates and signs on behalf of affiliates collective wage agreements	23.8
Negotiates and signs on behalf of affiliates collective agreements on non-wage issues	38.1
Co-ordinates collective bargaining of affiliates	95.0
Participates in the formulation of public industrial policy programmes	76.2
Implements public industrial policy programmes or participates in implementation	42.9
Participates in the formulation of public regional developement programmes	76.2
Implements regional development programmes or participates in implementation	42.9
Participates in the formulation of public occupational training programmes and active labour market policy	90.5
Implements occupational training programmes and active labour market policy or participates in implementation	57.1
Participates in the formulation of public research and development programmes	66.7
Implements public research and development programmes or participates in implementation	38.1
Formulates quality control programmes and/or standardisation of products or participates in formulation	47.6
Implements quality control programmes and/or standardisation of products, or participates in implementation	19.0

[1]Countries from Table 1, without nine minor Italian associations and one minor French association. Data source: ILC project.

If pure employer organisations do not adjust themselves to this interdependence through amalgamations with trade associations, they seem to incorporate selected product-market issues into their domain. A common property of all peak associations is that they engage much more in the formulation than in the implementation of policies. This can be traced to the problem of making the members comply with associational goals.

There is less difference in terms of activities between pure and mixed associations than among countries. Table 3 presents more detailed information on the principal peak association of each country. Among these associations pure organisations slightly outnumbered mixed ones in 1990. The CBI is the only organis-

TABLE 3

The functions and structure of the principal employer peak associations in Europe (1990)

Country and abbreviation for related employer association

	F	D	I	E	UK	A	B	DK	FIN	IRL	NL	P	S	N	CH
	CNPF	BDA	C	CEOE	CBI	WKÖ	VBO/FEB	DA	STK	FIE	VNO	CIP	SAF	NHO	ZSAO
Function (A)	P	P	M	P	M	M	P	P	M	P	M	M	P	P	P
Number of affiliates (B)	254[e]	56	212	97	207[c]	134[a]	n.a.	48	19	51[d]	95	79[b]	35	30	72[a]
Role in collective bargaining (C)	1 + 2	1	1 + 2	1	0	1 + 2	1 + 2	1 + 2	1	1 + 2	1	1	1 + 2	1 + 2	1

Explanatory note on measures: (A) P = pure employer organisations; M = mixed organisations
(B) Number of associations directly affiliated to the peak association
(C) 0 = no role; 1 = co-ordinating; 2 = negotiates and signs collective agreements n.a. not available
a = 1991, b = estimate, c = 1975; d = 1996 (for FIE's successor IBEC), e = data from Pestoff (1994); for abbreviation of countries and employer organisations, see Table 1 and appendix Data source: ILC project

ation that does not obtain any role in collective bargaining. This unique status accrues to the CBI not only in comparison with regard to the principal employer organisations but also to any national association from Table 2.

Generally, peak employer organisations represent a complex pyramid of associations of association which often relies on more than three hierarchical levels. In order to control for this vertical differentiation, Table 3 includes only those affiliates which are a direct member of the peak association. 'Lower-order' associations which are indirectly affiliated to the peak are excluded from this consideration. The number of affiliates can be taken as an indicator of the degree of domain differentiation under the umbrella of the peak association. The larger the number of affiliates the narrower the affiliates' domain tends to be. There is no correlation between the number of affiliates and country size. Since the 1970s the number of affiliates has declined. This trend was most pronounced in the Scandinavian countries, where the number of affiliates under the umbrella of the principal employer association fell by 44 per cent from the beginning of the 1970s to the end of the 1980s. The main reason for this is amalgamation, which in turn is related to analogous reforms of the collective bargaining system. For instance, DA's number of affiliates shrank in less than one year from 150 to 51. One main goal of this reform was to reduce the number of collective agreements from about 650 to 20 or even fewer (Due *et al.*, 1994, p. 206).

THE EUROPEAN LEVEL

As in general, so are employers less than employees interested in a collective regulation of the labour market, when it comes to European matters. In the context of the single market employers as the more mobile side of industry have a strategic advantage which the employees can compensate only by means of a pan-European regulation of working conditions. Employers' disinterest in such regulation is reflected by the functional differentiation of business associations at the EU level. Of the more than 300 associations the vast majority is pure trade associations.

While employer associations have maintained their interest in the status quo of low regulation, they had to change their strategy at the end of the 1980s. As long as decisions on social policy were bound to unanimity, employers could trust that social-policy initiatives would fail because of a veto by a sympathetic government in the Council of Ministers (Springer, 1992). In line with this, UNICE, the main representative of Europe's employers accepted only exchange of views as a form of direct dealing with the unions, but refused to enter into negotiations. At best, non-binding joint opinions could emerge from this limited kind of social dialogue. This position, however, became unsustainable, when initiatives to replace the unanimity rule with qualified majority voting gained momentum among EC member states (Buda, 1995). UNICE thus followed the Commission's invitation to elaborate with ETUC and CEEP a common proposal for the role of management and labour within the revised decision-making framework. In 1991 these associations arrived at an agreement which was then adopted as part of the Social Protocol on Social Policy annexed to the Maastricht Treaty. Accordingly, the social dialogue was institutionalised as a 'proto-corporatist' machinery, attributing to management and labour the right to participate in EU regulation of social and labour-market issues. The Protocol did not clarify what actors are to be recognised as representatives of management and labour. In its 'Communication concerning the Application of the Agreement on Social Policy' (COM [93] 600 final) the Commission laid down the general criteria for admission as a representative. In combination with a study on the representativeness of existing associations, these criteria served as the basis for listing those organisations to be recognised. In the case of management, this list differentiates between four groups. First, there is the group of general, interindustry associations referring to UNICE and CEEP. By the mid-1990s, 34 affiliates from 25 states were under UNICE's umbrella (Falkner, 1998, p. 328). Like all the other business associations listed by the Commission, UNICE is a mixed organisation. Correspondingly, it is open to both trade associations and employer organisations. This implies double membership of countries, where the associational system is differentiated in terms of pure employer and trade associations. The CEEP represents the employers of the public sector. The second group designates interindustry associations which represent special categories of management. This concerns UAPME which organises the craft sector and SMEs. Third, there is a group of specific organisations which currently includes the Eurochambres. The fourth group embraces sectoral Euro-associations such as Euro Commerce (representing retail, wholesale and international trades) and COPA, the association of agriculture.

While this list addresses relatively few of the several hundreds of existing associations, the practice of consultation according to the Social Protocol has even more narrowed down the number of participants. In the case of all issues dealt with under the Protocol, participation was confined to ETUC, UNICE and CEEP. This may be traced to the fact that all these issues were of general relevance. However, the question of what is a general issue has proved to be debatable. Euro Commerce and UAPME, for example, call for admission to all forms of consultation in which ETUC, UNICE and CEEP participate (Falkner, 1998). Both associations questioned the legitimacy of the agreement on parental leave because of their exclusion from participation. Moreover, UAPME appealed to the European Court of Justice to nullify the agreement and announced to proceed in the same way regarding atypical work. The Commission refused to meet the demand of these and other associations with the argument that participation in the social dialogue rests on mutual recognition of the associations rather than on official admission (Keller and Sörries, 1997, p.27). For obvious reasons, ETUC, UNICE and CEEP are not interested in extending the number of participants. The only concession UNICE offered to 'outsiders' was to participate in the negotiations about atypical work as observers. This was accepted by Euro Commerce but refused by UAPME (Falkner, 1998). Given that ETUC, UNICE and CEEP not only elaborated the terms of participation under the Protocol but also informally control access to it at the interindustry level, they have been developed into the principal Euro-associations at this level. Concerning employers, this means that the key role accrues to UNICE because of the declining weight of the public sector. Analysis of the practice of negotiations leads Falkner (1998, p.349) to the conclusion 'that there are in fact only two negotiating teams'; with a clearly minor importance of CEEP on the side of employers. Therefore, UNICE's goals will dominate employer politics in the interindustry social dialogue, most prominently its goal to prevent Euro-regulation. Under the new circumstances of the Protocol, this means that UNICE is willing to negotiate with labour only when an initiative of the Commission for legislation is regarded as a credible threat (Keller and Sörries, 1997, p. 22). This definitely rules out bipartite (i.e. 'state-free') agreements. Needless to say, UNICE's interest in non-regulation includes the sectoral level. This, however, is confronted with the problem that sectoral interests are not covered by UNICE's domain. The sectoral Euro-associations of business are not incorporated into UNICE. This arrangement contrasts with the national systems which are characterised by the affiliation of most sectoral associations to the general peak organisations. To bridge this gap, UNICE initiated an informal European Employers' Network in the early 1990s. Its aim is co-ordination of employer organisations in order to obviate incoherences in social-policy strategies (Hornung-Draus, 1994). This means avoiding breakthroughs by sectoral unions which are then to be generalised at the interindustry level. So far, this risk has been low, since the sectoral social dialogue is less developed than its interindustry counterpart. In a few sectors (e.g. retail, transport) joint committees and informal working groups which serve as a platform for exchange of views and formulation of joint opinions exist. A routine practice of negotiations aimed at arriving at binding agreements is not established (Keller and Sörries, 1997). The sectoral Euro-associations, seeing themselves as trade associations, hesitate to take on the task of an employer organisation. For instance, the WEM as the representative of the metal industry whose industrial relations are more organised than any other sector in the member states, has shown no interest in being listed as an association to be consulted under the Protocol (Keller and Sörries, 1997, p. 6). Despite the general disinterest of sectoral Euro-business in the social dialogue there may be nevertheless an increased need for employer co-ordination in the future. Social-policy issues will probably gain momentum due to growing economic integration. It is not mere coincidence that the social dialogue is most developed in sectors under a common Community policy. Furthermore, the unions will magnify their efforts to establish negotiations with employers. Given that the sector is the main arena of collective bargaining in the member states, such efforts will place special emphasis on this level. If there are pressures for negotiations, employers may prefer the sectoral over the interindustry level, since the former is more able to suit agreements to their specific product-market interests.

All in all, employer organisation at the EU level is still in a state of flux. This is manifested in both competition for representational domains and experiments with informal networks of inter-associational co-operation.

ACKNOWLEDGEMENTS

The author acknowledges the financial support of the Fonds zur Förderung der Wissenschaftlichen Forschung, Austria.

APPENDIX: LIST OF ABBREVIATIONS

BDA	Bundesvereinigung der Deutschen Arbeitgeberverbände (Federation of German Employer Associations)
BDI	Bundesverband der Deutschen Industrie (Federation of German Industries)
C	Confindustria-Confederazione Generale dell 'Industria Italiana. (General Confederation of Italian Industry)
CBI	Confederation of British Industry
CEEP	European Centre of Public Enterprises
CEOE	Confederación Española de Organizaciones Empresariales (Spanish Confederation of Employer Organisations)
CEYPME	Confederación Española de la Pequeña y Mediana Empresa (Spanish Confederation of Small and Medium-sized Enterprises)
CII	Confederation of Irish Industry
CIP	Confederacão da Indústria Portuguesa (Confederation of Portuguese Industry)
CNPF	Conseil national du patronat français (National Council of French Employers)
COPA	Committee of Agricultural Organisations in the EC
DA	Dansk Arbejdsgiverforening (Danish Employer Federation)
DI	Dansk Industri (Danish Industry)
ETUC	European Trade Union Confederation
FIE	Federation of Irish Employers
IBEC	Irish Business and Employers' Confederation
ISME	Irish Small and Medium Enterprise Association
KNOV	Koninklijk Nederlands Ondernemersverbond (Royal Dutch Entrepreneurs Confederation)
NAF	Norges Arbeidsgiverforening (Norwegian Employer Confederation)
NCOV	Nederlands Christelijk Ondernemers Verbond (Dutch Christian Entrepreneurs Confederation)
NHO	Naeringslivets Hovedorganisasjon (Confederation of Norwegian Business and Industry)
LTK	Liiketyönantajain Keskusliitto (Employer Confederation of Service Industries)
PT	Palvelutyönantajat (Employer Confederation of Service Industries)
SAF	Svenska Arbetsgivareföreningen (Swedish Employers' Confederation)

STK	Suomen Työnantajain Keskusliitto (Confederation of Finnish Employers)
UAPME	European Association of Craft, Small and Medium-sized Enterprises
UNICE	Union of Industrial and Employers' Confederations of Europe
VBO/FEB	Verband van Belgische Ondernemingen/Fédération des Entreprises Belgique (Federation of Belgian Enterprises)
VNO	Verbond van Nederlandse Ondernemingen (Confederation of Dutch Enterprises)
WEM	Western European Metal Trades Employers' Association
WKÖ	Wirtschaftskammer Österreich (Federal Economic Chamber of Austria)
VÖI	Vereinigung Österreichischer Industrieller (Federation of Austrian Industrialists)
ZSAO	Zentralverband Schweizerischer Arbeitgeber-Organisationen (Central Association of Swiss Employer Organisations)

REFERENCES

Buda, D. (1995) 'Auf dem Weg zu europäischen Arbeitsbeziehungen?' In M. Mesch (ed.) *Sozialpartnerschaft und Arbeitsbeziehungen in Europa*, Manz, Wien, pp. 289–333.

Der Spiegel (1997) No. 1, 29 December.

Due, J., Madsen, J. S., Jensen, C. S. and Petersen, L. K. (1994) *The Survival of the Danish Model*. DJØF, Copenhagen.

Due, J., Madsen, J. S. and Jensen, C. S. (1995) 'Adjusting the Danish Model: Towards Centralized Decentralization,' in C. Crouch and F. Traxler (eds) *Organized Industrial Relations in Europe: What Future?* Avebury, Aldershot. pp. 121–150.

Elster, J. (1989) *The Cement of Society*, Cambridge University Press, Cambridge.

Falkner, G. (1998) Towards a Corporatist Social Policy Community: EU Social Policy in the 1990s, University of Vienna, Habilitationsschrift.

Grant, W. and Marsh, P. (1977) *The CBI*, Hodder and Stoughton, London.

Hornung-Draus, R. (1994) 'Union der Industrie- und Arbeitgeberverbände in Europa UNICE', in W. Lecher and H.-W. Platzer (eds) *Europäische Union—Europäische Arbeitsbeziehungen: Nationale Voraussetzungen und internationaler Rahmen*, Bund, Köln, pp. 230–241.

Keller, B. and Sörries, B. (1997) 'The Sectoral Social Dialogue and European Social Policy', Universität Konstanz, Typescript.

Lash, S. and Urry, J. (1987) *The End of Organized Capitalism*, Polity Press, Oxford.

Lucio, M. M. (1992) 'Spain: Constructing Institutions and Actors in a Context of Change' in A. Ferner and R. Hyman (eds) *Industrial Relations in the New Europe*, Basil Blackwell, Oxford,' pp. 482–523.

Olson, M. (1965) *The Logic of Collective Action. Public Goods and the Theory of Groups*, Harvard University Press, Cambridge-London.

Pestoff, V. (1994) 'Employer Organizations: Their Changing Structures and Strategies in Nine OECD Countries', Stockholm University, Typescript.

Springer, B. (1992) *The Social Dimension of 1992—Europe Faces a New EC*. Praeger, New York.

Traxler, F. (1993) 'Business Associations and Labor Unions in Comparison: Theoretical Perspectives and Empirical Findings on Social Class, Collective Action and Associational Organizability', *British Journal of Sociology*, 44, 673–691.

Traxler, F. (1995) 'Farewell to Labour Market Associations? Organized versus Disorganized Decentralization as a Map for Industrial Relations', in C. Crouch and F. Traxler (eds) *Organized Industrial Relations in Europe: What Future?* Avebury, Aldershot, pp. 3–19.

Traxler, F. (1996) 'Collective Bargaining and Industrial Change: A Case of Disorganization? A Comparative Analysis of Eighteen OECD Countries', *European Sociological Review*, 12, 271–287.

Traxler, F. and Schmitter, P. C. (1995) 'The Emerging Euro-Policy and Organized Interests' *European Journal of International Relations*, 1, 191–218.

European trade unions in the mid-1990s

Jelle Visser

With the 20th century drawing to a close, European trade unions offer a mixed picture. In Western Europe unions have not yet recovered from a decade of distress, the 1980s, in which the return of large-scale unemployment, massive job restructuring, intensified international competition and the politics of neoliberalism sapped bargaining power, eroded their membership base and set in motion an unprecedented decline in workers' militancy. The 1990s were marked by the downfall of the communist command economies and the transition to democracy in Central and Eastern Europe, an international economic recession and the race towards Economic and Monetary Union as the three most significant macro events affecting trade unions. In Central and Eastern Europe it became possible, for the first time in half a century or longer, to build a democratic union movement, a task that was not and never could be easy. In Western Europe, the direct effects of the collapse of communism were most noticeable in Germany. Unification and the expansion of West Germany's organisational structures and industrial relations practices to the East, were followed by a severe labour market crisis, a sharp fall in membership and organisational turbulence in the German unions, the effects of which are felt by the European union movement in its entirety (Turner, 1996). The famous and rather unique stability of the German industrial relations system and its trade unions came to an abrupt halt. Its projection onto the European level became less obvious and its sponsorship of the European trade union movement less secure, paradoxically, at the same time that more unions (Italy, Ireland, even some major unions in France, Portugal and Spain) tried to imitate its features.

Persistent high levels of unemployment, declining rates of unionisation, dire union finances, pressures for a leaner welfare state and a better functioning labour market, together with a tighter framework for wage bargaining under the conditions for entry into the Economic and Monetary Union, have set the uneasy stage for most union movements in Western Europe in the mid-1990s. It is true that in 1995 and following years employment started to increase again, at a

Jelle Visser is Professor of Sociology at the University of Amsterdam.

© Blackwell Publishers Ltd 1998, 108 Cowley Road, Oxford OX4 1JF, UK
and 350 Main Street, Malden, MA 02148, USA.

modest rate, but from 1992 to 1995 five million jobs, more than half of all jobs created since the 1981–3 recession and the relaunch of Europe in the mid-1980s, were destroyed. By 1996–1997 the unemployment rate for the European Union as a whole had climbed to 11 per cent and still showed few signs of improvement.

MEMBERSHIP DEVELOPMENTS

Against the background of employment decline it is hardly surprising that in Western Europe trade unions lost 4.5 million, or nearly 11 per cent, of their employed members between 1990 and 1995, halting whatever signs of recovery there had been towards the end of the 1980s (see Table 1). In the first half of the decade the largest set-backs were felt by trade unions in Germany (−2,392,000 or 21 per cent), Great Britain (−1,581,000 or 18 per cent), and Italy (−531,000 or 9 per cent), but the number of employed union members also decreased in union strongholds like Sweden (−225,000 or 7 per cent) and Finland (−133,000 or 9 per cent). There were increases in the number of employed union members in Spain (+ 447,000 or +37 per cent until 1993, but the effects of the recession were felt the following years with a decline of 56,000 members), Denmark (+135,000 or 9 per cent), the Netherlands (+126,000 or 9 per cent), Norway (+79,000 or 8 per cent), and Ireland (+31,000 or 7 per cent). Incomplete returns for 1996 show further decline in union membership in Britain, Germany, Italy, Switzerland and Austria. In Central and Eastern Europe the set-backs for unions were much larger, amidst huge restructuring processes of industry, privatisation, and a sharp fall in employment. Membership levels have plummeted, but current levels presumably reflect more genuinely the kind of support that unions can muster among the populations in these countries than can have been the case in the past (ILO, 1997a,b). Levels of unionisation remain higher than elsewhere, but it remains to be seen whether this heritage of the past can last.

UNIONISATION TRENDS

One out of every three employed workers in Western Europe is a member of a trade union. What does this figure tell us; is the bottle half full or half empty? Thirty-one per cent (the exact figure for 1995) is more than twice the 14 per cent unionisation rate of the United States. But it is also nine percentage points below the post-war peak in unionisation in Western Europe at the end of the 1970s. Compared to the US and Japan union decline began later in Europe. In the 1980s the level of unionisation declined almost twice as much in the US than in Europe. In the 1990s, however, the reverse is true. The much faster decline in European unionisation is probably due to the sharp contraction of

TABLE 1
Union Membership, Employment and Union Density in the 1990s

	Members 1995	+/− 90–95	Employment 1995	+/− 90–95	Density 1995	+/− 90–95
North						
Sweden	3,101	−6.8%	3,540	−12.3%	87,6	+5.2
Finland	1,377	−8.8%	1,756	−16.3%	78,4	+6.4
Denmark	1,836	7.9%	2,319	−0.5%	79,1	+6.1
Norway	1,068	8.0%	1,851	4.8%	57,7	+1.7
West						
Ireland	455	7.3%	983	17.3%	46.2	−4.4
Britain	7,275	−17.8%	22,664	−2.5%	32.1	−6.0
Centre						
Belgium	1,585	1.5%	3,057	0.2%	51.9	+0.7
Netherlands	1,536	9.0%	5,987	8.1%	25.7	+0.2
Austria	1,287	−4.2%	3,226	10.1%	40.3	−5.6
Germany	9,284	−20.5%	31,998	−4.1%	29.0	−6.0
Switzerland	724	−9.3%	3,270	−3.8%	22.1	−1.4
South						
France	1,967	−4.1%	19,389	1.1%	10.1	−0.6
Spain	1,606	32.2%	8,620	−6.6%	18.6	+5.4
Portugal	800	−20.0%	3,173	−3.5%	25.2	−5.2
Italy	5,341	−8.9%	14,168	−3.2%	37.7	−2.4
Greece	430	−18.7%	2,060	5.8%	20.8	−6.4
Europe (W)	39,672	−10.4%	128,061	−2.1%	30.9	−2.9
EU	37,880	−10.8%	122,940	−2.1%	30.8	−3.0
Europe (CEE)						
Bulgaria	1,200	−45.5%	2,900	−17.9%	41.3	−21.0
Czechoslovakia	4,350	−24.2%	8,450	13.2%	51.5	−25.4
Czech Rep.	1,886		4,407		42.8	
Slovak Rep.	1,150		1,865		61.7	
Hungary	1,860	−38.0%	3,099	−17.0%	60.0	−20.4
Poland	3,420	−45.7%	10,124	−5.5%	33.8	−24.8
US	16,359	−2.2%	114,262	6.3%	14.3	−1.3
Japan	12,620	2.9%	52,630	8.9%	24.0	−1.3

Note: the Italian employment data for 1990 have been adjusted downward with 500,000 units (the estimated number of those aged 14 years) to allow comparison with the figure for 1995; Bulgaria 1991–1996; Czechoslovakia 1990–1993; Czech Republic 1995; Slovak Republic 1995; Hungary 1985–1995; Poland 1989–1995.

employment in the 1992–1993 recession, the rise in unemployment and the membership crisis in German unions following the aftermath of unification.

THE UNEMPLOYED

The membership figures mentioned above and shown in Table 1 do not include union members among the unemployed, self-employed and retired workers. They make up a total of 13 million members, or a quarter of all members of European trade unions, to be compared with nearly 40 million members in employment. The large majority are workers who have retired from the labour market, often before reaching the legal retirement age. The proportion of retired members now varies between 47 per cent in Italian unions to around 15–30 per cent in the main federations in Northern Europe, probably less (10 per cent) in Ireland and Britain. Unemployed members are a much smaller group. Only about two of the 18 million unemployed in the European Union are organised by the trade unions; most of them in Sweden, Finland, Denmark or Belgium, where unions run an unemployment insurance scheme or are involved in the decisions over its provision. Elsewhere, unions do organise small numbers of unemployed workers, but find it difficult to retain the membership of the long-term unemployed or attract the first-time job seekers, school-leavers and re-entering women who make up the bulk of the unemployed, especially in Southern Europe.

Movements of unemployed workers, outside the main unions, made their appearance in 1997 in France and Germany, and have in 1996 and 1997 been involved by the Irish Congress of Trade Unions in the re-negotiation and ratification of the Social Pact ('Partnership 2000') with employers and the Irish government. In some cases, notably in France, the claim of unions that they represent the unemployed in the governing boards of national insurance funds and other bodies, has been challenged. The current Socialist government of France seems set to allow separate representation of the unemployed, against the opposition of the CFDT which currently holds the presidency of the unemployment insurance fund.

THE CHALLENGE OF STRUCTURAL CHANGE

In the mid-1990s in Western Europe around 45 per cent of the employed membership of trade unions worked in the public or collective sector (including health, education and public transport); 40 per cent worked in mining, manufacturing and construction; and 14 per cent in private services. In terms of (dependent) employment, the three sectors—industry, private and public services—are nearly equal in size, each making up one-third of the total. The conclusion seems justified that trade unions have yet to make headway in organising the most dynamic sector of the economy, i.e. the private services. The large differences in union densities between industry and tradeable services, and between the private and public sector in all but two countries (Sweden and Denmark), are witness of a structural deficit (see Table 2).

The Achilles' heel of the trade unions, clearly, lies in the private service sector. This is especially evident if one looks at data on unionisation by firm size, employment contracts, tenure, and working hours. Such data, based on labour force sample surveys, are available, for instance, in the Netherlands and Britain,

TABLE 2
Union Density Rates by Gender, by Industry and Employment Sector

		Industry	Commerce & finance	Private sector	Public sector	Male	Female
Sweden	1995	99	61	78	93	81	85
Finland	1989	80		65	86	68	75
Denmark	1992	94	53	68	87	88	88
Norway	1989	74	18	45	83		
Ireland	1995			37	76		
Great Britain	1996	31	18	21	61	33	29
Netherlands	1996	37	14	19	45	33	20
Austria	1995	56	21	37	70	51	33
Germany	1992	45	12	25	56	40	21
Switzerland	1987	40	14	22	71		
France	1995	6	5	6	20		
Spain	1993	24	11				
Italy	1992	43	18	32	54		
Greece	1995			10	65		
EU	1992	40	15	25	25	37	30

Note: The EU figures are based on a weighted average for nine member states, i.e. Denmark, Norway, Sweden, Austria, West Germany, the Netherlands, Italy, Great Britain and France.

two countries which have made considerable progress with flexibilisation of the labour market. As expected, unions are under-represented in the most flexible segment of the labour market. This may also explain part of the sharp decline in unionisation among young people. Ageing of union members is a rather general phenomenon in European unions.

Similar conclusions apply with even greater force to Central and Eastern Europe. Here the role of public sector and heavy industry unionism was, and still is, overwhelming. In contrast, in the newly privatised sectors of the economy—notably services and distribution—union presence is feeble. One main problem for the new unions in these sectors is that they have no bargaining partner and that there is no basis for old style 'welfare' unionism either (MacShane, 1994).

It is a striking fact that in the Scandinavian countries (we have no data for Norway), women take up union membership in equal or larger numbers than men. This is closely related to the expansion of the public sector for social services which is much larger in these countries than elsewhere. The fact that many of these jobs are part-time, does not seem to discourage women from taking up union membership. Elsewhere, for instance in Britain and the Netherlands, where social services are much more organised through the market, female part-time workers do join unions in much smaller numbers than male and full-time employees.

Generally, female employees have made strides ahead in European unions. In all European countries for which we have data, all or nearly all membership growth during the past decade has come from women. The unionisation rate among women increased in all countries except Britain and Austria. Data for West Germany suggest a small rise, for East Germany a decline. There are no good data for the Central and Eastern countries, but the fact that women increasingly depend on jobs in the private service sector suggest that, as in East Germany, union membership becomes a less feasible option. Among men unionisation remained at the same level in Scandinavia and the Netherlands, but fell in Britain, Germany and Austria. Only in Britain this went together with a sharp fall of unionisation in industry. In the other countries unions have defended their position in industry, but often on the basis of a shrinking domain.

MATCHING THE NEW AND THE OLD

'Preserve the Old and Organise the New', this useful advice (Wever, 1996) is not easily implemented. Old and New, declining and growing segments of the labour market, are usually organised by different unions who rarely share resources. Often the richest unions are found in declining industries. Recent attempts, for instance in the Netherlands, to create 'conglomerate unions' which cross the boundaries between industry and services, address this problem (see below). Even the most powerful peak associations have hardly a say in where and how to spend money on recruitment drives, and are usually not allowed to set up direct membership services. Examples of failure abound (see Pankert 1993; Olney 1997 for overviews of the special recruitment programmes introduced, and abandoned, by a number of European union peak associations). In this sense, the traditional, federal structure of union movements suffers from the same 'conservative bias' and 'joint decision trap' as do federal states (Scharpf, 1988).

Matching the new and the old is of course also a matter of policy. This is nowhere clearer than in the discussion about so-called 'atypical work'. Even the preferred union term ('atypical') is quite ideological, as if the standard employment contract had not been the preserve of males, and as if this Fordist standard represents an ideal and norm for everybody even yesterday. This discussion is raging through all mainstream European unions, without producing a uniform pattern of response. These debates are directly reflected in the share of men working (voluntary) part-time, which is indeed very low in all but very few countries.

The TUC has initiated a 'New Unionism' campaign targeted at 'the new insecure world of work'. From the Message of John Monks, the TUC's general secretary, I cite: 'As trade unionists, we may not like the new labour market but we have to get to grips with it. Unions should never be an exclusive club for those in a full-time steady job'. Pleading for a joint effort, he adds: 'And the time when three or four unions could afford to waste time and effort chasing the same shrinking pool of members is long gone'. Unions in Germany, on the other hand, seem to do just that; they are still very reluctant to consider part-time work as acceptable and some defend that temporary jobs ought to be legis-lated out of existence. In contrast, Dutch unions have begun to promote part-time work as a work-sharing strategy and as a better way of combining work and care (for children or the elderly). From a Mori poll of British and Dutch employees we learn that the Dutch work far fewer 'unsociable hours', especially on Sundays, are less unhappy about working hours, and seem to have a greater say over the hours they work (TUC, 1998). Possibly, the 'one-and-a-half-job-per-household' model (Visser and Hemerijck, 1997) presents a new social opti-mum, with less full-time unemployment and better possibilities for the combi-nation of work and care. The implied 'privatisation' of social services, however, is still anathema to the Scandinavian unions. Today they may be the only ones not only willing but also able to defend a large collective sector for these kind of services.

Closely related is the debate over labour market flexibilty, or souplesse, as they say in France. Strict dismissal and job protection rights are often evaded, sometimes with the blessings of the law, by the creation of temporary jobs which carry no rights whatsoever and from which no or little social security or pension payments can be derived. In Western Europe, this kind of segmentation has nowhere been sharper than in Spain, where in 1995 one out of three jobs, and nine out of ten new jobs, were temporary. In countries without legislation making this possible, the informal sector and the sector of jobs under the 'social security contribution' threshold, plays a similar, less measurable role.

In Spain, the reality of the Spanish labour market has cornered the unions, which only organise the stable job segment in the declining internal labour mar-kets of large industrial firms and in the public sector. Their claim to fight for a unifying and solidaristic strategy, defending the employment opportunities and social rights of all workers, is increasingly at odds with the reality of wide-spread youth unemployment, the vast world of continuous temporary work, and entrenched segmentation. This predicament has led the two main unions, UGT and CCOO, to sign in April 1997 a Pact with the Spanish employers' associ-ations, in which dismissal protection is eased in the hope that more workers will gain a 'permanent contract' and temporary workers get a better deal. Despite considerable opposition in their own ranks, the agreement has been defended by the unions as a means to avoid legislation on flexibility by the conservative government (Richards and Gracla de Polavieja).

The Spanish compromise was modelled after a similar accord, signed in April 1996 and becoming the basis for subsequent legislation, between the Dutch unions and the employers federations. With this 'Flexibility and Security' accord, unions try to gain more rights for temporary workers by trading away some of the disincentives for employers to recruit more permanent staff. Whether this

unprincipled approach will help the unions to reorganise and reregulate the flexible labour market is yet to be seen; together with the pragmatic policies of
Dutch unions on business operating and working hours it has helped to boost
job growth. Working on Sundays remains taboo, however. On that issue the
Dutch unions have joined a large 'mixed bag coalition', with nearly all churches,
the opposition Christian parties and the left fringe, as well as shopkeepers, against
the '24 hours economy'.

From Table 1, I draw the conclusion that, for all the reasons mentioned above,
trade unions have a hard time to grow with employment (see: Ireland, the Netherlands, Spain or Austria). But they find it even harder to grow when employment
shrinks (the more usual case in Europe in the mid-1990s). Indeed, there is only
one case (Denmark) where employment contracts and membership increases, but
it represents a borderline case, given the availability of a union-administered
unemployment insurance scheme. The conclusion seems reasonable that, for their
own sake but above all for the good of the country, trade unions are well advised
to make the creation of more employment their first priority, like they did in
Ireland and the Netherlands. This advice is in line with Joel Rogers' hypothesis
that unions advance when they put forward practical programmes of action that
(a) benefit their members or potential members, (b) solve problems in the broader
society—often, problems of capitalists on whose well-being the rest of society
unfortunately depends, and (c) by doing both these things achieve the political
and social respect to secure support for their own organisation (cited in Wever,
1996). Through their qualified support for the European Monetary Union, and
the often painful measures to make membership of EMU possible, many mainstream unions in countries as diverse (but usually outside the D-mark zone) as
Italy, Spain, Ireland, and Finland are taking this lesson to heart (Foden, 1998).
The British TUC, although similarly supportive, has been denied such a role.
There was, and still is, no British government prepared to enlist union support in
this new game of 'competitive corporatism' (Rhodes, 1997) and like its German
counterpart, the TUC would probably not be allowed to play such a role of
'primus interparis' by its own mighty and divided unions.

RECRUITMENT POLICIES, SERVICES AND WORKPLACE ORGANISATION

As we already saw from the example of the TUC, the membership crisis has
caused many union leaders to reflect on how to better recruit, organise and retain
members. Nearly everywhere this has made them more conscious about the kind
of union services that must be offered in return for membership subscription,
especially in environments where a less supportive legal environment, a lack of
endorsement, or outright opposition, from employers, and the absence of social
pressure from colleagues, friends or families, has made trade union membership

a much less automatic or taken-for-granted decision than it has been, perhaps, in the past.

It must remain a matter of speculation whether employees are less motivated by collective values than, say, one or two generations ago. Research among union and non-union members in Britain and the Netherlands suggests that no large attitudinal differences exist between members and non-members (Klandermans and Visser, 1995; Gallie, 1996;). What certainly have changed are the type of labour markets and the nature of employment contracts, especially for new-comers, and it has definitely become more difficult for unions to reach workers. In the case of Britain it has been argued that the 'key explanation of non-member-ship appears to be the inability of unions to make contact with, or provide suf-ficient support to, potential members (Waddington and Whitston, 1997; p. 518). This also applies elewhere, notably in France or the Netherlands, where surveys show that two out of three workers find themselves in an environment where unions are virtually absent (Klandermans and Visser, 1995; Dufour and Nunes, 1998;).

From research among new members in Britain, Denmark and the Netherlands we learn that nearly three out of four of these new members mention 'support should I have a problem at work' as a motive for joining (Klandermans and Visser, 1995; Waddington and Whitston 1997;). This presupposes that unions are present in or near the workplace, and run an adequate legal service. Access to the workplace has become particularly important for unions with the disappear-ance of working-class neighbourhoods and the replacement of local dues collec-tion by centralised administrative procedures. Union representatives at the work-place are often the only direct means of contact between members and their union (except where unions administer or distribute social security benefits, as they do in, for instance, Denmark, Sweden, Finland or Belgium, and in some industries such as construction and agriculture elsewhere). Workplace organis-ation depends on the recognition and co-operation of employers, and tends to be restricted, by law or by collective agreement, to the one half of potential members who find regular employment in large firms. For the other, more dynamic, half, trade unions might need other methods of recruitment and servicing.

New members hardly ever mention financial reasons (extra discounts, credit cards and other gadgets, introduced by a number of unions following the Amer-ican example) as a reason for joining. Such techniques may however affect their decision to stay. Union recruitment is notoriously inefficient, since many new members leave the unions in the first years of their membership. In the Nether-lands, for instance two out of three new recruits leave the union within five years. Almost two out of five leavers mention disappointment with the union 'product' (no adequate help or support) as their main reason for leaving; 29 per cent no longer had use for the union after changing jobs, 24 per cent complained about the price of membership; 21 per cent disagreed with union policy. These exits are most frequent in the labour market segment of young people, women, workers on temporary contracts, and those holding part-time jobs (Klandermans and Visser, 1995). These employees may simply not get enough time to develop loyalty with their union. Given the lack of organisation in the workplaces where they work, it is unlikely that others will remind these workers of their 'duty' to organise. Centrally organised loyalty programmes may be the (costly) solution.

Few unions have experimented with new forms of insurance and it is not certain that unions can win the competition with the private insurance business without greater public support or voluntary support from lay officials (applying the method of the mutualism of the past). In the Netherlands trade unions have started to experiment with what has been called the 'capuccino' model—union insurance is supposed to provide the 'cacao', after the 'milk' from collective schemes negotiated with employers, and the 'coffee' based on mandatory minimum provisions. It is still too early to tell whether workers will like the taste.

The most promising area for unions appears to be the provision of legal advice to members in matters of employment and social security rights, but the requirement of greater professionalism and the increased casualisation and diversity of employment conditions makes it ever more expensive for unions to provide these services. In Belgium such advice extends to tax matters and housing; unions in the UK have also expanded legal advice into new areas; in Germany and the Netherlands burgeoning costs have led unions to draw instead narrower boundaries. The use of legal services has exponentially increased in both countries and has led to various rationalising attempts in the peak federations DGB and FNV. A possible way out is to charge members on the basis of their use of such services, or offer 'no claim' discounts, but there is considerable resistance against such attempts of 'marketisation' of the relations between unions and their members.

A final point relates to the organisational culture of unions. It may be that the image, if not reality, of unions as organisations of middle-aged men is simply too much for women and young people. Despite the advance of women among the membership, few women make it to the top of the union leadership. Even in a country like Sweden, where women make up half the membership, nine out of ten leadership positions are occupied by men. More unions now have programmes of affirmative action in place, or support quota rules for delegate conferences and executive office, like the CGIL in Italy or some of the main German and Dutch unions. Women presidents, like Nicole Notat of the CFDT in France, may be an important signal of change. In the Dutch FNV, a similar opportunity to elect a female president was wasted in 1997. And in this area too, positive policies also require a change in bargaining agendas with issues like breast cancer screening, parental leave, employment security, career breaks, part-time employment, and job-sharing.

INTEREST AGGREGATION AND UNION PLURALISM

The organisational landscape of unions in Europe is changing. In Eastern and Central Europe the monolithic union blocs of the past have been replaced by a plethora of rival, mostly weak and highly politicised unions, each vying for recognition, both nationally and internationally. MacShane (1994) distinguishes four sorts of union federations: the newly created, anti-communist, nationalist or free market unions like *Solidarity* in Poland, *Fratia* in Romania, *Prodkepa* in Bulgaria, and *Liga* in Hungary; the former communist unions that are taken over by a post-communist leadership, with the KOS federation in Czechoslovakia, in 1993 split up in a Czech and Slovak federation, as the prime example; the reformed communist unions, starting change in 1980s and accepting a Western style pluralism, as did MSzOSz in Hungary and CITUB in Bulgaria; and finally, the inheritors of communist unions, like the OPZZ in Poland. Further splits, based on politics and personalities, occurred in the 1990s and the tendency towards fragmentation has not yet stopped. Perhaps the admission into membership of the European Trade Union Confederation will help these unions to find better ways of mutual co-operation.

In Western Europe plural unionism is common as well. At one end of the spectrum we find Britain, Ireland, Austria, Germany and Greece. In these countries political and ideological divisions, if they exist, are internalised in one dominant federation, representing 80–100 per cent of all union members (see Table 3). Independent unionism may persist, but these do not combine in rival federations. Political conflict may be channelled through explicit factionalism, as in the Greek or Austrian federation, or be suppressed as in the German federation, still allowing it to express sympathy with the position of the Social Democratic Party. An interesting challenge to union monopoly has come from the extreme right in Austria, where Mr. Haider has founded a union, the first of its kind since 1945, which has been declared admissable under Austrian federal law.

At the other extreme we find the unions in Spain, Italy and France. Here the main union federation organises less than 40 per cent. In France the union landscape has further fragmented in recent years (Jefferys, 1996; Denis and Rozenblatt, 1998). CGT may have lost its traditional first place and is now clearly rivalled in size and leadership by the CFDT, which has developed into the moderate and responsible variant of French unionism, showing its willingness to compromise and enter dialogue with governments and employers. In this direction it may be followed by the Christian CFTC, the federation of senior staff, and a new federation of public sector unions. On its left wing there has been bloodletting, especially in the public sector where the SUD (Solidaire-Unitaire-Démocratique) unions, loosely combined in the 'Groupe de dix' offer a radical alternative. In the strike movement of 1995, the traditional arch-enemies of the French union movement, the communist CGT and the reformist FO, have moved

TABLE 3
Associational Monopoly and Affiliates of Main Confederation, 1996–7

	Main confederation	% of total membership	Number of affiliates
North			
Denmark	LO	66%	23
Sweden	LO	58%	20
Norway	LO	57%	28
Finland	SAK	52%	25
West			
Ireland	ICTU	94%	52
Great Britain	TUC	84%	74
Centre			
Austria	ÖGB	100%	15
Germany	DGB	81%	13
Netherlands	FNV	63%	15
Belgium	CSC	53%	25
Switzerland	SGB	50%	17
South			
Greece	GSEE	80%	53
Portugal	CNTG-IN	71%	150
Spain	UGT	39%	12
Italy	CGIL	38%	18
France	CFDT	26%	19

closer in their common opposition against the Juppé government. Whether the current fragmentation will lead to a duopoly around two variants of syndicalism, a rather Northern European model aspired by the CFDT and its allies, and the opposition model currently embraced by the CGT and FO alliance, with a social movement type of unionism on the fringe, remains unclear (see also Adam (1998) and the various debates, for instance between Bourdieu and Touraine, on the interpretation of the 1995 strikes).

The situation in the other Southern European countries is quite different. In Italy the three main confederations have again moved closer in recent years, without however making much progress towards unification. Independent union-ism in Italy is endemic, especially in the public sector. Its three main variants are always a current of occupational unions (traindriver, pilots, teachers, doctors) which may or may not combine in federations; rival political union federations, especially on the right, and a movement style of unionism, within and in oppo-sition of the main unions, especially in the CGIL. The latter current, most notably represented through the Cobas or Comitati di Base movement, seems to be over its zenith, as is the case with the 'coordinations' in France. The political project of creating a common union federation of the right, near to the political project of Mr. Berlusconi's Forza Italia, seems to have failed.

Spanish unionism has evolved towards a duopoly between UGT and CC.OO, nearly of equal size and influence. They work together and have together signed the Social pacts of recent years, as did the three main Italian federations. This is in sharp contrast with the position taken by the two main confederations in Portugal. CGTP-IN and UGT continue to pursue antagonistic social and political aims, they differ in their internal structure, and as a consequence produce very different patterns of union activity at all levels. In the 1990s the politicy of mutual boycott attenuated when the UGT gave up its veto to admit the majority CGTP-IN as member of the ETUC. CGTP-IN still excuses itself from participating in social concertation and did not sign the Social and Employment Pact of 1996.

Regional unionism plays hardly a role in Europe. There are separate regional organisations in the Basque country (ELA-STV) and in Galicia (INTG), but attempts to form such unions in Catalonia were as big a failure as the attempts of the Northern League to exploit union discontent and set up a Lombardian or Venetian union in Italy. It is interesting to note that there are no separate Northern Ireland union organisations; the two communities are largely represented by unions, combined in their own regional councils but with their home base in the Irish Republic and Britain, and affiliated with the ICTU and TUC respectively. In Belgium, the two main union federations—the Christian CSC and the socialist FGTB—organise across the two language communities, although there is a stronger base of the CSC in Flanders, and of the FGTB in Wallonia.

Finally, in the Scandinavian countries the traditional functional division between three federations—one for mainly blue-collar workers, one for employees, and one for higher-educated, managerial and professional staff—has survived, despite occasional tensions and border disputes. The main trend is the declining share of the main confederations in these countries; least affected seems to be the Danish LO, for the simple reason that it also organises lower ranking white collar staff. In the other countries, the time is near that the LO will become a minority organisation. The only way out would be a merger, across the collar-line, between unions of manual and non-manual workers. Despite talks about a new worker statute, in the context of new concepts of work organisation and workshop participation, particularly under debate in Sweden, there are still formidable obstacles for such a move.

Whether the traditional centralism in the Scandinavian union movements, always more prominent in Sweden and Norway than in Denmark, will last is also doubtful. In the export sector, Swedish unions joined with employers in 'cross-class coalition' with employers in their demand for more decentralisation and flexibility. The LO union in engineering looked for an answer to the siphoning off of skilled workers by its white-collar rival under centralised wage policy; and mounted at the same time opposition to the use of 'compensation clauses' (for wage drift) in public sector. There were several new co-ordination attempts below the level of the peak federations, between groups of unions in the export, domestic and public sector, each testifying to the declining authority of the LO as co-ordinator. Within and between peak associations 'unity appears more remote' (Kjellberg, 1983). The reluctance to let state mediators in, as proposed by the Swedish LO in 1997 and common in Norway and Denmark, is not helping either.

In Norway compulsory arbitration has been used to bring militant unions inside and outside LO in line, gag independent unions, and prevent conflict in so-called 'essential services'. A similar approach has been successfully used in Italy's public sector. The price seems to be the break-away of a new group of unions, called the 'Academics' from one of the federations. Whether they can gain a bargaining licence under Norwegian law remains uncertain.

MERGERS AND ORGANISATIONAL RESTRUCTURING

Declining membership and financial revenue, combined with increased demand for protection and services, has caused a spate of mergers and cost-reduction programmes in unions and federations throughout Western Europe. In the second half of the 1990s merger activity tends to lead to the formation of conglomerate (multi-sectoral and multi-occupational) unions, even in countries, like Germany or the Netherlands, with an established tradition of sectoral or industrial unionism (Streeck and Visser, 1997). These changes are driven by economics, not or not nearly as much by politics, or deliberate views of class unity, industrial governance, collective bargaining or European co-operation.

These merger movements have only just started. The Swedish LO has plans to reduce its number of affiliates to 8 or 13. Similar 'grandiose plans' failed however in Denmark, and both the Norwegian and Danish federation have settled for an intermediary solution by forming union bargaining cartels. In Switzerland, Germany, the Netherlands, Britain and Ireland the merger movement is in full swing, leading to the formation of conglomerate unions. It is likely that a similar process will bring the manual unions in Belgium and Austria together.

The logic behind all this is economic. As a rule, unions tend to suffer from the same inverse fluctuation of revenue and client needs as do most social security systems. The economics of union organising require that most members, most of the time, do not call upon the union's services except for the collective protection it offers. However, further decentralisation, increased diversity of needs and conditions, increased instability of employment and volatility of members, the availability of alternative providers of advice, and insurance, and not least a more self-conscious (potential) membership, increase the costs of union services while requiring a higher quality. Economies of scale may be the answer and create the conditions for greater professionalism, but mergers bring costs with them and may increase the (emotional) distance to and place greater strains on the union ideal of participative democracy.

It is furthermore striking that the international or European dimension is absent in the current restructuring process. Union mergers halt before national borders and thus testify to the national embeddedness of the European union movement. Cross-national mergers between unions from different countries have not yet occurred, although co-operation has increased between German chemicals' union and the GMB in Britain, between the printing unions of Germany, Austria, Switzerland and the Netherlands, or between the Christian union federations of Belgium and the Netherlands. In general, the international exchange of ideas or models of union reform plays a very small role. Moreover, the increase in ideosyncratic structures which differ from one country to the next, will make it increasingly difficult to match union organisations at the European level on a sectoral basis.

The consequences of multi-industry mergers will however be felt by the European union bodies that do exist. It is quite possible that the large conglomerate unions of the near future will erode the powers and functions of the national peak federations and will make their presence felt in Europe in a more direct way, bypassing the peak federations and creating a more complex environment for the European Trade Union Confederation which so far has rested, mainly, on these national peaks. The sectoral pillar of the European union movement— today organised around 14 European Industry Committees (metal, chemicals, food, construction, etc.)—will have to accommodate highly dissimilar and overlapping national unions. One might speculate that it is only a matter of time, once the potential for taking over smaller unions has dried up and the national market for union-mergers has cleared, before the new conglomerate unions will try international mergers. Such a development is the more likely, the less these unions' sole activity is collective bargaining and the more they specialise in services to members and to national and European works councils. Indeed, the first immediate effect of European Works Councils, established and negotiated under the relevant European Directive of 1994, is likely to be a closer, direct link between European unions and the development of a professional market for services and information-exchange for these councils and their members.

In the past few years, triggered by Maastricht and the revived Social Dialogue, international co-operation between unions has strengthened, especially at the level of peak federations. The relationships between unions from the Eastern and Western part of the continent have been reinforced. At its 1995 Congress in Brussels, the ETUC admitted many of the new unions of Central and Eastern Europe into its membership and at the same time strengthened its mandate for negotiations with European employers.

In contrast with the picture of membership decline stands the fact that in many corners of Europe, and in its core in Brussels and Strasbourg, trade unions share a place at the bargaining table with governments and with leading employers federations, while negotiating social pacts over wage moderation, welfare reform, labour market legislation, and employment (Pochet, 1998). Such pacts were concluded in recent years in Ireland, Italy, Spain, Portugal, Greece, and Finland; attempts to negotiate pacts were made, but failed, in Germany and Belgium. In Austria, Norway and the Netherlands unions and employers kept meeting at the highest level and set the framework for responsible wage policies and labour market change. In Denmark and Sweden central level wage negotiations were discontinued, but co-ordination at the sectoral level remained in place. Even in France, in spite of the internal rivalry among unions and misgivings in the employers' camp, and amidst shifting alliances with political forces and state intervention, a part of the union movement (CFDT, CFTC, FSU) was trying to involve itself, and create the conditions for, a process of political exchange. All these experiences, it seems to me, are a far cry from the tales of the 'End of Organised Capitalism', the 'Demise of Corporatism', or the 'Irrelevance of Trade Unions'.

REFERENCES

Adam, G. (1998) 'Vers un nouveau syndicalisme', *Droit Social*, February, 2, 107–9.
Ambrosini, M. (1995) 'Unionization, practical Models for Industrial Relations in the Private Service Industries in Europe', Rome: CISL-SindNova, dossier Soc94, 10064.
Armingeon, K. (1994) *Staat und Arbeitsbeziehungen. Ein internationaler Vergleich*, Opladen: Westdeutscher Verlag.
Bain, G.S. and R. Price (1983) 'Union Growth: Dimensions, Determinants and Destiny', in: G.S. Bain (ed.) *Industrial Relations in Britain*, Oxford: Blackwell, 3–33.
Barreto, J. and R. Naumann (1997) 'Portugal: Industrial Relations under Democracy', in: A. Ferner and R. Hyman, eds., *Changing Industrial Relations in Europe*, Oxford: Blackwell, 395–426.
Black, J., A-M. Greene, and P. Ackers (1997) 'Size and Effectiveness: A case study of a small union', *Industrial Relations Journal*, 28, 2, 136–148.
Boyer, R. (1995) The Future of Unions: Is the Anglo-Saxon model a fatality, or will contrasting national trajectories persist?', *British Journal of Industrial Relations*, vol. 33,4, 519–530.
Carrieri, M. (1997) 'I sindacati non confederali', in: CESOS, *Le relazioni sindacali in Italia. Rapporto 1994/95*, Roma: Centro di Studi Economici Sociali e Sindacali, 1997: 305–306.
Carrieri, M. and L. Tatarelli (1997) *Gli altri sindacati. Viaggio nelle organizzazioni autonome e di base*, Rome: Ediesse.
Cerdeira, M.C. (1997) 'Sindicalizaçao Portuguesa de 1974 a 1995', Sociedade e Trabalho, 1, october 1997.
Delsen, L. (1995) *Atypical Employment: An International Perspective. Causes, Consequences and Policy*, Groningen: Wolters-Noordhoff.
Denis, J.-M. (1996) *Les coordinations. Recherche désespérée d'une citoyenneté*, Paris: Syllepse.
Denis, J.-M. and Rozenblatt, P. (1998) 'L'institution d'un sindicalisme fédéré interprofessionel: le Groupe de Dix', in *Sociologie du Travail*, 40, 2, 263–277.
Dufour, C. and Nunes, C. (1998) 'Enquète auprès des sécretaires de comités d'entreprise', Paris; IRES/DARES.
Escobar, M. (1995) 'Spain: Works Councils or Unions?', in: J. Rogers and W. Streeck, eds., *Works Councils: Consultation, Representation, Co-ordination*, Chicago: University of Chicago Press, 153–188.
Esping-Andersen, G. (1990) *Three Worlds of Welfare Capitalism*, Princeton: Princeton University Press.
Ferner, A. and R. Hyman, eds. (1997) *Industrial Relations in the New Europe*, Oxford: Blackwell, second edition.

Gallie, D. (1996) 'Trade Union Allegiance and Decline in British Urban Labour Markets', in D. Gallie, R. Penn, and M. Rose (eds) *Trade Unionism in the Recession*, Oxford University Press, Oxford, 140–174.

Goetschy, J. and P. Rozenblatt (1992) France: The Industrial Relations System at a Turning Point?', pp. 404–44 in: A. Fermer and R. Hyman. eds., *Industrial Relations in the New Europe*, Oxford: B. Blackwell.

Green, F. (1990) 'Trade Union Availability and Trade Union Membership in Britain', *The Manchester School*, 58, 378–94.

Hancké, B. (1993) Trade Union Membership in Europe 1960–90. Rediscovering Local Unions', *British Journal of Industrial Relations*, 31, 4 593–613.

Heckscher, C. (1988) *The New Unionism*, New York: Basic Books.

Héthy, Lajos, 'Tripartism in Eastern Europe', in: R. Hyman and A. Ferner, eds., New Frontiers in European Industrial Relations, Oxford: Basil Blackwell, 312–337.

Jefferys, S. (1996) 'Down but not out: French unions after Chirac', *Work, Employment, and Society*, 10, 3, 509–527.

Jordana, J. (1996) 'Reconsidering union membership in Spain 1977–1994: Halting decline in a context of democratic consolidation', *Industrial Relations Journal*, 27, 3, 211–24.

Jordana, J. and H.-J Nagel (1995) 'Trade Unionism in Catalonia: Why unions do not join nationalism?', unpublished paper at conference 'Nationalist and Regionalist Dilemma's for Collective Action', Louvain, 7–8 December 1995.

Kjellberg, A. (1983) *Facklig organisering i tolv länder*, Lund: Arkiv.

Klandermans, P.G. and Visser, J. (1995) *De vakbeweging na de welvaartsstaat, Assen*: van Gorcum.

Labbé, D. (1996) *Syndicats et syndiqués en France depuis 1995*, Paris: l'Harmattan.

Lipset, S.-M. (1986) Labor Unions in the Public Mind', pp. 287–321 in: S.M. Lipset, ed., *Unions in Transition. Entering the Second Century*, San Francisco: ICS Press.

MacShane, D. (1994) The Changing Contours of Trade Unionism in Eastern Europe', in R. Hyman and A. Ferner, (eds), *New Frontiers in European Industrial Relations*, Basil Blackwell, Oxford, 337–367.

Mason, Bob (1995) 'Industrial Relations in an Unstable Environment: The case of Central and Eastern Europe', EJIR 1,3, 341–67.

Meer, M. van der (1997) 'Trade Union Development in Spain. Past currencies and Current Trends', Mannheim, Mannheimer Zentrum für Europäische Sozialforschung, working paper AB1/18.

Olney, S.L. (1996) *Unions in a Changing World*, International Labour Office Geneva.

Pankert, A. (1993) Adjustment Problems of Trade Unions in Selected Industrialised Market Economy Countries', *International Journal of Comparative Labour Law and Industrial Relations*, 9,1, 3–14.

Regini, M., ed. (1992) *The Future of Labour Movements*, London: Sage.

Rogers, J. and W. Streeck (1994) 'Workplace Representation Overseas: The Works Council Story', in: R.B. Freeman, ed., *Working Under Different Rules*, New York: Russell Sage Foundation.

Rothstein, B. (1992) Labour Market Institutions and Working-Class Strength', pp. 33–56 in: S. Steinmo, K. Thelen, and F. Longstreth, eds., *Structuring Politics. Historical Institutionalism in Comparative Analysis*, Cambridge, MA: Cambridge University Press.

Ruysseveldt, J. van. and J. Visser, eds. (1996) *Industrial Relations in Europe. Traditions and Transitions*, London: Sage.

Sinclair, D.M. (1995) 'The Importance of Sex for the Propensity to Unionize', *British Journal of Industrial Relations*, 33, 2, 173–90.

Stolaroff, A. and R. Naumann (1994) 'Der "Fall" Portugal. Zur Untersuchung des gewerkschaftlichen Organisationsgrades in einem Land der europäischen Peripherie', *WSI-Mitteilungen*, 2, 134–9.

Streeck, W. (1981) *Organisationsprobleme in der sozialstaatlichen Demokratie*, Königstein: Athenäum.

Tchobanian, R. (1995) 'France: From Conflict to Social Dialogue?', in J. Rogers and W. Streeck, eds., *Works Councils: Consultation, Representation, Co-ordination*, Chicago: University of Chicago Press, 115–152.

Visser, J. (1991) 'Trends in Trade Union Membership', pp. 97–134 in: *OECD Employment Outlook 1991*, Paris: OECD.

Visser, J. (1992) The Strength of Union Movements in Advanced Capitalist Democracies', pp. 17–52 in: M. Regini, ed., *The Future of Labour Movements*, London: Sage.

Visser, J. (1995) 'The Netherlands: From Paternalism to Representation', in: J. Rogers and W. Streeck, eds., *Works Councils: Consultation, Representation, Co-ordination*, Chicago: University of Chicago Press, 79–114.

Visser, J. (1996) Revisiting Union Growth. Recent trends in OECD countries', (CESAR), University of Amsterdam, research paper 96/2.

Waddington, J. and Whitston, C. (1997) 'Why Do People Join Unions in a Period of Membership Decline?', *British Journal of Industrial Relations*, 35: 4, 515–546.

European Community social law and policy: evolution or regression?

Catherine Barnard and Simon Deakin

A paper on the evolution of EC social policy requires, at the outset, some consideration of what constitutes 'social policy' in this context. Although both the EC Treaty and the Commission's White Paper of 1994 talk of a Community 'social policy', the traditional concept of social policy at national level, which encompasses social insurance, public assistance, health and welfare services and housing policy, is almost completely absent from Community social policy. In its place there exist rules relating to sex equality in the workplace (but not yet racial equality), health and safety, and protection in the case of corporate restructuring (transfers of undertakings, collective redundancies and insolvency). Therefore the terminology of 'social policy' masks what is in essence employment-related social policy—and an eclectic body of employment law at that (Freedland, 1996).

Nevertheless, the European Commission claims the existence of a 'European social model' based around certain shared values:

> These include democracy and individual rights, free collective bargaining, the market economy, equality of opportunity for all and social welfare and solidarity. These values ... are held together by the conviction that economic and social progress must go hand in hand. Competitiveness and solidarity have both been taken into account in building a successful Europe for the future.[1]

The central issue for the future of European Community social policy is whether these objectives are, indeed, complementary, or whether the forces which threaten to pull them apart will also, in due course, lead to the abandonment of attempts to regulate for social policy at European level. A formidable deregulatory agenda has been building against social policy, not just within certain member states (most notably but not exclusively the United Kingdom) but also as a consequence of the deepening of the single market programme of the Community itself. There is a real prospect of a 'negative integration' which flattens out national legislative differences in the name of freedom of movement for economic resources. But at the same time, Community law continues to be a vital means for the articu-

---

Catherine Barnard and Simon Deakin are both University Lecturers in Law and, respectively, Fellows of Trinity College and Peterhouse, University of Cambridge.
[1] White Paper on Social Policy COM(94)333, para.3.

lation of human rights within employment, particularly in respect of equal treatment. The Treaty of Amsterdam made some important further steps in the direction of a concept of European citizenship, and, in seeking to place employment policy on a firmer constitutional footing, opened up a potentially significant new area for social regulation and co-operation at transnational level.

The present review seeks to examine how these tensions have been expressed in some of the pivotal recent developments in European Community social law. We first examine the changes made by the Amsterdam Treaty before considering some key decisions of the European Court of Justice in the area of equal treatment. We then analyse in turn the relationship between flexibility and regulation; the role of economic jurisprudence within social policy; and the continuing debate over social dumping.

THE LEGAL FRAMEWORK FOR EC SOCIAL POLICY

From Maastricht...

The continued existence of some form of social policy was assured by the Maastricht Social Policy Agreement (SPA), from which the UK notoriously secured an opt-out. The SPA extended the areas of social policy in which the Community could legislate. More significantly, however, the SPA granted the possibility to the European social partners of negotiating European level social agreements which could then be adopted by the Community legislature. This revitalised the transnational role of the social partners and introduced a new, important set of actors into the European polity. The success of this approach has been mixed. The first attempt by the social partners to use their new powers—to negotiate an agreement on European Works Councils—ended in failure and the Commission had to step in.[2] However, they did succeed in negotiating two agreements on parental leave[3] and part-time work.[4] In a legislative process akin to the 'negotiated laws' which operate within certain member states, but which is unique within Community law, these agreements have been extended to cover all workers by means of a Directive.[5] The agreement is annexed to the Directive and, out of respect for the autonomy of the social partners, cannot be amended by the Council in the process of adopting the measure. The European Parliament is totally excluded from this process.

---

[2] European Works Council (EWC) Directive 94/95 (OJ L254, 30.9.94, p.64).

[3] The Directive on Parental Leave (Council Directive 96/34/EC of 3 June 1996 on the framework agreement on parental leave concluded by UNICE, CEEP and the ETUC (OJ L145,19.6.96, p. 4)).

[4] Council Directive 97/81/EC (OJ No. L14, 20.1.98, p.9).

[5] The English version of the SPA provided for a 'decision'. This has been interpreted to mean any legally binding instrument, including a Directive.

Allowing the social partners to produce negotiated laws in this way can be seen as a form of subsidiarity. At the same time, the social dialogue process highlights the multi-faceted nature of the principle of subsidiarity. Although the social partners are indeed negotiating, they are doing so at European level, at a time when decentralised collective bargaining is the trend in many states. However, the accords which result are inevitably framework agreements by their nature, which allows local level collective agreements and/or domestic legislation to flesh out the details following the model of 'decentralised centralisation' which has operated in a number of member states in the 1990s. Yet, as the social partners gain confidence in their ability to negotiate successfully, greater emphasis will be placed on their legitimacy and accountability, and on their representativeness. UEAPME, the organisation for small and medium sized enterprises has unsuccessfully challenged its exclusion from the negotiations on parental leave before the Court of First Instance.[5a]

At the same time the Court of Justice reinforced the role of the EC Treaty as a legal basis for social legislation, thus confirming the role of social policy within Community law. In the *Working Time* case, it ruled that Article 118a of the EC Treaty, which provides a jurisdictional basis for Directives and other measures in relation to the working environment and the protection of health and safety, should be given a broad interpretation, thereby vindicating the Working Time Directive (93/104) against the UK's challenge.[6]

... to Amsterdam and Beyond

A change of government in the UK in May 1997 led to a change of approach towards the Amsterdam Treaty negotiations. The UK agreed to opt-back into the Social Chapter. As a result, the SPA was merged with the Chapter on Social Policy (Articles 117–121) in the EC Treaty to form part of mainstream Community law (see Barnard, 1997). The Directives already adopted under the SPA are in the process of being (re)adopted under Article 100 EC to include the UK. With the exception of the provisions governing equal pay, little substantive change was made to the body of the SPA.

The most significant part of the Treaty of Amsterdam for social policy was the introduction of a new Chapter on Employment. According to Article 1 of this new Title in the Treaty, member states and the Community shall 'work towards developing a co-ordinated strategy for employment and particularly for promoting a skilled, trained and adaptable workforce and labour markets respon-

---

[5a] Case T-135/96, Judgment of 17 June 1998.
[6] Case C-84/94 *United Kingdom* v. *Council* [1996] ECR I-5755. Article 118a dates from the Single European Act of 1986; had the Court given that provision a narrow interpretation, the social policy provisions of the Maastricht Treaty would not have been immediately affected.

sive to economic change'. However, the principal actors remain the member states: according to Article 3 the Community is to support and, if necessary, complement their action. On the other hand Article 4 permits the Council to adopt certain labour market policies, albeit in the form of soft law, drawing up guidelines on employment. The Luxembourg European Council decided to put the new Title on Employment into effect immediately in order to implement the provisions on co-ordination of member states' employment policies from 1998.[7] The co-ordination is based on 'employment guidelines' drawn up by the Commission, structured around four 'pillars' of employability, entrepreneurship, adaptability and equal opportunities.

This new chapter on employment reflects the Community's concerns about high levels of unemployment across Europe. The initiatives begun in the Commission's 1994 White Paper on *Growth, Competitiveness and Employment*,[8] which set out a medium term strategy for creating jobs and adopting a more vigorous approach to tackling unemployment, and were followed up in the Essen summit which identified five priority fields of action to promote job creation,[9] and the Florence European Council which gave new impetus to job creation in line with the Confidence Pact for Employment proposed by the Commission. In essence, the inclusion of the Employment Chapter in the Amsterdam Treaty marks a constitutionalisation of these policies. It highlights a shift in emphasis from the enactment of employment law (the body of rules directly concerned with the employment relationship) to the creation of employment policy (measures directly concerned with the creation and maintenance of employment, including measures concerned with training) (see Freedland, 1996).

Why this change of emphasis? While the Commission and the Council have repeatedly expressed their concern about how to tackle high levels of unemployment and to address the threat to social cohesion which it poses, it proved easier to build political consensus around measures to tackle unemployment rather than employment law. Regulating for employment rights was seen as inherently more controversial in itself as well as touching on sensitive issues of national sovereignty. Such sensitivity helps to explain, historically, why Community social law enjoys such an ambivalent status in the EU.

The debates date back to the 1950s when at the time of the Treaty negotiations there were important differences in the scope and content of social legislation in force in the would-be member states. France, in particular, had a number of laws which favoured social protection, including legislation on equal pay for men and women, and rules permitting French workers longer paid holidays than

---

[7] Presidency Conclusions: Extraordinary European Council Meeting on Employment Luxembourg, 20 and 21 November 1997; http://europa.eu.int/en/comm/dgos/elm/summit/en/papers/concl.htm.
[8] Bull. Supp. 6/93.
[9] Bull. Supp. 12/94.

in other states. French workers were also entitled to overtime pay after fewer hours of work at basic rates than elsewhere. This raised concerns that the additional costs borne by French industry would make French goods uncompetitive in the Common Market (see Kahn-Freund, 1960, citing Katzenstein, 1957; Ellis, 1991). Consequently, the French argued that an elimination of distortions of competition was not enough, and that it would be necessary to assimilate the entire labour and social legislation of the member states, so as to achieve a parity of wages and social costs. The German government, however, was strongly committed to a minimal level of government interference in the area of wages and prices. The resulting compromise is reflected in the Treaty's social policy provisions. In the words of one commentator, Articles 117 and 118 on the need to improve working conditions and co-operation between states, even if textually broad, are legally shallow—at least when considered in isolation from Article 100 on the completion of the common market, which unlike Articles 117 and 118, does provide a concrete jurisdictional base for the adoption of directives (Forman, 1982, p. 17). Articles 119 and 120, by contrast, were from one point of view specific provisions designed to protect French industry (Barnard, 1996).[10]

It is striking that the emphasis in this debate is on Community social law as an adjunct to the law establishing and maintaining the single market, removing distortions of competition and eliminating social dumping. In this conception, Community social law completes or 'perfects' the market. It may be argued, however, that this approach misunderstands the very nature of *social* law, namely that it should serve a social welfare or employment rights purpose. From this point of view, Community law should interfere with the operation of the market to correct for social inequalities which would otherwise arise from its unfettered operation. In this conception, a tension exists between the 'market perfecting' and 'market correcting' rationales (see, for discussion, Streeck, 1995; Barnard and Hervey, forthcoming).

Even if some tension is inevitable, are the two perspectives irreconcilable? This debate has persisted from the earliest days of the Community: when the European Community project was first conceived its principal objective was economic in a quite specifically integrationist sense—the establishment of a European Economic Community on the basis of a common market. It is partly for this reason that social policy objectives were not among the primary purposes of the Community. Yet, as the Community has remoulded itself from an Economic Community, to the European Community and ultimately to the European Union, different priorities have asserted themselves, but within the framework of the old debates and, even now, many of the old institutions.

---

[10] According to the French Advocate General Dutheillet de Lamothe in Case 80/70 *Defrenne v Sabena* (No.1) [1971] ECR 445: 'It appears to be France which took the initiative, but the article [119] necessitated quite long negotiations'.

This tension is seen in respect of the relatively new concept of 'citizenship of the Union'. Introduced in order to encourage nationals of the member states to have some form of identification with the Union, the rights found in the citizenship provisions are still meagre, even after Amsterdam. Whereas in individual member states full social citizenship has come about through a process of historical development of individual rights starting with civil rights (basic freedoms from state interference), political rights (such as electoral rights) and most recently social rights, including rights to health care, unemployment insurance, and old age pensions—the rudiments of a welfare state (see Marshall, 1950)—the Community has neither the legal competence nor the resources to develop a model of full social citizenship along these lines (Shaw, 1995). Despite this, Community law purports to see the link between social rights and citizenship as crucial. This was demonstrated by the new section in the Amsterdam Treaty entitled 'The Union and the Citizen' which includes the Chapters on Employment and Social policy. Commentators have recognised that for citizenship not be 'trivialised' to the point of 'embarrassment' (Weiler, 1996, p. 65), it must draw on rights 'scattered' (Shaw, 1995) across the Treaty, commonly citing the social provisions as a key component (Reich, 1997; Shaw, 1997).

Therefore, if Community social policy cannot hope to replicate the complex web of national social policy, how might the Community develop the concept of social citizenship? One possibility is for the Community to develop some form of Bill of Rights to be included in the Treaty. This suggestion was made by the Commission's Comité des Sages which reported in 1996.[11] It argued that if the Union wishes to become an original political entity, it must have a clear statement of the citizenship it is offering its members. Inclusion of civic and social rights in the Treaties would help to nurture that citizenship and prevent Europe from being perceived as a bureaucracy assembled by technocratic elites far removed from daily concerns.[12]

The inclusion of social rights in this category would also be in harmony with the UN Covenant on Economic and Social Rights, the Conventions and Recommendations of the ILO, the European Social Charter of the Council of Europe and the Community's Social Charter of 1989. However, the practical difficulties of seeking agreement on what constitutes fundamental social rights might be vast. Another possibility would be for the Community to specialise—focusing its energies in areas with a transnational dimension and areas where it already has a strong foothold (Majone, 1993). Equal opportunities is a prime candidate,

---

[11] *For a Europe of Civic and Social Rights*, Report by the Comité des Sages chaired by Maria de Lourdes Pintasilgo, Brussels, October 1995–February 1996, Commission, DGV.

[12] The responses of the European Parliament, ECOSOC and the ETUC to the Commission's Green Paper on Social Policy also called for 'the establishment of the fundamental social rights of citizens as a constitutional element of the European Union'—COM(94)333, p.69. The *Molitor Report* (COM (95)288 final/2, 39) on legislative and administrative simplification also called for the adoption of a Bill of Rights.

for it is in this area that the Community has the most experience. Further, as we shall see, it is in the context of equality that the Court has developed the notion of fundamental rights.[13]

EQUAL OPPORTUNITIES AND HUMAN RIGHTS

The Community already has in place a large body of legislation designed to secure equal opportunities. Apart from Article 119 EC a number of Directives exist, most notably Directive 75/117 on equal pay, Directive 76/207 equal treatment in employment, and Directive 79/7 equality in social security. Further, the Court has recognised that equality serves a social as well as an economic function.[14] The Court has underlined the importance of the principle of equality in four recent cases—*P* v. *S*,[15] *Grant* v. *South West Trains*,[16] *Kalanke*[17] and *Marschall*[18] (see Barnard, 1998).

In *P* v. *S* the Court of Justice had to consider whether the principle of equal treatment between men and women contained in Directive 76/207 also applied to transsexuals.[19] The Court said that 'the Directive is simply the expression, in the relevant field, of the principle of equality, which is one of the fundamental principles of Community law'.[20] The Court then reasoned that since the right

---

[13] See, for example, Case 149/77 *Defrenne* v. *Sabena (No.3)* [1978] E.C.R 1365, 1378, Case 152/84 *Marshall* v. *Southampton Area Health Authority (No.1)* [1986] E.C.R 723, para. 36; see also Docksey, 1991.

[14] This ambivalence can be seen most clearly in Case 43/75 *Defrenne (No.2)* [1976] E.C.R 455: 'Article 119 pursues a double aim. *First*, ... the aim of Article 119 is to avoid a situation in which undertakings established in states which have actually implemented the principle of equal pay suffer a competitive disadvantage in intra-Community competition as compared with undertakings established in states which have not yet eliminated discrimination against women workers as regards pay. *Second*, this provision forms part of the social objectives of the Community, which is not merely an economic union, but is at the same time intended, by common action to ensure social progress and seek the constant improvement of living and working conditions of their peoples ... This double aim, which is at once economic and social, shows that the principle of equal pay forms part of the foundations of the Community' (emphasis added).

[15] *Case C-13/94 P* v. *S and Cornwall County Council* [1996] ECR I-2143.

[16] Case C-249/96 *Grant* v. *South West Trains* [1998] IRLR 165.

[17] *Case C-450/93 Kalanke* v. *Freie Hansestadt Bremen* [1995] ECR I-3051; [1996] All E.R.(EC) 66.

[18] *Case C-409/95 Hellmut Marschall* v. *Land Nordrhein-Westfalen* [1997] All E.R.(EC) 865.

[19] Transsexuals have been defined by the European Court of Human Rights in *Rees* v. *United Kingdom*, para.38, Series A, No.106, judgment of 17 October 1986 as 'those who, whilst belonging physically to one sex, feel convinced that they belong to the other, they often seek to achieve a more integrated, unambiguous identity by undergoing medical treatment and surgical operations to adapt their physical characteristics to their psychological nature. Transsexuals who have been operated upon thus form a fairly well-defined and identifiable group.' This definition was cited by the Court in *P* v. *S* at para.16.

[20] See also the Advocate General's Opinion at para. 22: 'The Directive is nothing if not an expression of a general principle and a fundamental right ... Respect for fundamental rights is one of the general principles of Community law, the observance of which the Court has a duty to ensure.'

not to be discriminated against on grounds of sex is one of the fundamental
human rights whose observance the Court has a duty to ensure, the scope of the
Directive could not be confined simply to discrimination based on the fact that
a person is of one sex or another.[21] It then said that in view of the purpose and
the nature of the rights which it seeks to safeguard, the scope of the Directive
applies to discrimination arising from the gender reassignment of the person
concerned, since 'such discrimination is based, essentially if not exclusively, on
the sex of the person concerned'.[22] It then added: '[t]o tolerate such discrimination would be tantamount, as regards such a person, to a failure to respect the
dignity and freedom to which he or she is entitled, and which the Court has a
duty to safeguard'.[23]

Such ideas did not, however, permeate *Grant* v. *South West Trains (SWT)*
where the Court was not prepared to use the fundamental rights argument to
extend the protection of the principle of non-discrimination to homosexuals. In
that case Ms Grant was refused travel concessions for her female partner on the
ground that these concessions could be granted only for a partner of the opposite
sex with whom the worker had a stable relationship. The Court, having reaffirmed
that the Directive prohibiting discrimination between men and women was simply the expression of the principle of equality, which is one of the fundamental
principles of Community law, said that the discrimination in *P* was in fact based,
essentially if not exclusively, on the sex of the person concerned. It then said:

> That reasoning, which leads to the conclusion that such discrimination is to be prohibited just as is
> discrimination based on the fact that a person belongs to a particular sex, is limited to the case of a
> worker's gender reassignment and does not therefore apply to differences of treatment based on a
> person's sexual orientation.

Perhaps extending the word 'sex' to include what the Court terms 'sexual orientation' was a bridge too far in terms of literal interpretation. But the real motivation appears to have been the Court's intention to put the matter into the hands
of the Community legislature. The new Article 6a introduced by the Amsterdam
Treaty now provides a legal basis for Community action to combat discrimination
based, inter alia, on sexual orientation.[24] This was expressly noted by the Court.

In *Marschall* the Court was prepared to breathe some life into Article 2(4) of
Directive 76/207 which allows for some forms of positive action. In the earlier
case of *Kalanke* the Court was much criticised (see Prechal, 1996; Schiek, 1996;)
for ruling that that national laws which guarantee women *absolute and uncon-*

---

[21] Paras. 18–19. The Court reached this conclusion even though Advocate General Tesauro pointed out
that it was indisputable that the *wording* of the principle of equal treatment laid down by the Directive
referred to the traditional man/woman dichotomy.

[22] Paras.20–21.

[23] Para.22.

[24] It could be argued that by placing sexual orientation under the same umbrella as sex, race, age etc, the
same principles should apply to it.

ditional priority for appointment or promotion go beyond promoting equal opportunities and overstep the limits of the exception in Article 2(4) of the Directive.[25] Therefore the Bremen law on positive discrimination which, in the case of a tie-break situation, gave priority to an equally-qualified woman over a man if women were under-represented,[26] contravened Community law.

In *Marschall* the facts were very similar to those in *Kalanke* except that the state law contained a saving clause: priority was given to the woman *'unless reasons specific to an individual [male] candidate tilt the balance in his favour'* (emphasis added). The Court distinguished *Marshall* from *Kalanke* on the grounds that in *Marschall* the state law contained a saving clause. It said that this national rule was compatible with Article 2(4) because

> ... even where male and female candidates are equally qualified, male candidates tend to be promoted in preference to female candidates particularly because of prejudices and stereotypes concerning the role and capacities of women in working life and the fear, for example, that women will interrupt their careers more frequently, that owing to household and family duties they will be less flexible in their working hours, or that they will be absent from work more frequently because of pregnancy, childbirth and breastfeeding.[27] For these reasons, the mere fact that a male candidate and a female candidate are equally qualified does not mean that they have the same chances.[28]

It therefore concluded that a state law with a saving clause might fall within the scope of Article 2(4) 'if such a rule may counteract the prejudicial effects on female candidates of the attitudes and behaviour described above and thus reduce actual instances of inequality which may exist in the real world'. The Court then added a proviso. The state rule did not breach Article 2(4) provided that

> in each individual case the rule provides for male candidates who are equally as qualified as the female candidates a guarantee that the candidatures will be the subject of an objective assessment which will take account of all criteria specific to the individual candidates and will over-ride the priority accorded to female candidates where one or more of those criteria tilts the balance in favour of the male candidate. In this respect it should be remembered that those criteria must not be such as to discriminate against the female candidates (para.33)

Despite the difficulties which the Community's social policy has encountered in other respects, the Court remains a powerful advocate of a place for human-rights analysis within employment law, building on the broad cultural consensus in support of the equality principle (Raz, 1986; Meehan, 1993).

---

[25] Para.22.

[26] Under-representation exists where women 'do not make up at least half the staff in the individual pay, remuneration and salary brackets in the relevant personnel group within a department'.

[27] See also the views of the Federal Labour Court when the *Kalanke* case (Nr226), Urteil; vom 5.3.1996 – 1 AZR 590/92 (A) returned to it. It said that it was impossible to distinguish between opportunity and result especially in the case of engagement and promotion because the selection itself was influenced by circumstances, expectations and prejudices that typically diminish the chances of women.

[28] Paras. 29–30.

FLEXIBILITY OR REGULATION?

The jurisprudence of human rights which the Court has been developing sits uneasily with the long-running debate over the place of labour flexibility within European social policy. The Social Policy Directorate of the Commission, building on its earlier contributions in the Green Paper of 1993 and White Paper of 1994, issued two documents on this theme in the second half of 1997, a further Green Paper, *Partnership for a New Organisation of Work*[29] and a Communication, *Modernising and Improving Social Protection in the European Union*.[30] Meanwhile the Court issued a series of rulings which widened the 'margin of discretion' for member states to exempt flexible forms of employment from employment protection standards, although this apparent move in favour of deregulation was counterbalanced by the conclusion of a framework agreement and Directive under the procedure of the Social Policy Agreement, providing for the removal of discrimination in relation to part-time work.

The two Commission documents are notable for their attempt to marry social and employment protection to an economic agenda based on the achievement of competitiveness through 'high trust' employment relations. According to the Partnership Green Paper, the challenge for social policy is 'how to reconcile security for workers with the flexibility which firms need'.[31] The answer lies in an 'improved organisation of work' which, although unable 'of itself to solve the unemployment problem', may nevertheless 'make a valuable contribution, firstly, to the competitiveness of European firms, and secondly, to the improvement of the quality of working life and the employability of the workforce'.[32] More specifically, 'the flexible firm could offer a sound basis for fundamental organisational renewal built on high skill, high productivity, high quality, good environmental management—and good wages'.[33]

To address this issue at the level of the regulatory framework, the Green Paper envisages what is, in effect, a two pronged approach. On the one hand, a certain softening of excessively rigid rules is required in order to accommodate new organisational developments which include 'downsizing, outsourcing, subcontracting, teleworking, net-working and joint ventures... for which traditional labour law provisions do not appear to have adequate answers'.[34] This implies 'the likely development of labour law and industrial relations from rigid and compulsory systems of statutory regulations to more open and flexible legal

---

[29] COM (97) 127 final.
[30] COM (97) 102 final
[31] COM (97) 127 final, Executive Summary.
[32] Ibid., para. 4
[33] Ibid., para. 24.
[34] Ibid., para. 42.

frameworks';[35] in practice, this means greater scope for derogations from legislative standards through not just collective agreements but also individual contracts of employment.[36] In a further nod to individualisation, the Green Paper stresses the benefits to be obtained from profit- and performance-related pay. Annualisation of working time and changes to thresholds for tax and social security contributions, aimed at equalising the tax treatment of different forms of work, are also mentioned in this connection.

On the other hand, the Green Paper falls a long way short of adopting an openly deregulatory agenda. Flexibility within organisations is to be encouraged, it suggests, by reinforcing mechanisms for employee participation at the level of the plant or enterprise; 'the role of workers in decision making and the need to review and strengthen the existing arrangements for workers' involvement in their companies will … become essential issues'.[37] This point is linked to the Commission's consultations on a new Directive concerning information and consultation of employees at national level (although these consultations have so far led to very little progress).[38]

Just as importantly, the Green Paper takes a sceptical view of the idea which featured in earlier Commission documents, in particular the White Paper on Social Policy of 1994, to the effect that deregulatory reforms should encourage the creation of low-paid, low-productivity 'entry jobs' as a way of combatting unemployment. High productivity remains the central objective:

> It has to be acknowledged that improvements in productivity can result in a reduction in employment in one part of the production chain. But improved productivity is necessary if real wages and profits are to be increased.[39] (para. 27.)

In similar sceptical vein, it is suggested that while SMEs are well placed to adopt flexible forms of organisation, nevertheless 'the informal nature of relationships in SMEs gives rise to a different set of problems in relation to work organisation: in particular the lack of resources necessary for systematic organisational planning tends to hinder long-term personnel development'.[40]

This tone is maintained in the Social Protection Communication which takes up a theme previously flagged by the Commission President Jacques Santer, namely the idea of 'social protection as a productive factor'. According to this point of view, attention should be paid to 'the links between social policy and economic performance', not least in the contribution of social protection to social

---

[35] Ibid., para. 44.
[36] Ibid., para. 43.
[37] Ibid., para. 44.
[38] In March 1998, the private sector employers' confederation, UNICE, refused to enter into negotiations with ETUC and CEEP: *European Industrial Relations Review*, vol. 291, April 1998, p. 1.
[39] COM (97) 127 final, para. 27.
[40] Ibid., para. 26.

and economic cohesion and political stability.[41] This is an area singled out for further research, building on work begun during the Dutch Presidency in the first half of 1997. More concretely, the Communication sees a role for structural reforms to the tax and social security systems, aimed at 'making social protection more employment-friendly'.[42] Reforms which could reduce the negative incentive effects of the unemployment and poverty traps include paying social security benefits on an individual rather than a household basis, introducing higher income ceilings for the means-tested benefits, and offering support to the long-term unemployed in the form of indirect income support such as publicly organised child care. The Communication also considers the adaptation of social protection provisions to the ageing of the population, to the changing gender-balance of work and employment, and to increased mobility of workers and families within the Union.

It may be said, then, that for DGV, at least, labour flexibility is far from synonymous with deregulation, at least as that term has come to be understood in the Anglo-American debate. The Directorate's line amounts to an argument for the *proceduralisation* of labour standards rather than for their abandonment. This involves an acceptance that the role of legislation should be predominantly facilitative, rather than prescriptive in nature. A similar shift can be observed within the labour law systems of most of the mainland member states over the past decade, where provisions for derogation from statutory standards, particularly in the areas of working time and the use of flexible forms of employment, have become widespread. However, this approach is not without its difficulties: these include the potential dilution of individual employment rights (in particular the right to equality of treatment) and the generation of inequalities between different categories of workers and between different workplaces and sectors. Above all, this strategy is critically dependent for its success on the successful development of new forms of employee participation and representation at enterprise level. Otherwise, there may be little to distinguish proceduralisation through enterprise-level bargaining from outright deregulation after all. From this point of view, the failure (to date) of the Commission's initiatives to extend information and consultation requirements below European works council level, thanks in part to the continuing political opposition of the United Kingdom government to advances in social policy legislation, is both worrying and curious, since such requirements have been in force since the 1970s in respect of collective redundancies[43] and transfers of undertakings.[44]

---

[41] *Modernising and Improving Social Protection in the European Union*, para. 2.1

[42] Ibid., para. 2.2

[43] Directive 75/129, implemented in the UK by the Employment Protection Act 1975 (now consolidated in the Trade Union and Labour Relations (Consolidation) Act 1992, ss. 188 et seq. as amended, in particular, by the Collective Redundancies and Transfer of Undertakings (Protection of Employment) Regulations, SI 1995/2587.

[44] Directive 77/187, implemented in the UK in the Transfer of Undertakings (Protection of Employment) Regulations, SI 1981/1974. (as amended, in particular, by SI 1995/2587)

The danger that flexibilisation will lead to a dilution of individual employment rights is evident from the case-law of the Court of Justice on the treatment of part-time workers. In judgments dating from the 1980s, the Court had established that legislative measures which discriminate against part-time workers, such as wage or hours thresholds which had to be crossed in order to qualify for employment protection, are likely to amount to unlawful sex discrimination in situations where women constitute the large majority of part-time workers (which is the case in most of the member states). A member state could nevertheless defend a measure of this kind via the 'justification' defence outlined in *Rinner-Kühn*. The Court ruled that the member state had to show that the means chosen met a necessary aim of its social policy and that the legislation was suitable for attaining that aim.[45] In *ex parte EOC* (1994),[46] the House of Lords, applying this formula without considering it necessary to make a reference to the Court, had decided that no adequate justification had been offered for the 8 and 16 hour thresholds which were then in force for the purposes of unfair dismissal and redundancy compensation under the Employment Protection (Consolidation) Act 1978; the thresholds thereupon became ineffective, and were later formally repealed.

By contrast, in its rulings in the *Nolte*[47] and *Megner and Scheffel*[48] cases towards the end of 1995, the Court took an approach which was much more tolerant of state-level exemptions of part-time work from protective legislation. It said 'it should be noted that the social and employment policy aim relied on by the German government is objectively unrelated to any discrimination on the grounds of sex and that, in exercising its competence, the national legislature was reasonably entitled to consider that the legislation in question was necessary in order to achieve that aim' (emphasis added).[49] The Court did not consider the question which the House of Lords had regarded as central to the litigation in *ex parte EOC*, namely whether there was any *evidence* that the thresholds had the positive job-creation effects which were being claimed for them. Further decisions on the relationship between part-time work and the principle of equal treatment have confirmed this 'softening' by the Court of the justification defence.[50]

The 1997 framework agreement on the removal of discrimination against part-time workers aims, among other things, to contribute to the 'flexible organisation

---

[45] Case 171/88 *Rinner-Kühn* [1989] ECR 2743.
[46] *R.* v. *Secretary of State for Employment, ex parte Equal Opportunities Commission* [1994] IRLR 176.
[47] Case C-317/93 [1995] ECR I-4625.
[48] Case C-444/93 [1995] ECR I-4741.
[49] *Nolte*, [1996] IRLR 225, 235.
[50] See Case C-457/93 [1996] ECR I-243 *Kuratorium für Dialyse under Nierentransplantation v. Lewark*; Case C-278/93 [1996] ECR I-1165 *Freers and Speckmann v. Deutsches Bundespost*, discussed by Barnard and Hervey, forthcoming.

of working time in a manner which takes into account the needs of employers and workers', as well as improving the quality of part-time work and facilitating the take-up of part-time work on a voluntary basis.[51] It contains a requirement of equal (or, where appropriate, *pro rata*) treatment between part-time and full-time workers, but this is subject to a defence where the difference in treatment is justifiable on objective grounds,[52] thereby bringing back in considerations of the kind which prevailed in the *Nolte* and *Megner and Scheffel* cases.

The agreement also considers the question of the movement of workers from full-time to part-time work, and vice versa. A worker's refusal to transfer from the one form of work to the other does not constitute, of itself, a valid ground for dismissal (this adds little to the domestic labour law of most member states); conversely, the employer must give consideration to requests by workers to transfer between full-time and part-time work and must provide information about opportunities for transfers, but is not required to accede to workers' requests.

In addition, member states and, within their spheres of responsibility, the social partners, are charged with the responsibility of identifying and, where possible, removing obstacles to part-time work.[53] This particular provision could be read as inviting the removal of protective legislation which, according to deregulatory thinking, may hinder opportunities for part-time work. Although it is too broadly phrased to amount to an instruction to deregulate, it could be prayed in aid by a member state to justify the exclusion of part-time workers from protective measures. The Directive therefore epitomises the uncertainty and ambiguity of much of contemporary social policy, which is seemingly unable to take a clear position on the merits or demerits of a deregulatory approach.

SOCIAL POLICY AND ECONOMIC JURISPRUDENCE

At the same time as social policy measures are increasingly affected by neoliberal considerations, one of the most important doctrinal developments of recent years has been the growing use by the courts of concepts drawn from competition policy to review, and sometimes to confine the scope of, social legislation. The increasing reach of competition policy has raised the possibility that social legislation can be viewed a distortion of competition or restriction on trade. Potential clashes between social policy and economic objectives arise in a number of different contexts under the EC Treaty. Outcomes tend to turn on the particular provision which is being considered rather than on any general principles (Deakin, 1996); nevertheless, the case-law is of wider interest for several reasons.

---

[51] Article 1.
[52] Article 4.
[53] Article 5.

Firstly, the type of reasoning employed by the Court can determine the validity of certain social policy measures which, from the point of view of the continuing programme of economic integration, are from time to time called into question. Secondly, the attitude of the Court to these issues directly affects the degree of freedom of the individual member states to act in the social policy field (and to a lesser extent the capacity of the Community legislature as well[54]). The general direction of social policy is therefore at stake, as much as the fate of existing measures.

In this context, the limited nature of the Community's jurisdiction to intervene in issues of social policy cuts both ways. On the one hand, the lack of a wider social policy 'treaty base' forms an obstacle to the goal of a Europe-wide social policy (although the new Social Chapter of the Amsterdam Treaty goes some way to addressing this problem). On the other hand, the autonomy accorded to the member states in the sphere of social policy affords them some protection against attempts to impose deregulation from the centre in the name of competition policy and freedom of movement. This is not a purely theoretical issue. The United States offers an example of a federal system (in this respect much further advanced, of course, than the Community) in which the 'pre-emption' principle has severely curtailed the capacity of the states to legislate in the area of social policy, resulting in a 'lowest common denominator' of provision in such areas as pension regulation. Within the European Union, state laws on Sunday trading, controls over working time, dock labour monopoly schemes, minimum wages, and redundancy compensation schemes have all been the subject of attacks since the mid-1980s; the weapons used have included Article 30 on the free movement of goods, Article 59 on freedom to supply services, Articles 85 and 86 on competition, and Articles 90–92 on state support for monopolies and state aids to employers.[55] Even if, on the whole, the attacks have been repulsed, this has not been without some judicial contortions and backtracking, and the law remains in a state of flux.

The issues involved were on display again in the Court's 1997 decision in *French Republic* v. *Commission.*[56] This case concerned the operation of French redundancy legislation, under which an employer proposing to make a minimum number of redundancies (10 employees in a 30-day period) was required to draw up a social plan with the aim of avoiding or reducing the redundancies, or assisting the redeployment or retraining of the workers concerned. The legislation provided for financial support to be given by the state through an agency, the Fonds National d'Emploi (FNE), the precise amount of which was to be

---

[54] See, for example, the Working Time case, Case C-84/94 *United Kingdom* v. *Commission* [1996] EC I-5755, discussed below.
[55] For recent reviews of this case-law, see Wedderburn, 1995, pp. 370–391; Davies, 1995; Deakin, 1996.
[56] Case C-241/94 [1997] IRLR 415.

negotiated with the employer concerned. The Commission argued that support given by the FNE in 1993, which amounted to 25 per cent of the cost of a social plan initiated by Kimberly Clark Sopalin in respect of redundancies at its works in Sotteville-les-Rouen, constituted a state aid under Article 92 of the Treaty. Under Article 92(1), 'any aid granted by a Member State or through state resources in any form whatsoever which distorts or threatens to distort competition by favouring certain undertakings or the production of certain goods shall, in so far as it affects trade between member states, be incompatible with the common market'. Although the Commission concluded that, in the event, the aid was not illegitimate, since it fell under a derogation or exception provided by Article 92(3)(c),[57] the French government challenged the Commission's initial finding that the payment by FNE came under Article 92 at all. The significance of the Commission's ruling, if correct, was that it would have to be notified of similar payments in future, and would also have the power to nullify them if they did not, in its view (subject to review by the Court), fall under the relevant derogation.

The pre-existing case law drew a distinction between measures of general application, which were not aid, and subsidies payable to particular undertakings, which were. According to Advocate General Jacobs,

> ...measures taken within the framework of employment policy are usually not state aid. However, where public funds are used to reduce the salary costs of undertakings, either directly (for example by recruitment premiums) or indirectly (for example by reductions in fiscal or social charges) the distinction between state aid and general measure becomes less clear. The existence of discretion serves to identify those financial measures promoting employment which are liable to distort competition and affect trade between member states.[58]

The Court followed this lead and concluded that since the French legislation gave the administration some discretion in the amounts of subsidy which it could grant to a particular employer, there was a state aid in the sense meant by Article 92(1). It also rejected the French government's argument to the effect that the principal beneficiaries in this case were the employees, and not the employer. Because the FNE met, in part, the costs of making employees redundant, there was assistance for the employers' aim of restructuring the plant in order to enhance its competitiveness: 'the Commission was entitled to consider that, as a result of the FNE intervention, Kimberly Clark had been relieved of certain legal obligations vis-à-vis its employees and that, accordingly, it was put in a more favourable position than that of its competitors'.[59]

---

[57] Article 92(3)(c) allows aid where it is made 'to facilitate the development of certain economic activities or of certain economic areas, where such aid does not adversely affect trading conditions to an extent contrary to the common interest'. Under Article 93, the Commission must be notified in advance of an intention to grant aid which falls under this derogation.

[58] [1997] IRLR 415, 417–418.

[59] [1997] IRLR 415, 423.

The decision can be seen as turning on the lack of specific criteria by which the financial assistance was to be disbursed. If the scheme had made state aid available on a clearly defined basis to all similarly-situated enterprises, it is possible that the outcome would have been different. Nevertheless, the decision is a reminder that social policy measures can be affected by competition policy provisions to which they may appear to have only a distant connection.

The opinions of the Court and of the Advocate General are also remarkable for the absence of any attempt to balance the potentially distortionary effects of the subsidy against not just the social but also the *economic* benefits (in the sense of enhanced competitiveness for the employer and improved re-employability for the redundant workers) which the scheme was intended to generate. In part, this omission arose because, in this case, the social and economic merits of such a subsidy were not an issue; they had been recognised by the Commission, when it accepted that the aid came under the derogation in Article 92(3)(c). At best, though, this aspect of the decision suggests that labour market policy measures at state level may be subject to increasing scrutiny and review by the Commission, which in this context means not DGV but the Competition Policy Directorate, DGIV.

The idea that social policy measures may contribute positively to productivity and competitiveness, although present as we have seen in some of the Commission's policy documents, has barely surfaced as yet in the case law. In the *Working Time* case, *United Kingdom* v. *Council*, the Court noted that 'were the organisation of working time to be viewed as a means of combating unemployment, a number of economic factors would have to be taken into account, such as, for example, its impact on productivity of undertakings and on workers' salaries'.[60] In other words, the Council (rather than the Court itself) would have had to make an assessment of this kind had it chosen to put the Directive forward as primarily an economic measure rather than a health and safety measure. It seems from the Court's assessment, later in its judgment, of the adequacy of the health and safety grounds actually offered by the Council, that the Court's role is, in such a case, largely confined to determining whether the grounds advanced by a legislative body are, *in principle*, sustainable, and not whether good evidence has *actually* been adduced in their favour.

Elsewhere in its judgment, the Court appears to adopt an unsatisfactory and unnecessary opposition between the 'restrictive' effects of social legislation on efficiency and competitiveness, on the one hand, and its 'beneficial' social consequences on the other. The United Kingdom argued that a Directive would fail the proportionality test which is implicit in Article 118a if 'the level of health and safety protection of workers which it establishes can be attained by measures

---

[60] para. 28.

which are less restrictive and involve fewer obstacles to the competitiveness of industry and the earning capacity of individuals'.[61] The Court replied that 'the Council must be allowed a wide discretion in an area which, as here, involves the legislature in making social policy choices and requires it to carry out complex assessments',[62] and concluded that in this case it had not acted on the basis of any manifest error. However, one reason for this was that the Working Time Directive contained exceptionally wide derogations from the basic limits to working time, as well as reference periods which softened the impact of those limits. The Court's judgment can be read as implying that had these derogations not been as wide as they were, the test of proportionality might not have been satisfied.[63]

SOCIAL DUMPING

A number of meanings can be attributed to the loose expression 'social dumping'; some of them have legal significance in the sense of providing a basis for Community-level intervention in the social policy sphere, others do not. One sense which is not particularly relevant from a legal point of view is the idea *that producers in low-cost or low labour-standard systems enjoy an inherent competitive advantage which must be countered by the imposition of a 'level playing field' in labour costs.* However, this view has not been used as the basis for legal intervention under the EC Treaty; it was, indeed, explicitly rejected at the outset of the Community's existence in the Ohlin Report and in Article 117 of the Treaty of Rome, which embodied the perhaps optimistic assumption that labour standards would, for the most part, 'level up' of their own accord once the common market was put in place. It was also assumed that, for the most part, wage levels were roughly matched with productivity, so that high-wage systems were protected against the effects of low-wage competition by virtue of superior technology and modes of economic organisation.

A second meaning of social dumping, which does have some legal resonance, would describe it *as unfair competition based on access to artificially cheap (or undervalued) labour.* This has some connection to the legally-relevant idea of a 'distortion of competition'. For example, the Ohlin Report accepted that producers based in states which lacked strong anti-discrimination laws would enjoy

---

[61] para. 52.
[62] para. 58.
[63] See, in particular, paras. 61–63 of the Judgment. A similarly strong contrast between 'restrictive' social legislation and the assumed economic benefits of flexibility arguably underlies the approach of the Advocate General and of the Court in the *Süzen* case (Case C-13/95 [1997] ECR I-1259) which significantly narrowed the definition of 'undertaking' under the Acquired Rights Directive, 77/187. See also Case C-298/94 *Hencke* [1996] ECR I-4989.

an artificial advantage, in the sense of being able to extract a surplus from under-valued labour which was not available to producers in states with stronger laws. On this basis, a transnational standard in relation to sex discrimination law could, exceptionally, be justified as countering a 'distortion of competition'. As we saw above, this argument was invoked by the French government to provide one of the bases for the inclusion of Article 119 (and also Article 120, concerning paid leave entitlements) in the Rome Treaty. However, if the argument was regarded as valid in relation to equal pay, it is not clear why it was not thought acceptable in other contexts, such as working time and flexible working arrangements.[64]

Since the 1950s, the social dumping debate has rumbled on without ever being clearly resolved. The issue was recently revived in relation to Directive 96/71 concerning the posting of workers in the framework of the provision of services, adopted by the Council in December 1996. The Directive provides that when workers are temporarily posted by their employer to work in a member state (the 'host state') other than that in which they are normally employed (the 'home state'), they must receive the protection of certain minimum labour standards which apply to employment in the host state. The background to the measure was mounting concern in certain northern member states, particularly France and Germany, of the effects of the subcontracting of construction work to employers based in lower-cost member states. The Directive had a long and uncertain gestation, having first been proposed as part of the 1989 Social Action Programme, after which it underwent numerous re-drafts. In addition to its potential signifi-cance for the construction trades and other industries where the cross-border supply of services is widespread, it has considerable implications for the relation-ship between social policy and the economic goals of the Union.

To see the full significance of the Directive, it is necessary to consider the law which applied to the cross-border supply of services prior to its adoption. On one view of the EC Treaty, it could have been argued that posted workers had the right to receive the same basic labour protections as other workers employed in the host state, by virtue of the principle of equal treatment of differ-ent EC nationals contained in Article 48(2) (an aspect of the freedom of move-ment principle). However, the Court held in a number of rulings that Article 48(2) did not apply to posted workers.[65]

Alternatively, the provisions of the Treaty dealing with the freedom of employers to provide services (Articles 57, 59 and 66) could have been invoked to have precisely the opposite effect: the imposition of basic labour standards on posted workers could have been regarded as constituting a barrier to the provision of cross-border services, by substantially raising the costs of employers

---

[64] For discussion, see Deakin and Wilkinson, 1994; Deakin, 1997.
[65] Case C-292/89, *Antonissen* [1991] ECR I-745; Case C-43/93 *Vander Elst* [1994] ECR-I 3803; Davies, 1997, p. 589.

coming from lower-cost states. This was the scenario in the *Rush Portuguesa* case:[66] a Portuguese subcontractor challenged the application to its (Portuguese) employees of French minimum wage legislation for the period in which they were posted to work in France. The Court held that the imposition by French law of the minimum wage was not contrary to Article 59, thereby saving the principle of the strict territorial application of domestic labour legislation.

After *Rush*, there was an uneasy compromise: host states could (and did[67]) regulate the terms and conditions of posted workers, but were not obliged to do so according to a common standard. The Directive can be seen as an attempt to introduce such a common approach to the treatment of posted workers. It applies in the following three situations: where undertakings in the home state and host state agree a contract for the supply of labour services between them; where the posting takes place through administrative arrangements made within a single group of companies (for example, where an employee of a group company based in the home state is seconded to a group company in the host state); and, where the posting takes place in the course of the supply of labour by an employment business/agency in the home state to an employer or agency in the host state.

The host state must then ensure that the workers concerned are covered by basic standards contained in laws, regulations and administrative provisions governing the following matters (listed in Article 3(1)): working hours, holidays, minimum pay, regulation of conditions of supply of labour by agencies, health and safety, protection of pregnancy and maternity, and equal treatment of men and women and 'other provisions on discrimination'.[68] In respect of the building and construction trades only,[69] the host state must also apply standards derived from collective agreements 'which must be observed by all undertakings in the geographical area and in the profession or industry concerned', or, in the absence of such agreements or awards, agreements or awards 'which are generally applicable to all similar undertakings' in the sector or area which have been concluded by 'most representative' trade unions and employers' organisations.[70]

The Directive goes on to state that host states *may* enlarge their regulatory competence in two ways:[71] firstly, by applying norms derived from collective

---

[66] Case C-113/89 [1990] ECR I-1417. See also Case C-3/95 *Reiseburo Broede* v. *Gerd Sanker* [1997] 1 CMLR 224 and Case C-272/94 *Guiot* [1996] ECR I-1905.

[67] A provision to this effect was introduced into the French *Code du Travail* (Art. L. 341–5) in 1993. In Germany, legislation (the *Arbeitnehmer-Entsendugsgezetz*) was enacted in February 1996.

[68] An obligation is also imposed upon the home state: its courts will be required to apply the minimum standards of the law of the host state for the period of the posting even if, in other respects, the contract is governed by the law of the home state. However, it is arguable that the relevant minimum standards here are cumulative, so that an employee cannot be made worse off by the application of the laws of the host state. This matter is unclear. See generally Davies, 1997, in particular at 578–579.

[69] The relevant sectors are defined in the Annex to the Directive.

[70] Article 3(8).

[71] Article 3(10).

agreements (as defined above) to posted workers other than those in the building and construction industries; and secondly, by applying to posted workers norms from laws, regulations and administrative provisions other than those contained in the list of compulsory items in Article 3(1) (such as unfair dismissal laws and laws relating to employee representation).

A proposal to exempt from the Directive all postings for less than three months, which had been included in an earlier draft, was removed from the final, agreed version. Three broad categories of exemptions remain.[72] Firstly, a host state *must* exempt certain workers involved in cross-border provision of instal- lation and/or assembly services, where skilled or specialist workers are required, and the posting does not exceed eight days. Secondly, in the case of postings for less than one month, the host state, after consulting the social partners, may exempt workers from the provisions of minimum pay laws; but this does not apply to agency-supplied labour. Thirdly, in the case of postings which are 'not significant', exemption from minimum pay and paid leave provisions is allowed; but again, this does not apply to agency-supplied labour.

The Directive can be seen as a vindication of the interests of the predominantly northern host states in limiting low-cost competition from elsewhere in the Union. It is less clear that it can be presented as a measure aimed at promoting the supply of cross-border services. However, Article 57, which constitutes the Directive's 'treaty base', authorises the Council by qualified majority voting to adopt harmonising directives not for protective purposes, but 'in order to make it easier for persons to take up and pursue activities as self-employed persons', and Article 66 duplicates this with regard to the freedom to provide services. So is the Directive a liberalising or a protective measure? Perhaps its protective intentions are compatible with the goal of regularising the position of posted workers: 'as a means of protecting both the established workforce in the higher paying country and the migrant worker, who is ignorant about the general level of costs in the new country, one could argue that the... full integration of workers from other Member States into the domestic labour regulation of the importing state is the correct policy' (Davies, 1997, p. 600). However, this may not prevent legal challenges to certain aspects of the Directive, in particular the application of its provisions to posted workers 'from day one' (ibid.).

CONCLUSION

The reasons for the failure of the European Community to generate a supra- national equivalent of the welfare state régimes of the individual member states are deeply rooted in the history of the Community over the past 40 years, in the

---

[72] Articles 3(2)-3(6).

political compromises which went into its making, and in the institutional structures to which they gave rise. It is now widely accepted that a more realistic
(and perhaps more desirable) goal would be a framework of *transnational social
regulation* which could mediate between the integrationist aims of the single
market and the preservation of diversity and autonomy within social policy
systems at national level (Majone, 1993; Streeck, 1995). The democratic articulation of fundamental social rights within Community law could become a central
part of this endeavour (Bercusson *et al.*, 1997). However, in the present state of
development of what has become the European Union, a *social constitution* of
this kind is very far from being realised. Indeed, the danger for social policy at
both European and national level is that the much more fully fledged *economic
constitution* of the EU, represented in competition policy and the law of free
movement, will lead to ever greater pressure for deregulation.

The Court's judgement in the *Working Time* case and the adoption of the
revised Social Chapter in the Amsterdam Treaty were important steps in the
formal recognition of the role of social policy within the European polity, and
at least cement into place most of the gains of the past 20 years. However, the
prospects of political agreement between the member states on new legal initiatives seem slim. What little progress is currently being made is thanks to the
process of transnational social dialogue, the hesistant development of a human
rights agenda by the Court, and the growing influence of an employment-orien-
tated labour market policy. It is along these pathways that, for the immediate
future at least, the painful evolution of Community social policy seems set to continue.

REFERENCES

Barnard, C. (1996) 'The Economic Objectives of Article 119', in T. Hervey and D. O'Keeffe (eds) *Sex
    Equality Law in the European Union*, Wiley, Chichester.
Barnard, C. (1997) 'The United Kingdom, the "Social Chapter" and the Amsterdam Treaty', *Industrial
    Law Journal*, 26, 275–282.
Barnard, C. and Hervey, T. (1998) 'European Union Employment and Social Policy Survey 1996 and
    1997', *Yearbook of European Law*, forthcoming.
Barnard, C. (1998) 'The principle of equality in the Community context. *P, Grant, Kalanke* and *Marschall*:
    four uneasy bedfellows?' (1998) *Cambridge Law Journal*, forthcoming.
Bercusson, B., Deakin, S., Koistinen, P., Kravaritou, Y., Mückenberger, U., Supiot, A. and Veneziani,
    B. (1997) *A Manifesto for Social Europe*, ETUI, Brussels.
Davies, P. (1995) 'Market Integration and Social Policy in the Court of Justice', *Industrial Law Journal*,
    24, 49–77.
Davies, P. (1997) 'Posted Workers: Single Market or Protection of National Labour Law Systems?'
    Common Market Law Review, 34, 571–602.
Deakin, S. (1996) 'Labour Law as Market Regulation: the Economic Foundations of European Social
    Policy', in P. Davies *et al.* (eds) *European Community Labour Law: Principles and Perspectives*,
    Clarendon Press, Oxford.
Deakin, S. and Wilkinson, F. (1994) 'Rights vs. Efficiency? The Economic Case for Transnational Labour
    Standards', *Industrial Law Journal*, 23, 289–310.

Docksey, C. (1991) 'The Principle of Equality between Men and Women as a Fundamental Right in European Law', *Industrial Law Journal*, 20, 258–280.

Ellis, E. (1991) *European Community Sex Equality Law*, Clarendon Press, Oxford.

Forman, J. (1982) 'The Equal Pay Principle under Community Law', *Legal Issues in European Integration*, 1, 17–36.

Freedland, M. (1996) 'Employment Policy', in P. Davies *et al.* (eds) *European Community Labour Law: Principles and Perspectives*, Clarendon Press, Oxford.

Kahn-Freund, O. (1960) 'Labour Law and Social Security', in E. Stein and T. Nicholson (eds) *American Enterprise in the European Common Market: A Legal Profile*, University of Michigan Law School, Ann Arbor.

Majone, G. (1993) 'The European Community between Social Policy and Social Regulation', *Journal of Common Market Studies*, 31, 153–170.

Marshall, T.H. (1950) *Citizenship and Social Class*, Cambridge University Press, Cambridge.

Meehan, E. (1993) *Citizenship and the European Community*, Sage, London.

Prechal, S. (1996) 'Case note on Case C-450/93 *Kalanke* v. *Freie Hansestadt Bremen* [1995] ECR I-3051' *Common Market Law Review*, 33, 1245–1259.

Raz, J. (1986) *The Morality of Freedom*, Clarendon Press, Oxford.

Reich, N. (1997) 'A European Constitution for Citizens: Reflections on the Rethinking of Union and Community Law', *European Law Journal*, 3, 131–164.

Shaw, J. (1995) *Citizenship of the Union: Towards Post-National Membership*, specialised course delivered at the Academy of European Law, Florence, July.

Shaw, J. (1997) 'The Many Pasts and Futures of Citizenship in the European Union', *European Law Review*, 22, 554–572.

Schiek, D. (1996) 'Positive Action in Community Law', *Industrial Law Journal*, 25, 239–246.

Wedderburn, Lord (1995) *Labour Law and Freedom*, Lawrence & Wishart, London.

Weiler, J. (1996) 'European Citizenship and Human Rights', in J. Winter *et al.* (eds), *Reforming the Treaty on European Union*, Kluwer/Asser Institute, Deventer.

European Community employment law: key recent cases

Ramsumair Singh

European Union law is now a dynamic force in industrial relations generating a large and increasing volume of case law. A steady stream of cases in the employment field are now referred to the European Court of Justice by national courts particularly in the context of sex equality, equal pay, pensions and social security.

Moreover, the British courts, most notably the House of Lords, have shown themselves very receptive to arguments based on EU law. This has permitted cases to be decided nationally rather than being referred to the European Court of Justice (ECJ). This trend is to be welcomed as it may take a couple of years for the ECJ to hear a reference.

There are problems relating to the comparatively long gestation period for a case to be heard by the ECJ, and, not surprisingly, the ECJ has given guidance in dealing with some of the urgent cases. In *Zuckerfabrick Süderdithmarschen AG v Hauptzollamt Itzehoe Joined Cases C-143/88 and C-92/89 [1991] ECRE—415* the ECJ ruled that national courts may suspend the enforcement of a national administrative measure adopted on the basis of a Community regulation provided certain conditions are satisfied.

Most importantly, the national court must entertain serious doubts as to the validity of the measure, and if the contested measure is not already at issue before the ECJ, the national court must refer the question to it, since the ECJ is the only court with jurisdiction to declare a Community regulation invalid. The national court must, however, respect previous decisions of the ECJ.

There are some fundamental principles recognised by the ECJ as inherent in, and inseparable from, the system of Community law. They include the protection of fundamental human rights and the principles of administrative legality including proportionality and non-discrimination.

EMPLOYMENT CASES

Almost all the cases relating to employment have been the result of Art. 177 references from national courts under Art. 177(2). Where a question as to the

---

Ramsumair Singh is Lecturer in Industrial Relations at the University of Lancaster.

interpretation of the Treaty or concerning an act of one of the community institutions is raised before a national court or tribunal, if the latter considers that a decision on the issue in question is necessary to enable it to give a judgement, it may request the European Court of Justice to give a ruling on the issue. Before the ECJ can give a ruling it has to consider whether the Court has jurisdiction to hear the issue.

Under Article 177 there is a clear separation between the functions of national courts and tribunals and the ECJ. This fact is often stressed by the ECJ (*Zabala Erasun v Instituto Nacional de Empleo Joined Cases C-422–424/93 [1995] All ER (EC 758)*. The separation of functions is based on the premise that national courts have more intimate knowledge of the Acts and circumstances of the case in question, and are therefore in the best position to decide whether a ruling from the ECJ is necessary in order for the national court to decide the case. Generally speaking, where the issue being referred is related to the interpretation of Community law, the ECJ is bound to give a ruling.

Within recent years, however, the ECJ has attempted to exercise some control over the number and type of cases on which it is prepared to give a preliminary ruling. For example, the ECJ stipulated that national courts must give some explanation as to why it is necessary to refer the particular issues for interpretation, and as to the link between the issues in question and the national legislation applicable to the particular dispute. (*Criminal Proceedings against Gran Gumis Case C-167/94 [1995] All ER (EC) 668.*) Moreover, a national court cannot refer a question to the ECJ, unless a case in which the issues are raised, is pending before it. The spirit and purpose of the ECJ is to assist in the administration of justice in member states, and not to give opinions on hypothetical questions.

The question as to which court or tribunal can make a reference to the ECJ is of fundamental importance, particularly for the United Kingdom. Under Art. 177(2) any court or tribunal may make a reference, but there is guidance that, in general, it should be the court of last resort. In the UK there has been consideration from time to time as to whether the Court of Appeal or the House of Lords is the court of last resort. As a guiding principle, the House of Lords is the court of last resort, but the Court of Appeal is the court of last resort in cases where leave to appeal from a decision of the Court of Appeal to the House of Lords is denied.

Attention has been drawn to the fact that national courts and tribunals, of necessity, apply EU laws in cases coming before them. In this review of cases, therefore, cases coming before the ECJ, and those before the national courts and tribunals especially the Court of Appeal and the House of Lords, will be the subject of review. In an exercise of this nature it is, moreover, inevitable that a selection has to be made and it is hoped that the cases selected will have policy implications for industrial relations.

REMEDIES AGAINST THE STATE

The case of *Dillenkoffer and Others v Federal Republic of Germany, Joined Cases C-178/94, C-189/94, C-189/94 and C-190/94, [1997] IRLR 699* raises points of general importance concerning the financial liabilities of member states to individuals who have suffered loss as a result of the state's failure to implement a European Community Directive. The UK, German and Netherlands Governments argued that a state can incur liability for late implementation of a Directive only if there has been a serious breach of Community law for which it can be held responsible. This, it was contended, depends on the circumstances which caused the period for transposition to be exceeded.

Article 7 of Council Directive 90/314 provides that an organiser and/or retailer of a package holiday must provide security in the event of insolvency for the refund of money paid over, and for the repatriation of the consumer. Member states were required to implement the Directive by 31 December 1992. Germany did not implement the Directive until 1 July 1994.

The plaintiffs bought package holidays from German travel firms during 1993 and, as a result of the insolvency of the firms, were either unable to take the holiday or had to return from the holiday destination at their own expense, and did not succeed in obtaining reimbursement of the sums already paid.

The Regional Court of Bonn referred a number of questions relating to the case to the ECJ for a preliminary ruling. Among the questions of general public importance were:

(1) Does the mere fact that the time-limit specified in Article 9 of the Directive has been exceeded suffice to confer the right to compensation involving state liability as defined in the *Francovich*[1] judgement of the Court of Justice, or can a member state put forward the objection that the period for transposition proved to be inadequate.

(2) Does it follow from the *Francovich* judgement of the Court of Justice that the right to compensation on grounds of breach of Community law is not dependent on a finding of fault in general, or at any rate of wrongful non-adoption of legislative measures, on the part of the member state?

(3) Does liability on the part of the member state for an infringement of Community law presuppose a serious, that is to say a manifest and grave, breach of obligation.

The European Court of Justice held:

(1) A failure by a member state to take any steps to transpose a Directive into national law within the period laid down by the Directive is sufficient *per se* to be a breach of Community law so as to afford individuals who have suffered injury a right to damages if the result prescribed by the Directive entails the

---

[1] *Francovich and others v Italian Republic, joined cases C-6/90 and C-9/90 [1992] IRLR 84 ECJ.*

grant of rights to individuals, the content of those rights is identifiable on the basis of the Directive's provisions and a casual link exists between the breach of the State's obligation and the loss and damage suffered by the injured party. No other conditions need to be taken into consideration.

(2) When a member state fails to take any of the measures necessary to achieve the result prescribed by a Directive within the period it lays down, that member state manifestly and gravely disregards the limits of its discretion. Reparation of the loss and damage suffered by the injured parties does not depend on the existence of intentional fault or negligence on the part of the organ of the State to which the infringement is attributable, or on a prior finding by the European Court if an infringement of Community law attributable to the State.

(3) The German Government's contention that the period prescribed for the transposition of the Directive was inadequate could not justify its failure to transpose the Directive within the prescribed period. If the period allowed for the implementation of a Directive proves to be too short, the only step compatible with Community law available to the member state concerned is to take the appropriate initiatives within the Community in order to have the competent Community institution grant an extension of the period.

STATE AID—HANDLING REDUNDANCIES

The Case of French Republic v Commission of the European Communities, Case C-241/94 [1997] IRLR 415 concerned a decision by The European Commission to classify as state aid contributions by the French Fonds National de l'Emploi (FNE) (National Employment Fund) to redundancy and redeployment costs incurred by Kimberley Clark Soplain in implementing a social plan.

Article 92(1) of the EC Treaty provides

> save as otherwise provided in this Treaty, any aid granted by a member state or through state resources in any form whatsoever which distorts or threatens to distort competition by favouring certain undertakings or the production of certain goods shall, in so far as it affects trade between member states, be incompatible with the common market.

French redundancy legislation provides that where an undertaking with at least 50 employees proposes to dismiss at least 10 employees in a 30-day period, it must draw up a social plan, with the aim of avoiding or reducing the redundancies and of facilitating redeployment of those whose redundancy cannot be avoided. The social plan can include measures which, by agreement with the FNE may be jointly financed by the state.

In 1993 Kimberley Clark restructured its factory in Solteville-les-Rouen, leading to 207 proposed redundancies. Twenty-five per cent of the total cost of the social plan of FF109 million was borne by the state by way of FNE agreements. The European Commission, after receiving information from the French

Government, took a decision on 27 June 1994 classifying the contributions by the FNE as state aid. France brought an action seeking annulment of the Commission's decision. It argued that an FNE contribution was not state aid within the meaning of Article 92(1), but was a general measure for the benefit of employees designed to fight unemployment.

The European Court of Justice held:

(1) The system under which the French National Employment Fund (FNE) contributes to the implementation of social policy drawn up by employers in accordance with French legislation on redundancy met the conditions for classification as state aid and incompatible with the common market within the meaning of Article 92(1) of the Treaty, notwithstanding its social objective ....

(2) Since, as a result of FNE intervention, an employer is relieved of certain legal obligations to its employees, and since the FNE enjoys a latitude enabling it to adjust its financial assistance, the system is liable to place certain undertakings in a more favourable situation than that of their competitors, thus meeting the conditions for classification as aid. Accordingly, the Commission was entitled to conclude that, as a result of the social plan drawn up in collaboration with the state, Kimberley Clark had received state aid within the meaning of Article 92.

GENDER DISCRIMINATION

The ambit of EU discrimination law and whether it could apply beyond a straight male–female comparison continues to give rise to litigation.

In *Grant v South-West Trains Case C-249/06; The Times 23/2/98*; the ECJ had to consider whether an employer's refusal to grant travel concessions to an employee's partner of the same sex, where they were allowed to the spouse or partner of the opposite sex of an employee, did not constitute discrimination contrary to Community law.

By employees' contracts of employment and regulations adopted by the employer, South-West Trains Limited, free and reduced-rate travel concessions were granted to employees and also 'for one legal spouse' and 'for one common law opposite sex spouse of staff ... subject to a statutory declaration being made that a meaningful relationship has existed for a period of two years or more ...'

The applicant employee, Lisa Jacqueline Grant, applied for concessions for her female partner, with whom she declared she had had a meaningful relationship for over two years, but was refused on the ground that for unmarried persons concessions were only grantable for a partner of the opposite sex.

A Southampton industrial tribunal referred the issue to the ECJ under Article 177 of the EC Treaty. The tribunal sought an answer to the questions whether the refusals constituted discrimination prohibited by article 119 of the Treaty, on equal pay for men and women, and Council Directive 75/117/EEC of February

10, 1975 on the approximation of the laws of member states relating to the application of the principle of equal pay for men and women (*OH 1975 L45 p.19*). In essence, three questions fell to be answered and the ECJ dealt with them *seriatim*.

The first was whether a condition such as that at issue constituted discrimination based directly on the sex of the worker. The condition that the worker had to live in a stable relationship with a person of the opposite sex in order to benefit from the travel concessions applied regardless of the sex of the worker, so that concessions were refused to a male person living with a male just as to a female worker living with a female. Since the condition applied in the same way to female and male workers, it did not constitute discrimination based on sex.

The second question was whether Community law now required stable relationships between two persons of the same sex to be regarded by all employees as equivalent to marriages or, stable relationships outside marriage between two persons of opposite sex. Ms Grant submitted that the laws of the member states, as well as those of the Community and other international organisations, increasingly treated the two situations as equivalent. The ECJ noted that the European Parliament had indeed declared that it deplored all forms of discrimination based on a person's sexual orientation, but the Community had not as yet adopted rules providing for such equivalence.

The European Commission of Human Rights, for its part, considered that despite the modern evolution of attitudes towards homosexuality, stable homosexual relationships did not fall within the scope of the right to respect for family life under Art. 8 of the Convention on Human Rights. National provisions for the purpose of protecting the family, and which accorded more favourable treatment to married persons and persons of opposite sex living together as man and wife than to persons of the same sex in a stable relationship were not contrary to Article 14, which prohibited discrimination on the ground of sex. In another context, the European Court of Human Rights had interpreted Article 12 as applying only to traditional marriage between two persons of opposite biological sex. It followed that, in the present state of Community law, the two situations were not regarded as equivalent, so that employers were not required to treat them as such.

The third question was whether discrimination based on sexual orientation constituted discrimination based on the sex of the worker. Ms Grant submitted that it followed from (*PVS Case—13/94 [1996] ALL ER (EC) 397; [1996] ECR I-2143*) that differences in treatment based on sexual orientation were included in the 'discrimination based on sex' prohibited by Article 199 of the Treaty. In that case the ECJ was asked by a Truro industrial tribunal whether a dismissal based on the change of sex of a worker was to be regarded as discrimination on the ground of sex. The ECJ held that the dismissal of a transsexual for a reason related to a sex change was contrary to Article 5(1) of the Equal Treatment

Directive. The Court's reasoning leading to the conclusion that there was discrimination was limited to the case of a worker's gender reassignation and did not apply to differences of treatment based on sexual orientation.

Ms Grant referred to the International Covenant on Civil and Political Rights of 19 December 1996 (*United Nations Treaty Series, Vol. 999, p. 171*) in which, in the view of the Human Rights Committee established under article 28 of the Covenant, the term 'sex' was to be taken as including sexual orientation. The ECJ stated that the Covenant was one of the international instruments relating to the protection of human rights of which the ECJ took account in applying the fundamental principles of Community law, and respect for the fundamental rights which formed an integral part of those general principles was a condition of the legality of Community Acts. Yet those rights could not in themselves extend the scope of treaty provisions beyond the competencies of the Community. Furthermore, in the communication referred to by Ms Grant, the Human Rights Committee—which is not a judicial institution and whose findings have no binding force in law—does not in any event appear to reflect the interpretation generally accepted of the concept of discrimination based on sex which appeared in various international instruments. It could not constitute a basis for the Court to extend the scope of Article 119 of the Treaty.

The Scope of Article 119 was to be determined having regard only to its working and purpose, its place in the scheme of the Treaty, and its legal context. It followed from these considerations that Community law did not cover sexual orientation.

The Court observed, however, that the Treaty of Amsterdam signed on 3 October 1997 provided for an insertion into the EC Treaty of an Article 6a which, once the Treaty of Amsterdam had come into force, would allow the Council to take action to eliminate discrimination based on sexual orientation.

The Court ruled that:

> The refusal by an employer to allow travel concessions to the person of the same sex with whom a worker has had a stable relationship where such concessions are allowed to a worker's spouse or to the person of the opposite sex with whom a worker has had a stable relationship outside marriage, does not constitute discrimination prohibited by Article 119 of the EC Treaty and Council Directive 75/117/EEC of February 1975 on the approximation of the laws of the Member States relating to the application of the principle of equal pay for men and women.

This is an important decision and goes a long way to clarifying the law relating to sexual orientation in relation to same sex couples in the field of employment. The question must be whether the issue could become live again after the incorporation of the proposed article in the Amsterdam Treaty to eliminate discrimination based on sexual orientation.

PREGNANT WORKERS

In *Handels-OG Kontorfunktion/Ærernes Forbund v Dansk Handel & Service Case—400/95 (1997) IRLR 643,* a case emanating from Denmark, the ECJ was asked to rule on the rights of women to pregnancy leave.

Ms L informed her employers that she was pregnant in August 1991. During her pregnancy she was on sick leave. When her statutory maternity leave of 24 weeks came to an end she went on annual leave. However, as she was still receiving treatment for her illness, she again went on sick leave.

The employer gave notice to terminate the contract of employment on the grounds that 'it is scarcely likely that you will at any time in the future—on grounds of health—be again in a position to carry out your work in a satisfactory manner'. Ms L claimed that her dismissal while on sick leave was contrary to the Equal Treatment Directive in as much as her illness began during her pregnancy and continued after the expiry of her maternity leave.

The Danish Supreme Court referred the following question to the European Court of Justice for a preliminary ruling.

Does the Equal Treatment Directive—Directive 76/207/EEC of 9 February 1976—on the implementation of the principle of equal treatment for men and women as regards access to employment, vocational training and promotion and working conditions, cover dismissal as a result of absence following the end of maternity leave if the absence is attributable to an illness which arose during pregnancy and continued during and after maternity leave, it being assumed that the dismissal took place after the end of the maternity leave.

The European Court of Justice held:

(1) The Equal Treatment Directive does not preclude dismissal on the grounds of periods of absence due to illness attributable to pregnancy or childbirth, even where that illness first appeared during pregnancy and continued during the period of maternity leave ... The only question is whether a woman is dismissed on account of absence due to illness in the same circumstances as a man.

(2) The Equal Treatment Directive does not, however, preclude account being taken of a woman's absence from work between the beginning of her pregnancy and the beginning of her maternity leave when calculating the period providing grounds for her dismissal under national law.

(3) The Pregnant Workers Directive 92/85 provides for special protection to be given to women, by prohibiting their dismissal during the period of pregnancy to the end of their maternity leave, save in cases unconnected with their condition. It is clear from the objective of that provision that absence during the protected period, other than for reasons unconnected with the employee's condition, can no longer be taken into account as grounds for subsequent dismissal. However, Directive 92/85 had not been adopted when the applicant in the current case was dismissed.

It should be noted that similar issues on pregnant workers have recently been raised in the Court of Appeal. See *Kwik Save Stores Limited v Janet Greaves; Heather Ellen Crees vs Royal London Mutual Insurance Society Limited, EATRF 97/0533/B, Lexis.*

HEALTH AND SAFETY AT WORK: WORKING TIME DIRECTIVE

The decision by the ECJ in *United Kingdom v European Council (C84/94) [1997] ICR (2) 443; [1997] IRLR (3) 30* is perhaps one of the most important cases concerning health and safety over recent years. The point at issue is the validity of the Working Time Directive.

The UK applied for annulment of Council Directive 93/104. This directive obliged member states to implement measures to ensure workers' entitlement to minimum rest periods, as a means to improve health and safety in the working environment under the Treaty of Rome 1957 Art. 118a (2). The Directive provided for a 24 hour uninterrupted rest period for every seven day period. It included 11 hours daily rest, which in principle included Sunday, and an overall restriction that the average time worked in each seven-day period, including overtime, should not exceed 48 hours. The UK contended that the choice of legal basis for the Directive was erroneous and that the principle of proportionality had not been observed.

The ECJ dismissed the UK's application. It pointed out, however, that the Court's powers of review were limited to considering the legality of the Directive and not its merits. The main purpose of the Directive was the protection of the health and safety of workers and therefore Art. 118a was its proper legal basis even though it might have some effect on the workings of the Single Market. The principle of proportionality had not been infringed as the Council was entitled to set standards higher than the minimum established by different member states for protecting the health and safety of workers and had a wide discretion in social policy matters which involved complex evaluation. However, the provision that the minimum weekly rest period must include Sunday would be annulled because the Council had not explained why Sunday should be treated as more important than any other day of the week in the context of the health and safety of workers.

There is an interesting case on the failure to implement the Working Time Directive emanating from Northern Ireland: *R v Attorney General for Northern Ireland ex P. McHugh (Current Law Cases, Ref. 97/Sept).*

M was appointed through a temping agency to work for a government department in Londonderry, Northern Ireland. Both the temping agency and the government department refused to accept that they were M's employer. She received no terms and conditions of employment. M commenced a Francovich action against the government for non-implementation of the Working Time Directive. The government acknowledged that they had failed to implement the terms of the Directive in breach of the Treaty of Rome 1957 and that they intended to implement the Directive as soon as possible.

EQUALITY BETWEEN MEN AND WOMEN

European law figures prominently in the cases on employment law both in the House of Lords and in the Court of Appeal, and perhaps one of the most prominent issues is the question of equality between men and women in the employment sphere. The decisions of the House of Lords in recent cases relate to issues raised by women seeking to establish rights under Community Law.

In *R vs Secretary of State for Employment, ex parte Seymour-Smith and Another [1997] 2 All ER 273* the House of Lords had to consider whether judicial review was available to challenge the validity of the Unfair Dismissal (Variation of Qualifying Period Order 1985), by which the Secretary of State had extended the qualifying period for unfair dismissal claims from one year to two years' employment.

In 1991 the two applicants, both of whom were female, were dismissed from their employment after working between one and two years. They wished to make a complaint to an industrial tribunal but were unable to do so because they had not been continuously employed for two years as required by the 1985 Order. The applicants applied for judicial review to quash the 1985 Order on the grounds that it was contrary to Art. 5 of Council Directive (EEC) 76/207 on the implementation of the principle of equal treatment for men and women with regard to employment and working conditions.[2]

The applicants contended that the two-year qualifying period discriminated against women because a smaller proportion of women than men qualified under the 1985 Order to bring unfair dismissal claims. The applicants contended that the resulting discrimination was unjustified and that it contravened the principle of equal treatment for men and women which the 1985 Order required to be implemented in United Kingdom law.

The Divisional Court dismissed the application and the applicants appealed, contending further that the right to compensation for unfair dismissal constituted 'pay' for the purposes of Art. 119 of the EC Treaty and that the making of the 1985 Order was a breach by the United Kingdom of its obligations under Art.

---

[2] Article 5 states 'Application of the principle of equal treatment with regard to working conditions, including conditions governing dismissal, means that men and women should be guaranteed the same conditions without discrimination on grounds of sex'.

119 to uphold the principle of equal pay for equal work.[3] The Court of Appeal held that the applicants had sufficient standing to rely on the Equal Treatment Directive to bring judicial review proceedings challenging the validity of the 1985 Order; that the order was discriminatory but it would be inappropriate to quash the order. The applicants were, however, entitled to declaratory relief to the effect that provisions whereby the right not to be unfairly dismissed did not apply to employees who had not been continuously employed for a minimum period of two years at the date of their dismissal were incompatible with the Equal Treatment Directive. The Court further held that the question of whether the right to compensation for unfair dismissal constituted 'pay' for the purposes of Art. 119 of the EC Treaty was not acute claire but it was not necessary to decide the issue.

The Secretary of State appealed against the grant of the declaration and applicants cross-appealed against the refusal to grant relief under Art. 119.

Lord Hoffman, giving the unanimous judgement of the House of Lords noted that 'this is an exceptional case' (p. 281). The House held:

(1) It was acute claire that a council directive, as such, had no effect on the private rights of parties such as employees and employers. An individual had no right to mandamus against the state in his national court requiring that a directive be implemented. Accordingly, except in proceedings which brought into question the legal relations between the individual and the state or its emanations, directives did not give rights or restrictions which without further enactment were required to be given legal effect. The European Communities Act 1972 did not enable directives to affect the validity or construction of domestic legislation such as the 1985 order. The declaration made by the Court of Appeal would not enable the applicant employees to pursue their cases in the industrial tribunal. The declaration would accordingly be discharged.

(2) On the issue of compatibility with Art. 119 of the EC Treaty, a person claiming as a matter of private law to compensation for unfair dismissal ordinarily had to bring proceedings in the industrial tribunal, even if they raise an issue of incompatibility between domestic and Community law. However, in the exceptional circumstances of this case, where all the issues and relevant evidence were before the House, it would entertain the appeal.

The House would, however, seek preliminary rulings from the European Court of Justice on whether the award of compensation for breach of the right not to be unfairly dismissed under national legislation such as the Employment Protection

---

[3] Article 119 provides 'Each Member State shall … maintain the application of the principle that men and women should receive equal pay for equal work. for the purposes of this Article "pay" means the ordinary basic or minimum wage or salary and any other considerations … which the worker receives … in respect of his employment …'.

(Consolidation) Act 1978 constituted 'pay' within the meaning of Art. 119 and certain related question on the construction of Art. 119 before giving judgement.

This case raises a number of issues not only in employment law, but also in administrative law. Clearly, the rulings from the ECJ would certainly clarify the law in a contentious area of industrial relations.

FREEDOM OF MOVEMENT

During the period under review there has been a number of cases relating to the freedom of movement of workers within member states.

In *Secretary of State for Social Security and Another v Remilien; and Chief Adjudication Officer v Wolke [1998] A11 ER129* the House of Lords had to rule on the freedom of movement of two EU non-British nationals, and on their eligibility for income support in Britain.

W and R were single mothers and nationals of member states of the European Community living in England and claiming income support. They received letters from the Home Office informing each of them that the Secretary of State was not satisfied that they were lawfully resident in the United Kingdom under Community law in view of the fact that they were present in a non-economic capacity and had become a burden on public funds and that they should make arrangements to leave. An adjudication officer, decided, in each case, that W and R were not entitled to income support, as they were required by the Secretary of State to leave the United Kingdom. The adjudication officer's decision against W was quashed on her application for judicial review and R's appeal to the Commissioner, following the Social Security Appeal Tribunal's decision upholding the adjudication officer's decision, was successful. The Chief Adjudication Officer appealed to the Court of Appeal against both decisions. The Court of Appeal (by a majority) allowed the appeals on the ground that the letters from the Home Office constituted a requirement to leave the United Kingdom which ended W and R's entitlement to income support. W and R appealed to the House of Lords.

The House (Lord Slynn of Hadley dissenting) ruled that a person would be required to leave the United Kingdom by the Secretary of State, thereby terminating any entitlement to income support, only if he had been placed under a legal obligation to do so by the Secretary of State. Such an obligation would only arise from an act having legal consequences, such as a deportation order or an act for removal under the Immigration (European Economic Area) Order 1994. Since the letters to W and R did not impose the necessary legal obligation, W and R had not been 'required to leave' so as to end their entitlement to income support. Accordingly, the appeals would be allowed.

In *Joined Cases Jacquet v Land Nordrhein-Westfalen [(C65/96) The Times,*

11 August 1997] the ECJ clarified the employment rights of spouses of a non-member state married to nationals of a member state.

The ECJ ruled that a national of a non-member state who was married to a national of a member state was not entitled to rely on Council Regulation 16 12/68 Art. 11 to challenge the validity of a law of that country which placed limitations on the length of an employment contract where the worker had never exercised the right to freedom of movement within the community. Free movement rights under Art. 11 were not intended to apply to wholly internal situations where there was no link with EC law, and in such circumstances it was irrelevant that the national law was incompatible with the Treaty of Rome 1957 Art. 48 (2).

In *Tetik v Land Berlin [Independent* February 5 1997] the ECJ was asked to rule on the freedom of movement of Turkish workers, and their right to reside in a member state whilst seeking new employment.

Under the Treaty of Rome 1957 and subsequent agreements a Turkish national has a right of abode in a member state whilst seeking employment. T, a Turkish national, had been legally employed on German ships for about eight years, and had obtained successive resident permits, each for a specified period and limited to employment in shipping. When T left his job as a seaman, he applied to the German authorities for an unlimited residence permit to enable him to seek employment on land. His application was refused and, on appeal, the matter was referred to ECJ for a ruling on the interpretation and effect on the Council of the EEC/Turkey Association Decision No 1/80 Art. 6.

The ECJ held that:

(1) Decision 1/80 did not give full freedom of movement to Turkish workers, but it did confer rights to lawful entrants who had worked legally for more than a certain period.

(2) Pursuant to Article 6 (1) the worker had not only the right to respond to a prior offer of employment but also the unconditional right to seek and take up any employment he chose, without any possibility of priority being given to workers from member states.

(3) A Turkish worker must be entitled to reside in a member state, in which he has worked for four years or more, for a reasonable period whilst seeking new employment, since his access to any paid employment of his choice within that provision would otherwise be deprived of substance.

(4) The worker in this case was therefore entitled to reside in Germany for a reasonable period, provided that he continued to be registered as belonging to the German labour force and complied with the relevant requirements of domestic employment legislation. The length of that reasonable period was to be determined by the authorities or the courts in the host member state, but had to be sufficient so as not to jeopardise the worker's prospects of finding new employment.

COMPATIBILITY OF GERMAN CIVIL SERVICE LAW WITH COMMUNITY LAW

In *Helmut Marschall v Land Nordrhein-Westfalen Case C-409/95 [1997] All ER 865* there was a reference by a German Court to the European Court of Justice for a preliminary ruling under Art. 177 of the EC Treaty as to whether German Civil Service Law preferring women for appointment to a higher grade post where there are fewer women than men in such posts was contrary to EC Council Directive (EC) 76/297 on equal treatment for both sexes.

The ECJ held that:

(1) Such a rule preferring a female candidate over an equally well qualified male candidate had to provide a guarantee that candidates would be subject to an objective assessment of the criteria specific to each candidate.

(2) Such an assessment had to be capable of overriding the priority accorded to the female candidate where one or more of the criteria tilted the balance in favour of the male candidate.

(3) The specific criteria must not be such as to discriminate against women.

It is essential that this decision is seen in its social, economic and political context. In the United Kingdom and indeed, in other member states contemporary research shows that equality in terms of pay and conditions between men and women is still some way from achievement in many sectors of employment. The Commission has not only recognised this problem, but has attempted to address it as is evidenced in the *Fourth Medium-Term Action Programme on Equal Opportunities for Men and Women (1996–2000)*. An important observation of the Court, which is consistent with the recommendations in the Action Programme, is that existing EU legal provisions on equal treatment are inadequate for the elimination of all existing inequalities and it is therefore essential that parallel action is taken by member states, both sides of industry, and other bodies concerned to counteract the prejudicial effects on women in employment which are from social attitudes, structures and processes.

The purpose of Directive 76/207 is to put into effect in member states the principle of equal treatment for men and women as regards, amongst other things, access to employment, including occupational mobility. Art. 2(1) states that 'there shall be no discrimination whatsoever on grounds of sex directly or indirectly'. Article 2(4) lays down that the Directive is to be 'without prejudice to measures to promote equal opportunity for men and women, in particular by removing existing inequalities which affect women's opportunities in the areas covered by the Directive.

In 1995 the legality of many positive measures to advance the goal of substantive equality was put into question when it was seen that Court's ruling in *Kalanke [Case C-450/93, Kalanke v Freie Hansetadt Bremen [1995] ILRL, 660 [1996] All ER (EC) 66)* was subject to two possible interpretations. It could be regarded as applying only to a national rule of the Bremen type which, without its protective 'saving clause' exceeded the 'opportunities' term of Art. 2 (4) and, by leading to an automatic precedence for women, aimed to achieve equality as regards results or representation. Such a narrow interpretation, it was felt, would not therefore endanger other positive measures such as programmes focusing on professional training, goals and action timetables.

A broader interpretation of *Kalanke* was however possible based on the Court's general statement when it said that 'National rules which guarantee women absolute and unconditional priority for appointment or promotion go beyond committing equal opportunities and overstep the limits of the exception in Art. 2(4) of the Directive' (para. 22).

The Court's ruling on *Marschall* does not support the broader interpretation of *Kalanke*, and should be considered in the light of the *Amsterdam Treaty*. Art. 119(4) provides that 'with a view to ensuring full equality in practice between men and women in working life, the principle of equal treatment shall not prevent any member state from maintaining or adopting measures providing for specific advantages in order to make it easier for the under-represented sex to pursue a vocational activity or to prevent or compensate for disadvantages in professional careers'.

It would seem that, to some extent, the way is open for positive discrimination in member states. The policy implications of this development are, of course, immense.

Another case from Germany related to the application of the Equal Treatment Directive to part-time employees: *Gerster v Freistaff Bayern (C1/95) [1997] IRLR 699.*

G, an employee of the Bavarian State Civil Service who worked over half of normal hours, applied for promotion. Under Bavarian Civil Service rules promotion was to be based on length of service. Periods of employment during which the hours worked were between one half and two thirds of normal working hours were to be treated as equivalent to two thirds. G asked that her employment be treated as full-time employment for the purposes of calculating her length of service, but her application was refused. G brought proceedings against the State on the grounds that the rejection of her candidature was contrary to the Treaty of Rome 1957, Art. 199, Council Directive 75/117 and Council Directive 76/207 Art. 3. She contended that, as her case concerned a system or the classification of salaries, it fell within the scope of the term 'pay' as used in Art. 119, and further, that since the majority of part-time employees in G's department were women, the selection process for promotion resulted in indirect discrimination.

The ECJ held that while the principle of equal pay for men and women enshrined in Art. 119 applied to employment in the public service, Art. 119 did not extend to aspects of employment other than those referred to. [The ECJ followed the ruling in *Defrenne v Sabena (C149/77) [1978] ECR 1365, [1978] CLY 1291.*] Since the Bavarian rule relating to promotion concerned access to career advancement and was only indirectly linked to pay, it did not fall within the ambit of Art. 119 or Council Directive 75/117. However, Council Directive 76/207 Art. 3, precluded such a rule unless it was justified by objective criteria unrelated to any sex discrimination and it was for the national court to determine whether the measure in question could be objectively justified or not.

PENSIONS

On 28 September 1994 the European Court of Justice ruled that the right to membership of an occupational pension scheme fell within the scope of Art. 119 of the EC Treaty. It further ruled that any exclusion of part-time workers from such schemes which affected a much greater number of women than men and which could not be justified objectively by an employee on other grounds, amounted to discrimination on grounds of sex in contravention of Art. 119.

Following that ruling, a number of part-time workers brought proceedings claiming to have been excluded from, or unfairly dealt with by, such schemes. A group of test cases came before the industrial tribunal concerning certain provisions of the Sex Discrimination Act 1979 and the Sex Discrimination Act 1975 and their relationship with Art. 119 of the Treaty. [*Preston and Others v Wolverhampton Healthcare NHS Trust and Others; Fletcher and others v Midland Bank plc [1998] 1 All ER 528.*] The Tribunal decided that the six month time limit 52(4) of the Equal Pay Act did apply to the cases, and that its application in the context did not render the workers' exercise of rights under Art. 1190 'impossible' or 'excessively difficult" in accordance with the test laid down by the European Court of Justice. It also decided that a claim could not be brought in respect of a period of employment which was more than two years before the claim, as provided by 5 2(5) of the 1979 Act and that the requirement also met the ECJ's conditions. On appeal, the Employment Appeals Tribunal and the Court of Appeal both upheld the decisions of the industrial tribunal. The workers appealed to the House of Lords.

A referral to the European Court of Justice was made by the House of Lords under Act 119 of the Treaty in respect of two questions: (1) whether the time limits laid down in S2(4) and 52(5) of the 1970 Act did pass the 'impossible' or 'excessively difficult' tests; and (2) whether the different time limits for binding claims laid down by other national statutes and the domestic law of contract was in breach of the principle that procedural rules for breach of a Community principle should be no less favourable to a complainant than those which applied to similar claims of a domestic nature. The House of Lords ruled that it was not possible to claim in respect of previous contracts unless proceedings had been instituted within six months of their termination.

CONCLUSION

It is abundantly clear that the European Court of Justice as the final arbiter over issues concerned with the European Union is playing a central role in the development of employment law in member states. However, the long gestation period poses real problems for workers exercising their rights under European law. Moreover, as judgements of the ECJ have to be applied in all member states it is sometimes difficult to interpret and apply the decision within a national context.

Yet the Court has provided solutions to very complex problems in the field of industrial relations. The cases referred to in this review bear ample testimony to the competence and deep understanding of the employer–employee relationship and its many manifestations within the diverse cultural contexts of member states. In Britain where the 'old' and the 'new' industrial relations exist side by side and with the symbiotic tie between common law and statute, the ECJ has shown a remarkable understanding of the traditions and circumstances of Britain, and indeed of all member states with their special characteristics.

ACKNOWLEDGEMENTS

The author is grateful for the assistance he received from Ms Lesley Dingle of the Squire Library, University of Cambridge, and that from Michael Dunn and Brian Kirtley of University of Lancaster Library who assisted with obtaining material and commented on drafts of this article. Alan Airth and Dr Catherine Singh also gave the benefit of their comments.

REFERENCES

Barnard, C. (1997) 'The United Kingdom, the "Social Chapter" and the Amsterdam Treaty', *Industrial Law Journal*, 26, 275–282.

Davies, P. (1995) 'Market Integration and Social Policy in the Court of Justice', *Industrial Law Journal*, 24, 49–77.

Davies, P., *et al.* (eds) (1996) *European Community Labour Law: Principles and Perspectives*, Clarendon Press, Oxford.

Schiek, D. (1996) 'Positive Action in Community Law', *Industrial Law Journal*, 25, 239–246.

Singh, R. (1997) 'Equal Opportunities for Men and Women in the EU: A Commentary', *Industrial Relations Journal*, 28, 1, 68–71.

Watson, P. (1995) 'Equality of Treatment: A Variable Concept?', *Industrial Law Journal*, 24, 33–48.

Szyszczak, E. (1995) Future Direction in European Union Social Policy, *Industrial Law Journal*, 24, 19–32.

Cases Referred to in Review

Criminal Proceedings against Gran Gomis, C-167/94 [1995] A11 ER (EC) 668.

Defrenne v Sabena (C419/77, [1978] ECR 1365 [1978] O.L.Y. 1291)

Dillenkoffer and Others vs Federal Republic of Germany, Joined Cases C-178/94, C-188/94, C-189/94 and C-190/94, [1997] IRLR, 699.

Francovich and Others v Italian Republic, joined cases C-6/90 and C-9/90 [1992] IRLR 84 ECJ.

French Republic v Commission of the European Communities, Case C-241/94 [1997] IRLR 415.

Grant v South-West Trains, Cases C-249/96; *The Times*, 23/2/98; [1998] IRLR 165. Also, Lexis transcript of judgement.

Gerster v Freistaff Bayern (C1/95) [1997] IRLR 699.

Handels-OG Kontorfunktion/Ærernes Forbund v Dansk Handel & Service Case – 400/95 [1997] IRLR 643.

Hellmut Marschall v Land Nordrhein-Westfalen (C-409/95) [1997] A11 ER 865.

Jacquet v Land Nordrhein-Westfalen (C69/96); *The Times*, 11 August 1997.

Kalanke v Freie Hansestadt Bremen [1995] ECR I-3051; [1996] A11 ER (EC) 66.

Kwik Save Stores Limited v Janet Greeves; Heather Ellen Crees v Royal London Mutual Insurance Society Limited, EAST RF97/0533/B, Lexis.

P v S Case-13/94 [1996] A11 ER (EC) 397; [1996] ECJ I 2143.

Preston and Others v Wolverhampton Healthcare NHS Trust and Others; Fletcher and Others v Midland Bank plc [1998] 1 A11 ER 528.

R v Attorney General for Northern Ireland, ex parte McHugh (Current Law Cases, Ref 97/Sept.).

R v Secretary of State for Employment, ex parte Seymour Smith and Another [1997] 2 A11 ER 273.

Secretary of State for Social Security and Another v Remilien; and Chief Adjudication Officer v Wolke [1998] 1 A11 ER 129.

United Kingdom v European Council (C84/94) [1997] ICR (2) 443; [1997] IRLR (3) 30.

Zabala Erasun v Instituto Nacional de Empleo Joined Cases C-422–424/93 [1995] A11 ER (EC) 758.

Zuckerfabrick Suderdithmarschen AG v Hauptzollamt Itzehoe Joined Cases C-143/88 and C-92/89 [1991] ECRE-415.

Industrial relations in Central and Eastern Europe in the late 1990s

Roderick Martin

This paper provides a bird's eye view of industrial relations in Central and Eastern Europe in the late 1990s. The aim is twofold: to summarise the major trends in industrial relations in the region, and, secondly, to provide a baseline for evaluating future trends. With the redefinition of the boundaries of Europe as a political entity which has followed the fall of Communist regimes in 1989 and the impending accession of an as yet unknown number of countries of the region to the European Union within the next decade it is important to assess developments in the region in any review of 'European' industrial relations.

Following this brief introduction, this paper outlines the economic context within which industrial relations are developing, focusing on trends in employment, unemployment, labour productivity, wages and prices. The economic performance of different countries within the region varied widely, with the Polish economy at one extreme developing strongly by the mid 1990s, and at the other the Bulgarian economy experiencing financial collapse in 1996. Economic performance was linked closely with political developments. This paper provides a brief survey of major institutional developments in the region, sketching trends in employers' organisations and trade unions, emphasising in particular the continuing importance of relations between the state and the industrial relations parties. A major theme is the slow progress in bringing about the 'depoliticisation' of industrial relations. The paper then examines developments at the enterprise level, and the impact of the processes of privatisation and restructuring upon industrial relations. It concludes with an assessment of regional industrial relations in the light of the anticipated expansion of the European Union eastwards.

Underlying analyses of specific national systems of industrial relations is the issue of convergence between industrial relations systems, either within the region itself or between systems in the region and Western models (Thirkell *et al.*, 1994). Is there a regional model? The paper argues that there are common themes within the region, and that many of these themes are shared with systems

---

Roderick Martin is Professor of Organisational Behaviour at the University of Glasgow Business School.

in Western Europe (if less so with the UK). Labour markets are developing in a West European direction. Similarly, the themes of tripartism, corporatism, micro-neo-corporatism are as relevant to Central and Eastern Europe as to Western Europe. However, there is not a single regional model. Moreover, the likelihood of such a model occurring is declining as the residues of the Communist period grow weaker. Rather, common materials are combined in different ways, according to different 'recipes', to develop systems meeting specific national requirements. This process is occurring through a mixture of direct borrowing, partial imitation and, primarily, independent national institutional development. The sources from which national systems are being built include international agencies, most importantly the International Labour Organisation (ILO), missions from national and international trade unions and trade union organisations such as the British TUC and the European TUC, international seminars for government and trade union officials as well as national historical traditions. International financial institutions have played a significant role in the type of industrial relations system emerging, especially the World Bank and the International Monetary Fund: both have urged the development of collective bargaining systems as an integral part of marketisation, whilst recognising the importance of securing trade union support by developing tripartite institutions.

Crouch (1993) suggests that there are four stages in the development of industrial relations systems in their political aspects. First, contestation, characterised by master/servant relations, high levels of state regulation and embryonic trade unionism. Second, institutionalised collective bargaining at the national, sectoral or enterprise level, on the Anglo–American model. Third, neo-corporatism, involving tripartite institutions and concerted action between state, employers' organisations and trade unions at both macro and micro level. Fourth, human resource management, involving a focus on managerial strategies at the enterprise level, and viewing employees primarily in individual terms, as units of human capital. Traces of all four stages are evident in industrial relations systems in the region. Countries in the region share experience of over 40 years of Communist rule. But the widely differing economic and institutional structures which preceded Communism, the varying ways in which the Communist system operated in practice and the different trajectories of the exit from socialism mean that the emergent capitalist industrial relations systems differ. This is to be expected.

ECONOMIC CONTEXT

The economies of Central and Eastern Europe experienced a catastrophic decline after 1989. The extent of the decline differed between countries, being particularly steep in Bulgaria and Romania and the Russian Federation. The trends in GNP between 1990 and 1993 which illustrate this collapse are summarised in

TABLE 1
Trends in GDP for Selected Countries, 1990–93

	Percentage GDP change on previous year			
	1990	1991	1992	1993
Bulgaria	−9.1	−11.7	−7.3	−1.5
Czech Republic	−1.2	−11.5	−3.3	0.6
Hungary	−3.5	−11.9	−3.1	−0.6
Poland	−11.6	−7.0	−2.6	3.8
Romania	−5.6	−12.9	−8.7	1.5
Russian Federation	−3.0	−5.0	−14.5	−8.7
Slovakia	−2.5	−14.5	−6.5	−3.7
Slovenia	−4.7	−8.9	−5.5	2.8
Ukraine	−2.6	−11.6	−13.7	−14.2

Source: *Business Central Europe: Key Data 1990–97.*

Table 1. The collapse in output was due to several factors, including the collapse of intra regional trade associated with the disintegration of the Council for Mutual Economic Assistance (CMEA), the severe international competition in domestic markets which followed trade liberalisation and the disruption of established supply chains. In addition to such general developments, Balkan countries (especially Bulgaria) suffered disproportionately from the effects of the war in Yugoslavia and the UN sanctions against Serbia. However, the process of recovery was underway in many countries by 1997 and, as Table 2 shows, the majority of countries had resumed a growth path. In 1994–5 the region began to experience a small scale export led boom, mainly due to revived demand in Western Europe, especially for raw materials, metals, chemicals and intermediate goods. The overall growth rates for 1994–7 are summarised in Table 2.

TABLE 2
Trends in GDP for Selected Countries, 1994–97

	Percentage GDP change on previous year			
	1994	1995	1996	1997
Bulgaria	1.8	2.1	−10.9	−7.4
Czech Republic	2.7	4.8	3.9	1.0
Hungary	2.9	1.5	1.3	4.0
Poland	5.2	7.0	6.1	7.0
Romania	3.9	7.1	4.1	−6.6
Russia	−12.7	−4.2	−4.9	0.4
Slovakia	4.9	6.8	6.9	6.5
Slovenia	5.3	4.1	3.1	2.9
Ukraine	−23.0	−11.8	−10.0	−3.2

Source: *Business Central Europe: Key Data 1990–97.*

Employment

The size of the labour force in the region declined in the early years of the transition, with voluntary withdrawals from the labour force, including early retirement, rising levels of sickness, women not returning to work after childbirth and emigration. The workforce declined through attrition. Between 1990 and 1993 overall employment fell by 16 per cent (although overall real GDP declined by 23 per cent). In 1994–5 output began to recover, but employment continued to decline, although at a slower rate. Economic growth did not involve increasing employment, but rather involved bringing spare capacity back into use. In 1995 and 1996 small numbers of new jobs began to be created in Poland, the Czech Republic, Slovakia and Romania. The decline in employment throughout the 1990s was especially marked for female and older workers.

There was also a change in the structure of employment. During the Socialist period there was a high level of concentration of employment in agriculture in Bulgaria, Hungary, Poland, Romania, and Russia and in industry in every country in the region. In the 1990s there was a significant shift towards the service sector, with expansion in retail distribution, and especially in banking and financial services: employment in industry declined markedly (Table 3). Reductions in the role of the state and privatisation brought about a reduction in the public sector.

Changes in the structure of employment were associated with changes in the size of employing units. In the Socialist period employing units had been either very large or very small; there were high levels of employment concentration, and few medium sized enterprises. During the transition the average size of employment unit declined and the number of small and medium sized employing units increased. This trend continued in 1997.

TABLE 3
Cumulative Changes in Employment Levels in Selected Countries, 1990–95

	Total employment 1990–95	Employment in industry 1990–95
Bulgaria	−24.1	−43.2
Czech Republic	−7.2	−22.9
Hungary	−27.4	−37.5
Poland	−13.3	−23.8
Romania	−13.3	−34.6
Russia	−12.1	−24.7
Slovakia	−14.6	−28.4
Slovenia	−20.7	−35.9
Ukraine	−6.7	−20.8

Cumulative change over period.
Source: *UN Economic Survey 1996–7*, p. 113 (modified).

Throughout the 1990s there has been a decline in activity rates, with a reduction in the number of jobs and dislocation in the labour market. However, this type of labour market dislocation, brought about by an excess supply of labour, may prove to be short-lived. In the medium term the low birth rate—and continuing emigration—may result in a labour shortage.

The overall effect of employment changes in the region is a limited convergence towards a Western European pattern: the growth of the service sector and in the number of small and medium sized enterprises parallels earlier developments in Western Europe. However, the level of employment in the service sector remains below Western European levels and the proportion of employment in the industrial sector greater.

Unemployment

Regional international comparisons of trends in unemployment rates are summarised in Table 4. The figures are based on registrations, and significantly understate the level of unemployment. Figures based on labour force surveys show higher levels of unemployment in most (but not all) countries (UNECE, 1997, pp. 115–116). In view of the catastrophic drop in output, unemployment levels did not rise as high as expected during the early years of the transition. The level of unemployment remained especially low in the Czech Republic until 1996, before rising rapidly to reach levels comparable to other countries in the region. Unemployment rates in Hungary were notably high throughout the period. The reasons for the lower than expected level of unemployment throughout the region reflected the social welfare traditions of the Socialist period, political circumstances and, primarily, the motivations of managers and employees. Management had strong incentives in the short run to retain labour, since a large workforce provided political leverage (especially if concentrated in an isolated

TABLE 4
Unemployment Rates (per cent) in Selected Countries, 1990–97

	1990	*1991*	*1992*	*1993*	*1994*	*1995*	*1996*	*1997*
Bulgaria	1.7	11.1	15.2	16.4	12.8	11.1	12.5	13.7
Czech Republic	0.8	4.1	2.6	3.5	3.2	2.9	3.5	4.5
Hungary	1.9	7.8	13.2	13.3	11.4	11.1	10.7	10.8
Poland	6.3	11.8	13.6	16.4	16.0	14.9	13.6	10.5
Romania	0.4	3.0	8.2	10.4	10.9	9.5	6.3	8.8
Russia	n.a.	0.1	4.8	5.7	7.5	8.8	9.3	10.0
Slovakia	0.8	4.1	10.4	14.4	14.8	13.1	12.8	12.5
Slovenia	4.7	8.2	13.4	15.4	14.2	14.5	14.4	14.8
Ukraine	0.0	0.0	0.3	0.3	0.3	0.6	1.6	2.5

Source: *Business Central Europe: Key Data 1990–97.*

community). Similarly, employees had strong incentives to remain with their enterprises, even with very low wages or compulsory unpaid holidays. There was little prospect of alternative employment, and the enterprise continued to provide important social welfare benefits; indeed, the impoverishment of state budgets led to increased reliance upon the enterprise for social welfare in many circumstances (Rein *et al.*, 1997).

Four trends were evident in unemployment throughout the region. First, the sharp increase in unemployment in the early 1990s was due to major structural changes in the economy. However, by 1997 the major structural changes were already underway in the majority of Central and East European countries and unemployment was beginning to reflect cyclical factors, for example in Hungary and Poland. Second, the unemployment rate was higher for female than for male workers, especially in the Czech Republic and Poland (as in the former GDR). For example, up to 60 per cent of the unemployed were female in the Czech Republic. Third, the rate of youth unemployment was high, up to 2 or 3 times the overall average rate. Fourth, the proportion of the unemployed who were long term unemployed increased throughout the period. By 1997 50 per cent of the unemployed were long term unemployed.

Labour Productivity

During the first stage of the transition productivity declined sharply, the steep fall in output being accompanied by a much more gradual decline in employment. By 1995 the process of adjustment was underway, with output rising and employment either continuing to decline slowly or to rise gradually. Import liberalisation and the redirection of exports to more competitive Western markets required extensive industrial restructuring, especially to improve product quality: low labour costs and continued subsidisation of energy prices ensured competitive prices. In the judgement of the UN Economic Report, countries in the region needed to upgrade their physical capital stock, adopt more modern management techniques and improve the human capital stock (UNECE, 1997). The negative conclusions of the UN report underestimate the current quality of human capital and the extent of the management changes already underway and show little sensitivity to the particular characteristics of the region. However, capital shortage represented a major constraint on improvements in productivity: domestic capital formation was low, external capital flows, especially portfolio investment, remained small, whilst the terms of World Bank loans precluded lending to enterprises which continued in public ownership (although in the short run they represented the best prospects for substantial exports) (Amsden *et al.*, 1995). The multinational corporation became critical for improvements in productivity, both directly through investment in wholly owned subsidiaries or joint ventures and indirectly as exemplars of international best practice. Productivity in Western subsidiaries and joint ventures normally matched West European standards—as German managers said of the Volkswagen investment in the Skoda Motor plant in the Czech Republic, German productivity at East European wages.

Overall improvements in productivity varied widely between countries, being especially strong in Hungary and Poland. In Hungary, by 1996 the productivity of industrial labour was 40 per cent above its 1990 level, although output was 9 per cent lower: employment in the sector had declined by 37 per cent. There was an even steeper increase in productivity in Poland; productivity was 66 per cent above its 1990 level, whilst output exceeded 1990 levels and employment in the sector declined by 20 per cent (UNECE, 1997, p. 112). Developments in the Czech Republic and Slovakia followed a different path: employment levels were maintained, at the expense of declining productivity. In the Czech Republic industrial labour productivity in 1996 was below the 1990 level, whilst employment had declined by 20 per cent. Experience in the Russian Federation matched that of the Czech Republic rather than Hungary: in 1996 real GDP was 45 per cent below its 1989 level, whilst employment was 12 per cent lower.

In view of the continuing capital shortage, changes in management practices, including the management of labour, played a major role in improving productivity. Changes in management practices reflected changing political, social and cultural conditions, rather than economic ones. Hence the improvements in productivity in Hungary reflected partly the higher level of foreign investment than elsewhere, but also the greater flexibility and adaptability of Hungarian management. Hungarian managers and employees had shown much ingenuity in developing the second economy during the Socialist period, and continued to show the same flexibility in the post Socialist period.

Prices

By 1997 the high levels of inflation of the early 1990s had been moderated in most, but not all, countries in the region. Trends in inflation are summarised in Table 5. As Table 5 shows, in 1997 inflation was less than 10 per cent only in the Czech Republic, Slovakia and Slovenia. However, the rate of inflation was lower in most countries than it had been in previous years. The major exceptions were Bulgaria, where the financial system collapsed in 1996 following loose lending policies by major banks, and Romania, where the process of restructuring remained slow. Prices rose faster for services than for manufactured goods, reflecting the relative weakness of foreign competition in services as well as the relative scarcity of skills.

Wages

Comparative data on wages, productivity and unit labour costs for selected countries for 1995–6 are summarised in Table 6. Again, experience differed

TABLE 5

Inflation Rates (per cent) in Selected Countries, 1990–97

	1990	1991	1992	1993	1994	1995	1996	1997
Bulgaria	23.8	338.5	91.2	72.8	96.0	62.1	123.0	1083.0
Czech Republic	10.0	56.6	11.1	20.8	10.0	9.1	8.8	8.5
Hungary	28.9	35.0	23.0	22.5	18.8	28.2	23.6	18.3
Poland	553.6	70.3	43.0	35.3	32.2	27.8	19.9	15.3
Romania	5.1	170.2	210.4	256.1	136.8	32.3	38.8	154.8
Russia	5.6	92.6	874.7	307.4	197.4	47.6	14.7	11.5
Slovakia	18.0	61.2	10.0	23.2	13.4	9.9	5.8	6.1
Slovenia	549.7	117.7	201.3	32.3	19.8	12.6	9.9	8.4
Ukraine	n.a.	1210.0	1210.0	5371.0	891.0	376.8	80.2	16.0

Source: *Business Central Europe: Key Data 1990–97.*

TABLE 6

Wages and Unit Labour Costs in Industry in Selected Countries, 1995–96: Annual Average per cent Change

	Real product wages[a]		Labour productivity[b]		Real unit labour costs[c]	
	1995	1996	1995	1996	1995	1996
Bulgaria	7.3	−10.5	6.6	6.2	09.7	−15.7
Czech Republic	9.5	12.2	8.6	7.6	0.9	4.3
Hungary	−5.7	−0.7	10.5	3.9	−14.6	−4.4
Poland	4.7	11.6	6.0	9.9	−1.2	1.5
Romania	14.0	2.3	16.2	13.8	−1.8	−10.1
Russia	−33.2	−1.8	4.5	−2.8	−36.1	1.0
Slovakia	5.5	10.3	8.3	2.5	−2.6	7.5
Slovenia	4.0	6.0	5.8	7.6	−1.7	−1.5
Ukraine	−4.7	−22.0	−3.9	3.0	−0.8	−24.3

[a]Nominal wages deflated by producer price index.
[b]Gross industrial output deflated by industrial employment.
[c]Real product wages deflated by productivity.
Source: *UNECE: Economic Survey of Europe in 1996–7*, p. 127 (modified).

between countries. Average real wages increased in 1996 in the Czech Republic (12.2 per cent), Poland (11.6 per cent), Romania (2.3 per cent) and Slovakia (10.3 per cent). However, real wages declined in Bulgaria (−10.5 per cent), Hungary (−0.7 per cent) and the Russian Federation (−1.8 per cent). Wages trends reflected changes in output and productivity as well as macro-economic policy (see UNECE, 1997).

To summarise, the economic trauma of the early 1990s was surmounted in most countries of Central and Eastern Europe by 1997, at considerable cost. The problems of transition were giving way to the problems of capitalism. In economic performance, as measured by growth in GDP, level of inflation and level of unemployment the Czech Republic, Hungary, Poland, Russia and Slovakia were beginning to experience economic cycles similar to those experienced by open economies in Western Europe. However, the economies remained fragile, as indicated by the economic crisis in the Czech Republic in 1997. Moreover, earnings remained substantially below West European levels, especially in the Russian Federation. In March 1997 average monthly earnings in the Czech Republic had reached 383 USD, Hungary 369 USD, Poland 339 USD, Slovakia 315 USD and the Russian Federation 152 USD (Business Central Europe, April 1998, p. 69). Two major countries remained outside the pattern, Romania and Bulgaria. Although Romania reported growth of 4.1 per cent in real GDP in 1997, inflation was running at 76.2 per cent; although unemployment was reported at 7.1 per cent, average real monthly wages were only 146 USD (which declined further to 139 USD per month by March 1998). The Bulgarian economy fared even worse. Year on year inflation reached 476.6 per cent in April 1997, with average monthly wages of 57 USD: in March 1998 year on year inflation was still 383.1 per cent, with average monthly real wages of 108 USD.

INSTITUTIONAL DEVELOPMENTS

The uniform pattern of industrial relations institutions of the Socialist period disappeared in the transition; for an indication of the variety see the special issue of the *European Journal of Industrial Relations,* 1997. However, four trends were apparent by 1997. First, the involvement of the state in industrial relations on a continuing basis, primarily through tripartite arrangements. Industrial relations remained politicised. Second, with regard to trade union developments, tension continued between the 'successor' unions descended from the trade unions of the Communist period and the reform trade unions often modelled on the early Solidarity movement, against a background of overall declining trade union membership. The successor unions consolidated their institutional position. Third, employers' organisations emerged only hesitantly, against the background of dominant managerialism. Fourth, the embryonic status of the regulation of private sector industrial relations.

The mode of industrial relations governance emerging in Central and Eastern Europe may be described as 'directive corporatism', i.e. a system in which the state defined the relationships amongst interest groups, including trade unions and employers' organisations, and between interest groups and the state. The role of the state extended far beyond establishing 'the rules of the game'. The extent and form of the corporatist institutional arrangements varied, being especially elaborate and regulated in Bulgaria, less significant and less regulated in Poland and Russia. Tripartite bodies involving government, employers and trade unions were established throughout the region. In Hungary, the National Council for the Reconciliation of Interests was initially established in 1988, and re-launched as the Interest Reconciliation Council (IRC) in 1990. (The term 'reconciliation' implied more than consultation, but less than the right of veto. 'Reconciliation does not mean the right to consent, but it is more comprehensive than listening to the views of others. Reconciliation comprises the outlining of the views, the confrontation of the views and the efforts to harmonise the views to the maximum possible extent' (Lado, 1996, p. 163).) Councils of Economic and Social Agreement were established in the Czech and Slovak Republics in 1991; the National Council for the Co-ordination of Interests was established in Bulgaria in 1990, and placed on a firm legal basis in 1993; the National Negotiating Commission was established in Poland in 1993. Tripartite institutions provided a mechanism for discussing three main areas of concern: industrial relations issues specifically, especially wages, broader public policies, especially regarding social security, and nationally significant industrial disputes. According to some critics such tripartite arrangements are merely window dressing; Lajos Hethy, for example, saw the Hungarian IRC as a relic of the unitarist assumptions of the Socialist period, of some short-term political benefit but no long-term economic importance (Hethy, 1994). However, even if tripartism and concerted action have only limited effect on macro-economic performance, they provide a means for reconciling interests, increasing institutional integration, enhancing regime legitimacy and assisting in reducing industrial conflicts.

In addition to its role in stimulating tripartism, the state continued to set the legislative framework for industrial relations. Comprehensive Labour Codes continued to be promulgated; the formal commitments to extending the role of collective bargaining were placed within an extensive legal framework. The politicisation of industrial relations was further reflected in the continuing political role of trade unions, both the former Communist successor unions and the new anti-Communist reformist unions such as Podkrepa in Bulgaria, although survey evidence suggests that, at least in Poland, union members and the general public believed that trade unions should concentrate upon their economic role (Cichomski et al., 1998, p. 175).

During the Socialist period trade union membership was almost universal: union dues were deducted at source and trade unions were major social welfare organisations. Union membership remained high in the 1990s, with up to 80 per cent in Bulgaria, 60 per cent in Hungary, and 50 per cent in the Czech Republic in 1991 although not all nominal members paid their dues and the trend in union membership was downwards (Hethy, 1994, p. 90). Membership was especially high in the state and the privatised sectors; union membership became rare in the private sector, where union recognition was unusual. Although membership density remained high in many countries in comparison with West European levels, levels of satisfaction with union performance were low, according to case study research at the enterprise level (Martin *et al.*, 1998). The objective of pro-market advocates was to create politically independent unions who would concentrate on collective bargaining to secure direct economic benefits for their members. However, trade unions retained a significant political role, which served the interests of both politicians and union leaders. For politicians, trade unions provided a national organisation, capable of mobilising electoral support—especially required by non-Socialist parties without access to the residues of Communist Party organisation at local level. For union leaders, political influence represented the easiest way of following traditional centripetal policies, whilst compensating for organisational weakness at the enterprise level. The politicisation of trade unions is especially evident in Bulgaria and Poland, where they have respectively brought down and participated in government. In Poland, Solidarity split between its leadership active in government and in the Sejm and the rank and file concerned with economic issues. In Bulgaria Podkrepa was associated with the Union of Democratic Forces and the Confederation of Independent Trade Unions was identified with the Socialists, although its leadership was ostensibly non-political (Martin *et al.*, 1996).

The emergence of new trade union movements organised on the model of Solidarity—including the Democratic League of Independent Trade Unions in Hungary, Fratia in Romania, Podkrepa in Bulgaria—did not result in a new form of union organisation; like the successor unions, they were initially organised on a top–down basis, with strong political motivations and only limited organisational strength at shop floor level. The new movements were initially anti-Socialist. However, by 1997 such reformist unions were co-operating with former Socialist unions to secure economic objectives, although the alliances remained fragile. The Socialist trade unions consolidated their position. It was initially expected that the post 1989 successor unions to the Communist trade unions would be discredited and lose their membership and influence. However, by 1994 the successor unions had consolidated their position, both in membership and in influence. In Hungary, Bulgaria, the Czech Republic, Slovakia and even in Poland the successor unions secured more members than the anti-Communist unions. The former Communist unions restructured their organisation to create more decentralised structures, widened their democratic base and adopted an explicitly non-party political stance (although without achieving full credibility in this stance). The success of the former Communist unions reflected their commitment to seeking to protect deprived social groups, especially pensioners and the unemployed, their support for maintaining the social wage, institutional strength based on their maintaining a degree of control over the assets inherited from the Socialist period and the decline of anti-Communism as a guiding political force. Throughout the period the successor unions took the lead in campaigning for the protection of employment levels and the social wage, with varying success in Europe if not in the Russian federation; reformist unions faced great difficulty in dealing with liberal governments, with whom they were ideologically aligned. However, where unions sought to control strikes in key sectors, as in the miners' strikes in Russia, they achieved only limited success. Union success in defending the social wage reflected the political importance of trade unions as guarantors of social peace, not their strength at enterprise level.

Employers' Organisations

Industrial associations and trade associations were an integral part of the Socialist system, but played no role in industrial relations. After 1989 employers' organisations emerged rapidly, partly due to autonomous trends and partly due to government stimulus through the development of tripartite structures which required employers' organisations to balance trade unions. The variety in the forms of ownership (state, corporatised, privatised, municipal, co-operative, as well as private) as well as the breadth of sectoral influences, resulted in a fragmented structure of employer representation. The Hungarian Industrial Reconciliation Commission, for example, included nine employers organisations (not including the state itself); the National Federation of Consumers Co-operatives, National Federation of Craftsmen's Associations, National Federation of Industrial Co-operatives, National Federation of Retail Traders, National Association of Employers, Hungarian Chamber of Agriculture, Manufacturers' National Association, National Federation of Agricultural Producers and Co-operatives, and the National Association of Entrepreneurs. Foreign owned multinationals formed their own association, outside the tripartite structure. In the Czech Republic the employers' side of the Council of Economic and Social Agreement comprised seven employers' associations. The Bulgarian National Council for the Conciliation of Interests included three major employers, associations and a smaller fourth one, who rarely agreed with each other. The role of employers' organisations in regulating industrial relations is important at the national tripartite level, although of limited importance at the enterprise level. Employers' associations have little authority over their members, as Hungarian commentators have stressed (Lado, 1996) (but nor do British employers' organisations). Within the state sector, the employer interest is directly represented by the state and sectoral wage policies reflect national priorities, not necessarily the interests of the state as employer. In the privatised and private sector wages are determined at the enterprise level, primarily in relation to the market conditions of the specific enterprise. As the German analyst Wiesenthal commented in 1996, 'not until economic sectors become more consolidated in the process of commercialisation (which is of more importance than formal privatisation) will associations be seen as representatives of important social interests with autonomous resources, valuable knowledge and strategic competence' (Wiesenthal, 1996, p. 51).

ENTERPRISE LEVEL INDUSTRIAL RELATIONS

Enterprise restructuring involved changing work organisation and the mode of managing labour. Traditionally, management practices had combined formal bureaucratic centralisation with paternalism at the supervisory level. Levels of work effort varied between enterprises and between sections of enterprises, as well as with the seasons ('storming' at the year's end to meet or exceed plan targets was normal). The overall level of work effort required was low (as the common phrase had it, 'we pretend to work and they pretend to pay us'), although much flexibility and ingenuity was often required to operate antiquated machinery or to compensate for lack of spare parts (Clarke, 1996). The transition involved work intensification and increasing flexibility, for example to cope with greater variety in the length of production runs. The principles underlying work organisation in the Socialist period had been those of Taylorism, involving strict division of labour and precise specification of work tasks. Authority resided with line management, and the role of the personnel function was limited. The same principles were followed during the transition, with more vigour. Work intensification followed the gradual reduction in employment from 1990, becoming particularly pronounced with the revival of output after 1994. Real wages increased, as did work effort.

The administrative allocation of labour has been replaced by the labour market. However, the process of developing the institutions required to enable the labour market to operate effectively has been slow. International missions, including missions from the British Department for Employment, have assisted in the establishment of regional and local employment exchanges and social welfare offices, which appear to be used more widely by state than by private organisations. With the collapse of output in the early 1990s recruitment declined, and enterprises paid little attention to recruitment issues. (Although even during the precipitous decline in output in Russia enterprises continued to recruit, largely using informal methods.) The growth of the labour market has led to a concern with assessment of abilities, skills, qualifications and experience, in place of the heavy reliance upon formal qualifications characteristic of the Socialist period. However, informal connections remain of major importance for both state and, especially, private sector jobs. Western companies may adopt professional recruitment practices for expatriate staff, but remain dependent upon local connections for the recruitment of local staff.

Training was a short-term casualty of the transition. Theoretical education in mathematics, science and engineering had been well developed during the Socialist period, but the link between theoretical training and employment had been limited and little attention had been paid to systematic on-the-job training. In the early years of the transition the previous training system collapsed as firms were preoccupied with survival. However, even during the early 1990s public and especially private provision for training in business and management expanded rapidly, with especial emphasis on expertise in finance, accounting and marketing. A major contribution of the European Union has been the funding of training schemes for management education, although curricula initially showed little sensitivity to the particular requirements of the region. By 1997 indigenous firms were using managers trained in Western management methods. Multinational corporations are a second source of skilled management, although there is little evidence yet on the extent to which there is mobility between Western and indigenous firms.

In the Socialist period wages had been determined by national systems of job assessment and qualifications and centrally determined coefficients of wage differentiation, relying heavily upon the formal qualifications required for specific jobs. The scope for enterprise level variation was limited, although output bonuses could be important for favoured workers. Elements of central wage determination continued in the transition period, to different degrees in different countries, and for different sectors. Hungarian pay determination is less central-ised that the Bulgarian or even the Czech system. The following account of the Czech system illustrates the influences upon plant level wage determination (Lado, 1996). There are three levels of collective bargaining. The National Tri-partite Commission is the highest level. The Tripartite Commission concludes an annual General Agreement, setting wage guidelines for the following year, through a process of tripartite negotiation. Collective bargaining at the national level involves four basic components: setting indicative real wage growth levels, defining minimum wages, negotiating real wage growth limits and making spe-cific agreements covering employees in the state sector. National level bargaining is supplemented by sectoral and regional as well as enterprise level bargaining. Supplementary sectoral agreements were concluded in the majority of industries according to research carried out in 1994, but their significance varied between sectors. Similarly, the majority of enterprises concluded enterprise level agree-ments. Similar structures existed in other countries in the region, although the precise role of the national level agreements and the enterprise level collective agreements varied (Neumann, 1997).

Two contrary principles were involved in wage determination. The first was the continuation of the principles of relatively egalitarian wage policies of the Socialist period, with a high level of 'social' wage. The second was the need to provide incentives for the acquisition of skills and for work effort, as well as to reflect the market scarcity of particular types of labour. The outcome of the tension between the different principles was a widening of income differentials. The major differential is between employment in the private sector and in the state sector: earnings in the private sector are higher than in the state sector. In Poland, for example, the average income in the private sector was 41 per cent higher than in the state sector in 1995 (and there is no reason to believe that the trend has reversed) (Cichomski *et al.*, 1998). Professional specialists such as engineers and technicians were particularly highly paid in the private sector, earning almost three times the salaries of their colleagues working in state enterprises, whilst skilled workers earned 30 per cent more. Differences in ownership type have become more important than differences in industrial sector; within comparable enterprises in the electronics sector in Poland average monthly pay in the private enterprises was 60.3 per cent higher than in the state enterprise and 44.0 per cent higher than in the enterprise with mixed ownership (partly state owned). Overall, in the process of widening differential the positions of supervisors and managers improved most; in 1985 the income of the group was 27 per cent higher than that of blue collar workers in Poland, in 1995 41 per cent higher. Traditional patterns of earnings differentials appeared more resilient in state than in private enterprises, with technicians doing less well than managers and blue collar workers.

The pattern of differentials reflected national policies and the operations of the labour market, rather than local level trade union power. Trade unions remained weakly organised at the enterprise level, especially in the private sector; a Czech survey reported that only 22 per cent of employees in the private sector were trade union members, although opinion polls reported that 53 per cent of all 'economically active' Czechs were members of trade unions. Historically, workplace union organisation had reflected the structure of the enterprise and the requirements of the personnel department (with the important exception of Solidarity in Poland). Workers' interests were represented at a collective level through different forms of participatory structures, such as the Workers Collectives in Bulgaria in the late 1980s. Workers' individual interests were represented by first level supervision. The union acted as an ancillary social welfare arm to the personnel department through arranging vacations and assisting in the allocation of housing, and as a 'transmission belt' for Party policy (Pravda and Ruble, 1986). After 1989 it was anticipated that workshop level union organisation would develop with marketisation, the devolution of decision-making responsibility for wages to the enterprise, the increasing economic rather than political role of the union and voluntary rather than compulsory union membership. Responding to membership opinion required an effective workplace presence. This conception of trade unionism was enshrined in international advice, for example by the International Labour Organisation, and reflected in national legislation, for example in the 1991 Collective Bargaining Act and the Labour Code in the Czech Republic. However, the severity of the economic crisis in the early 1990s and apathy about organisational activities made it difficult to persuade rank and file members to assume plant level responsibilities and to become shop floor representatives, despite the legislative support for plant level activity. Moreover, the unions themselves had too few resources to provide effective professional support at local level. There was therefore little enterprise level union organisation or local level bargaining. It is therefore unsurprising that there was a high level of criticism of trade unions by their members in the plant level research in the electronics sector. Trade union leaders were perceived as being out of touch with their members; first level supervision continued to be seen as a more accurate reflection of members' opinions and more capable defenders of their interests than union officials.

CONCLUSION

Employment relations in Central and Eastern Europe are a kaleidoscope, reflecting four different stages in the development of industrial relations systems. In some circumstances unions continue to retain their role as means of mobilisation in support of political objectives, which may be pro-government or oppositional; this is a role assumed by a major faction of Solidarity in Poland and by Podkrepa in Bulgaria. This corresponds to the first stage in Colin Crouch's schema, the confrontational stage. Secondly, there are elements of free collective bargaining, as in the Czech Republic and Hungary, although the reality of the bargaining process differs sharply from that envisaged by its ILO advocates, with state regulation and individual bargaining continuing to play a major role. Thirdly, there are elements of neo-corporatism, with unions participating in tripartite decision-making on major economic and social issues, as in Bulgaria, at times the Czech Republic and to a lesser extent Hungary. Finally, there are elements of human resource management policies, especially in multi-national corporations operating in the Czech Republic and Hungary, with a strong emphasis on individual pay determination (Pollert, 1997 for the Czech Republic). The systems which are developing are divergent, as the influence of the Socialist template diminishes: the systems reflect longer term historical structures as well as the strength of union influence and contemporary market requirements.

The pattern is heavily influenced by political and economic developments. The state continues to play a major role even in the countries seen as being furthest along the road to marketisation. In part this reflects the continuing size of the state budget labour force. More broadly, the state continues to influence the institutional arrangements for industrial relations through Labour Codes as well as wages policies, for largely macro-economic reasons. This state influence has been directed partly at creating the institutions which would replace the state, but which lack the supporting social infrastructure, for example shop floor union organisation. State influence is reflected in wages policies, which are directed at two objectives: controlling inflation and maintaining broad ranging public support through maintaining a realistic minimum wage, which has been achieved in some countries but not in others (Standing, 1997). However, there is increasing income differentiation, between occupations, between sectors and between ownership groups. Managers and professional specialists, especially in the private financial sector, are prospering. Such differentials reflect labour market scarcity rather than union organisation. Trade unions have not yet developed the institutional structures to operate effectively in collective bargaining at sectoral and enterprise level, although they have maintained their influence at national level. Assessment of the effectiveness of unions is largely negative, as reflected in declining membership levels as well as in the results of opinion poll surveys. However, membership levels remain high by Western European standards.

Ownership changes have not resulted in the creation of a privately owned capitalist market economy throughout the region. The process of transferring productive assets out of state ownership is largely complete in Hungary, the Czech Republic, Poland and Russia. Voucher privatisation, as followed in the Czech Republic, Russia and to a degree Poland, with or without preferential treatment of managers and employees of the firm, has transferred effective control of the enterprise to the management. The withdrawal of state ownership rights has not been replaced by the discipline of the capital market or other external agents (Frydman *et al.*, 1996). The form of privatisation followed has resulted in the major power residing with enterprise managements; external corporate governance mechanisms on the Anglo-American or even the German model have not emerged. This has encouraged continuity in management—labour relations in practice with the Socialist period, if within a different institutional framework.

Employers and trade unions are formally engaged in processes of collective bargaining at national, sectoral and enterprise levels. However, the state retains a major influence at national level, whilst sectoral and local agreements are negotiated within parameters set at national level, and in extreme cases are merely re-written versions of agreements made at a higher level. The private sector is an important exception, both legally and in practice; in the Czech Republic private companies with more than 30 per cent foreign participation are specifically excluded from the provisions of the Wages Act. In the private sector wages appear to be determined by market principles, with collective bargaining playing only a limited role. Price inflation, income differentials and earnings are higher in the private sector than in the state sector.

Major states in Central and Eastern Europe are scheduled to join the European Union within the next decade; it is not yet clear which states will join, or when. As discussed earlier, the economic performance of different states within the region has varied sharply, and the state which appeared to have adjusted most rapidly to the new economic situation, the Czech Republic, experienced a financial crisis in 1997. However, by 1997 the Czech Republic, Hungary, Poland and Slovakia, as well as smaller states such as Slovenia, had established market economies. The problems of the transition from socialism have been replaced by the problems of adjusting to capitalism, including adjustments to fluctuations in the trade cycle. There remain varying levels of state participation in the economy, as in Western Europe. Romania and Bulgaria have not yet developed market economies, whilst the Russian federation remains a special case. With regard to industrial relations specifically, different states have adopted different structures in detail, but the variety of systems is no greater than in Western Europe. The state retains a major influence on employment relations, but within a framework of collective bargaining structures. Participation of the major countries of the region within the European Union would broaden the range of industrial relations systems, as did earlier expansions of the European Community.

REFERENCES

Amsden, A.H., Kovhanowicz, J. and Taylor, L. (1994) *The Market Meets its Match: Restructuring the Economies of Eastern Europe*, Harvard University Press, Cambridge, Mass.
Business Central Europe, April 1998.
Cichomski, B., Kulpinska, J. and Morawski, W. (1998) 'Employment, Commitment and Trade Unions: Continuity or Change in Poland 1985–1995', in R. Martin, A. Ishikawa, C. Makó and F. Consoli (eds), *Workers, Firms and Unions*, Peter Lang, Frankfurt.
Crouch, C.J. (1993) *Industrial Relations and European State Traditions*, Oxford University Press, Oxford.
European Journal of Industrial Relations, 3:2, June 1997.
Frydman, R., Gray, C.W. and Rapaczynski, A. (eds) (1996) *Corporate Governance in Central Europe and Russia: Vol. 1, Banks, Funds and Foreign Investors; Vol. 2, Insiders and the State*, Central European University Press, Budapest.
Hethy, L. (1994) 'Tripartism—its chances and limits in Central and Eastern Europe', in T. Kauppinen and V. Kogkka, *Transformation of the Industrial Relations in Central and Eastern Europe*, Finnish Labour Relations Association: IIRA, Helsinki.
Lado, M. (1996) 'Continuity and Changes in Tripartism in Hungary', in A. Agh *et al.* (eds), *Parliament and Organized Interests: The Second Steps*, Hungarian Centre for Democracy Studies, Budapest.
Martin, R., Hill, S. and Vidinova, A. (1996) 'Constrained Collective Bargaining: Industrial Relations in Transition Economies: the case of Bulgaria', *British Journal of Industrial Relations*, 34:1.
Neumann, L. (1997) 'Circumventing Trade Unions in Hungary: Old and New Channels of Collective Bargaining', *European Journal of Industrial Relations*, 3:2.
Pollert, A. (1997) 'The Transformation of Trade Unionism in the Capitalist and Democratic Restructuring of the Czech Republic', *European Journal of Industrial Relations*, 3:2.
Pravda, A. and Ruble, B.A. (eds) (1986) *Trade Unions in Communist States*, Allen and Unwin, Boston.
Rein, M., Friedmann, B.L. and Worgotter, A. (eds) (1997) *Enterprise and Social Benefits after Communism*, Cambridge University Press, Cambridge.
Standing, G. (1997) 'Labour Market Governance in Eastern Europe', *European Journal of Industrial Relations*, 3:2.
Thirkell, J., Scase, R. and Vickerstaff, S. (1994) 'Labour Relations in Transition in Eastern Europe', *Industrial Relations Journal*, 25:2.
United Nations Economic Commission for Europe (1997) *Economic Survey of Europe in 1996–7*, United Nations, Geneva.
Wiesenthal, H. (1996), 'Organized Interests in Contemporary East Central Europe', in A. Agh *et al.* (eds), *Parliament and Organized Interests: The Second Steps*, Hungarian Centre for Democracy Studies, Budapest.

European industrial relations in 1997: chronicle of events

Mark Gilman and Tina Weber

This article chronicles industrial relations throughout the EU in 1997. All of the information is gained from articles contained within the European Industrial Relations Observatory (EIRO).[1] Throughout, the articles are referenced numerically corresponding to record numbers within the database, so as to allow the reader easy access to the materials contained within EIRO which give greater detail of the events mentioned.

Developments in European Union (EU) level policy with a direct impact on industrial relations were influenced by a number of key trends and events, many of which are set to continue to be of relevance in the policy debate in 1998:

(i) the persistence of the phenomenon of jobless growth;
(ii) the countdown towards the deadline for Economic and Monetary Union (EMU);
(iii) the announcement, without prior workforce consultation, of the closure of the Renault plant at Vilvoorde;
(iv) the review of the development of the European social dialogue process;
(v) the conclusion of the Inter-governmental Conference and the conclusion of a new draft Treaty in Amsterdam;
(vi) the special Employment Summit in Luxembourg.

In the face of the persistence of jobless growth in most EU member states, the European policy agenda continued to be dominated by the question of how to achieve greater employment creation, particularly for disadvantaged groups in the labour market. Co-operation on employment policies and the achievement of job creation are among the concerns of the new Chapter on Employment included in the new Treaty negotiated at the Amsterdam summit in June 1997 (EU9707135f). Support for employment creation was also at the heart of the

---

Mark Gilman is a Research Fellow at the Industrial Relations Research Unit, University of Warwick; Tina Weber works for the research organisation Ecotec.
[1]EIRO is based at The European Foundation for the Improvement Of Living and Working Conditions in Dublin. Both of the authors work for national centres writing on behalf of EIRO. The EIRO database can be accessed on the World Wide Web in the following location *http:*www.eiro.eurofound.ie

first-ever special summit dedicated to the issue of employment, held under the Luxembourg Presidency in November 1997 (EU9711168f). The Summit discussed, among other things, employment guidelines to be translated into action plans by the member state governments. The debate surrounding the drawing up, and the review of the implementation of these action plans will doubtless be a centrepiece for the employment debate at the national and EU level in 1998 (EU9712174n).

Hand in hand with this debate went discussions among policy makers, social partners and other interest groups on the contribution that new forms of work and working time organisation could make to the twin goals of employment creation and the achievement of greater competitiveness. This debate was stimulated by a Green Paper on new forms of work organisations issued by the European Commission in April 1997 (EU9705131n).

In the year which was to act as the benchmark for fulfilling the criteria for EMU, increasing attention was accorded to the impact of economic and monetary union on the industrial relations sphere, and increasingly voices were being raised, particularly among the trade union movement, of the detrimental effects of budgetary stringency enforced in order to meet these criteria on employment and working conditions in the European Union and the lack of preparation for this event.

The impact of restructuring on employment, and in particular the role played by employee information and consultation in this process was also high on the policy agenda, in the aftermath of the decision by French car maker Renault to close its plant at Vilvoorde without prior consultation with the workforce (EU9703108f). The year 1997 saw the revival of the debate on the European Company Statute (EU9705128n), agreement on the inclusion of the UK under the provisions of the European Works Councils (EWC) Directive, as well as a renewed debate on European Union regulation in the area of national employee information and consultation legislation (EU9803193n).

The year also saw ever-increasing attention being accorded to the role of the social partner organisations in decision making. This was boosted by the intersectoral framework agreement on part-time work (EU9706131f), key sectoral agreements and finally the inclusion of the social partners in the Council troika (the meetings between the current, previous and following Council presidencies).

COLLECTIVE BARGAINING AND INDUSTRIAL ACTION

Despite a slow convergence through the application of EU social policy, and the establishment of European Works Councils, collective bargaining in each economy still remains distinct. Only a small number of exceptional European Works Councils agreements make any provision for negotiation at the European level, which could be perceived as a step towards a Europeanisation of collective bargaining. Nevertheless, the sympathy action generated by the announcement of the closure of Renault's Vilvoorde plant, has been argued by some observers to mark the birth of the Euro-strike. A recent seminar on European Works Councils (EU9803191f) has indicated the increasing co-operation of employee representatives from different countries, which, albeit currently often limited to unofficial channels, could provide an example for an increasing push for the development of common goals and strategies, not only at the level of the peak organisations, but also at the company level. However, in the context of continuing high unemployment and budgetary stringency, common trends in collective bargaining tended to be dominated by management's desire for greater flexibility. There are clearly common denominators which ran through all systems during 1997 such as the desire to increase flexibility and decentralise collective bargaining, and a widening of the bargaining agenda to include issues such as employment, working time, pensions and so on. A country by country analysis of key trends in collective bargaining also shows an emphasis on wage restraint and a comparatively peaceful bargaining round.

Austria

Minimum wages and salaries rose, on average, by 1.7 per cent in 1997, with awards ranging between 1.5 per cent and 3.0 per cent. While such sectors as manufacturing averaged increases of 2.0 per cent (AT9709130F) minimum salaries in the civil service remained unchanged. These sectors also saw the continuation of a trend (AT9705112F) to reform salary grades. The aim being to reduce the impact of seniority on incomes while maintaining lifetime incomes and keeping stable enterprises' total salary bill. A novel element was the introduction of a distribution option in a number of collective agreements (AT9710138N, AT9801155F) allowing the salaries of designated groups to be increased, particularly young or female or key personnel, outside seniority considerations.

Pension reform (AT9711144F, AT9712152N) was the only issue in several years that led to strike action in Austria (AT9706117F, AT9707124N, AT9709132N). The civil service experienced the greatest conflict, triggered by the pensions reform issue and by the government's intention to drastically reduce the number of tenured positions. Industrial action, though in the form of public protest, information campaigns and staff meetings, also took place in the tourism industry (AT9706120N, AT9704111F).

Belgium

In the absence of agreement between the social partners concerning the 1997–98 biennial inter-industry agreement (BE9702101F), the government laid down the basis for negotiations at sector and firm level including: a ceiling on wage increases; measures to reduce employers' contributions in firms which redistribute jobs; specific measures for target groups; and development of community services through return-to-work schemes for unemployed.

At sector level, most agreements favoured job redistribution (BE9706205F). The insurance sector is the only one to have chosen the reduction of working time in exchange for more flexibility (BE9707111N).

At firm level, agreements to reduce working time have been concluded in some firms, as part of government measures to maintain or create jobs by reducing labour costs and working time. These measures are limited to firms which apply for them (BE9705106N).

At regional level the scope of the negotiations between regional social partners is theoretically limited to matters covered by employment and training policies. But in practice they have their own economic policies and their collective negotiation practices are different.

The Flemish Region

In the Leuven Declaration signed in July 1997, the social partners stated that their common objective was to reduce unemployment by half by the year 2000 (BE9710220N). The Flemish region's employment policy is aimed at stimulating demand by means of economic aids and support for in-company training. Job creation is promoted in the voluntary and public works sector and workers are encouraged to reduce their working-time voluntarily by the granting of subsidies (BE9707214N).

The Walloon Region

The social partners have signed a joint declaration committing themselves to collaborate actively in the economic development of the Walloon region within the Economic and Social Council of the Walloon, a tripartite regional body.

The region promotes training and development projects in SMEs, the re-integration of low-qualified unemployed persons in jobs in the voluntary and public sector and training schemes through subsidies. It also supports projects in firms to reduce working time to increase jobs (BE9711123F).

In the *Brussels–Capital Region* there is a continuous dialogue between regional social partners on employment and vocational training. The region is preparing a series of projects to support firms that reduce working time to increase jobs.

Denmark

Two key results came out of the 1997 collective bargaining round in Denmark; the introduction of a new salary scale system in the public sector; and the introduction of unsynchronised one-, two- and three-year collective agreements.

In February, a two-year collective agreement offering a 4.25 per cent pay increase, wage adjustment schemes, and improved pension and maternity leave provisions was approved by employees in the public sector. There was also what has been described as 'a peaceful wage revolution', introducing a more flexible and decentralised salary-scale system.

The 1997 collective bargaining round in the private sector concentrated on the issue of the duration of agreements, with a return to a common expiry date being the major issue. The Danish Employers' Confederation (Dansk Arbejdsgiverforening/DA) proposed that the various agreements in the private sector should be arranged so that they expire in 2000. This strategy was based on the assumption that bargaining sectors outside the domain of DA would have to accept a change in the length of the agreements if the pattern of synchronised bargaining were to be re-established in 2000.

The Confederation of Danish Trade Unions (Landsorganisationen i Danmark/LO) opposed any change in the duration of the agreement, arguing that the employers had upset the pattern, so it was therefore their responsibility to revert to the existing pattern by entering into a one-year settlement for 1998 or a three-year agreement, so that a common expiry date could be agreed for the all-industry collective agreement in either 1999 or 2001. Unsynchronised one, two and three-year collective agreements ensued resulting in a failure of the DA's strategy.

1997 was a relatively peaceful year, with fewer conflicts on the Danish labour market. According to statistics from DA the number of lost working days due to industrial action in 1997 was significantly lower than in 1995 and 1993, but this was mainly due to the fact that only half of the private sector conducted collective bargaining in 1997. More than half of the lost working days (44,000) in 1997 were due to secondary strikes and other conflicts that had backgrounds other than disputes over wage related conditions.

Finland

In December 1997, the Finnish social partners signed a central bi-annual incomes policy agreement. The agreement covers 98 per cent of wage earners and provides for wage increases which will raise average labour costs by about 2.6 per cent in 1998 and 1.7 per cent in 1999. The accord also includes measures to enable older employees to combine part-time work with a partial pension. Despite the relatively smooth conclusion of the central agreement many local disputes arose, particularly in relation to the increasing tendency towards contracting out and outsources. Strikes were concentrated in the public sector and transport in particular.

The economic recession of the early 1990s left a strong impression on the industrial relations sphere in Finland, with high unemployment placing traditional negotiating mechanisms under pressure. It is assumed likely that the very central-ised negotiations process will become diluted and further decentralised.

France

The National Conference on Employment, Wages and the Working Week held on 10 October 1997 ended in a breakdown of negotiations, the main stumbling block having been the introduction of the 35-hour week.

The prevailing tendency in France is for the existence of a wide spectrum of unions with very little joint action among the larger confederations. However, it should be noted that low membership and union fragmentation does not mean social apathy. This was demonstrated by industrial action mounted first at SNCF and then by the truckers. During industrial action in these sectors, the unions demonstrated an ability to increase public awareness, and to bring the conflict to a successful end.

Germany

In 1997, the collective bargaining round was overshadowed by the question of how to preserve or create employment. On the one hand trade union leaders declared that the very moderate wages increases in recent years had not led to new employment. On the other hand the employers associations demanded a continuation of *wage moderation* in order to further reduce labour costs (DE9711236F), including a much more differentiated wage structure. According to figures from the WSI Collective Agreements Archive, collectively agreed basic wages and salaries in western Germany rose on average about 1.4 per cent in 1997, which meant an average decrease of real wages of about 0.4 percentage points. In eastern Germany, collectively agreed basic wages and salaries rose on average about 2.7 per cent in 1997, in comparison to 5.0 per cent in 1996 (WSI Collective Agreement Archive). In the meantime average wages in the east have reached about 89.2 per cent of the western levels. However, since east Germany has lower yearly bonus payments and longer working hours the actual income gap between east and west Germany is still wider.

All in all, about 47,300 collective agreements had officially been registered by the German Ministry of Labour in 1997 (1996: 45,000), and 1997 was marked by a further differentiation and decentralisation of branch-level collective agree-ments (DE97093229F). An important example was the introduction of a new clause in the national pay framework agreement of the west German chemical industry in June 1997 (DE9706216F), which allows companies to reduce the collectively agreed wage by up to 10 per cent within a limited period of time to safeguard jobs and improve competitiveness. So far, however, a similar agree-ment was concluded only by the east German construction industry

(DE9707126N). Negotiations have also begun in the German metal industry for further reforms of branch-level collective agreements (DE9712240F). Since the metal industry is still the most important collective bargaining area and still represents the notion of a 'German model', the outcome of these negotiations will have major consequences for the future of German collective bargaining.

Greece

Traditionally, collective bargaining in Greece has been centralised, and based on annual negotiations. However, a trend started in the 1990s towards National General Collective Agreements for two year periods, continued in 1997. Changes to the institutional framework broadening the agenda of negotiations to include issues in addition to purely economic ones (GR9702101F) also allowed further agreements to be reached at branch and company level. The year began with the implementation of the second part of the 1996–1997 National General Collective Agreement, and an unprecedented wave of strikes, in both the public and private sectors, in opposition to the government's economic austerity policy (GR9702103N). There was also a marked shift in the sources of conflict signalled by the broader demand framework of the Greek General Confederation of Labour (GSEE) for the National General Collective Agreement (GR9801151N), to include institutional issues such as working time employment and working conditions and so on. This shift, however, has not eliminated conflict over economic issues (see GR9711139N and GR9710129F).

Ireland

Since 1987, nationally negotiated wage agreements have been a significant factor underpinning the growth in output and employment that has characterised the Irish economy. The year 1997 began with agreement on the fourth national pact since 1987, *Partnership 2000 (P2000)*. *P2000* encompasses a broader range of economic and social policies than its predecessors, and new participants, especially those representing marginalised or disadvantaged groups, have entered the consultative process. *P2000's* pay provisions provide roughly the same increase of 9.25 per cent for private and public sector employees. The main difference between private and public sectors relates to the phasing of the increases and the 'local bargaining element' worth 2 per cent.

While most deals on a plant-by-plant basis appear to be largely conforming to the terms of Partnership 2000, there have been a small number of companies who have gained concessions over wage cuts and new work organisation. There have also been other sectors such as pharmaceuticals and chemicals who have paid increases above the terms of the national agreement.

One example of industrial unrest that attracted considerable attention during the year was the Irish Life dispute in which sales staff resisted fundamental changes in how their work is performed. Other than this, the nurses' pay dispute in February, and the current Ryanair dispute over union recognition, there have been no other significant disputes.

Italy

February 1997 marked the renewal of the industry-wide agreement for metal-working (IT9702202F). Negotiations were long and were finally resolved through government mediation. The difficulties experienced in the negotiations re-opened a debate defined in the 1993 tripartite agreement, over the two level bar-gaining structure.

In the banking sector, negotiations began on how to manage redundancies resulting from ongoing sectoral restructuring (IT9704304F, IT9706115N).

In the transport sector, three trade union representatives joined the Board of Directors, following an agreement on the reorganisation of Alitalia, the Italian national airline (IT9706306F), while an agreement that envisages the use of early retirements as a means of avoiding redundancies was signed in regard to the restructuring of the state railways (IT9712316F, IT9705305F).

An innovation was the creation of supplementary pension funds (IT9705205F), through collective bargaining, especially in chemicals and metalworking.

While industrial action declined in general, the transport sector experienced the majority of conflict due to its 'unordered' nature (IT9707209F).

Luxembourg

The minimum wage rose by 3.3 per cent in January 1997, and all salaries went up by 2.5 per cent in February 1997 in line with automatic statutory indexation.

The social partners agreed to be bound by moderate wages; this undertaking has been generally adhered to. The National Conciliation Office has had a quiet year, although it has been argued that it would be wrong to draw hasty con-clusions from this.

The Netherlands

In mid-November 1997, the social partners united in the Labour Foundation (Stichting van de Arbeid—STAR) reached a new agreement on the agenda for future collective bargaining. This agreement reaffirms the importance of wage moderation and the employability of the labour force. Although this is in line with government policy and contributes to the preservation of the so-called Dutch consultation economy, the first rounds of collective bargaining are progressing with difficulty. Training and wage demands appear to be the main stumbling blocks.

In general, one can perceive a shift in the collective bargaining agenda. In the past, wage moderation was usually traded off for shorter working hours, but now unions have put training issues and workloads squarely on the agenda, while the employers wish to increase flexibility and performance-based pay.

Strikes remain rare but have recently taken place by those participating in the Melkert job-creation and labour pool schemes, with the aim of raising wages to above 120 per cent of the minimum wage. With the exception of the docks, industrial action appears to occur mainly in the public sector, against deregulation and privatisation plans.

Norway

Wage growth for 1997 was estimated at 4.25 per cent. The growth in real wages after taxes is estimated to be 1.8 per cent. Most of the wage agreements in Norway are of two-year duration and expire in 1998. The 1997 wage settlement was therefore a mid-term settlement where the parties mainly negotiated over remuneration levels. In addition, an agreement was reached making it possible to retire from the age of 62 years (NO1008EN).

Portugal

In 1997, 409 agreements were negotiated, of which 68 per cent were sector-level agreements, 26.4 per cent company-level agreements, and 5.6 per cent adoption agreements.

Although collective bargaining may be spreading to the police force and other areas where conditions of work are traditionally regulated by administrative instruments, in general there has been a relative decline in collective bargaining.

There were 313 strikes in 1997. Conflict at individual companies accounted for 77 per cent while a further 9 per cent involved entire sectors.

Spain

Consensus between the social partners led to two intersectoral agreements on 'collective bargaining' and 'filling the gaps in regulation', which encourage universal collective bargaining and the basing of company-level bargaining around the nationwide sectoral collective agreements. For the unions, these agreements constitute an extremely important point of reference because they have cleared up some of the ambiguities of the 1994 labour reforms. These gave greater autonomy to the social partners in collective bargaining but at the same time introduced a greater degree of vulnerability which meant that agreements on the regulation of working conditions were often restricted to the company level (ES9712137F). As a consequence of a greater degree of autonomy there has also been a noticeable trend toward the negotiation of 'special clauses' on geographical mobility, regulation of overtime, temporary jobs and social benefits such as pensions (ES9711231F).

Sweden

As collective agreements in most of the larger sectors are of two years or more duration, collective bargaining was limited to a few sectors in 1997. In these sectors negotiations were difficult, with boycotts and strikes more frequent than usual. The main issue of contention was working time rather than pay. The unions' calls for reductions in working time were rejected by the employers. In return, unions refused to discuss employer demands for a more flexible organisation of working time.

Average pay increases were 2.5–3 per cent, which was less than expected. A change in the industrial relations climate occurred in 1997, seemingly as a result of high unemployment and the Government's resolution to keep inflation down. A mutual understanding was reached between employers' organisations, trade union confederations and the Government that nominal wages must not increase as much as they had done in the past years, if unemployment is to be reduced. They also agreed that there might be a need to change the procedural rules for collective bargaining and mediation if wages are to be kept at a level where they will not increase inflation.

A new national agreement for industry committed the social partners to avoiding industrial action, since such action is illegal as long as an agreement is running. In reality it only allows postponement of any action for 14 days. The rules are intended to work through the moral obligation that the parties to the agreement have committed themselves to.

UK

Average earnings growth fluctuated within the range 4.25–4.75 per cent, with average pay awards remaining at around 3 per cent for most of the year, but moving towards the 4 per cent mark in the last quarter (UK1100).

The UK system of collective bargaining remains largely decentralised, with a continued decline in the coverage of collective bargaining (UK1026). In the public sector the government continued the former policy of a pay freeze on the overall wage bill, with any further pay increases having to be found from efficiency savings (UK1004/1070).

The summer of 1997 saw a number of disputes (UK1053) which led to speculation of possible upsurge in militancy. However, it seems that fears were unfounded as after a rise in industrial action for 1996 (UK1044), in 1997 figures settled down again. In the 12 months to September 1997 the number of stoppages recorded were 211, with a total of 259,800 workers involved and 414,800 working days lost. This is compared with 239; 25,400 and 1,244,700 respectively for the same period in 1996.

EMPLOYMENT CREATION AND NEW FORMS OF WORK ORGANISATION

Although many member states experienced a fall in unemployment figures in 1997, the number of jobseekers chasing each vacancy increased in most countries. The 1997 Employment in Europe report shows that a majority of the jobs created were either part-time or temporary. Despite the persistent concerns about high levels of unemployment and the impact this would have on the perception of EMU among European citizens as the deadline for monetary union approaches, the Intergovernmental Conference and the Amsterdam Summit were very much dominated by negotiations over the adaptations of the internal structures of the Union in the light of the impending accession negotiations. Another pre-occupation was with the finalisation of steps towards EMU. As a result, the new Amsterdam Treaty, the draft of which was agreed at the Amsterdam Summit on 17 June 1997, brought only limited advances for employment and social policy at EU level, which essentially place practices previously established under the Essen recommendations on a Treaty footing. Nevertheless, the Treaty brought some advances in the area of employment and social policy. The Union's attachment to fundamental social rights was confirmed by the inclusion of this commitment in a new paragraph added to the Preamble of the TEU. In addition, the principle of non-discrimination on the basis of sex, racial and ethnic origin, religion or belief, disability, age and sexual orientation is confirmed by Article 6a and the objective of achieving equality between men and women was added to Article 2 of the TEC outlining the general principles to be promoted by the Community.

A new Title on Employment was included in the TEC under Title VI which sets the objective of working towards the development of a co-ordinated strategy for employment and particularly for promoting a skilled, trained and adaptable workforce and labour markets responsive to economic change. Member states are called upon to co-ordinate their actions in this area. The process of encouraging co-operation, drawing up of employment guidelines and annual progress monitoring (a process informally established post-Essen) is strengthened by inclusion in the Treaty. In light of the new UK government's commitment to sign up to the Social Protocol, this is to be repealed and included into the Treaty with some alterations (EU9707135f).

Because of the domination of the Amsterdam Summit by issues other than employment, and in response to increasing disenchantment by many citizens with the inability of the Union to take steps to combat the problem of high unemployment in the run-up to EMU, it was agreed that a special summit on employment was to be held under the Luxembourg Presidency in November 1997. Prior to the Summit, the Commission drew up draft employment guidelines to be implemented by the member states and set targets for job creation and the inclusion of young people and the unemployment in training and other job creation programmes (EU9710159n). The emphasis of the Summit was placed by the Luxembourg Presidency on the formulation of achievable targets, and the measures agreed by heads of state consequently remained more limited that what was initially envisaged by the Commission. For example, the Commission had envisaged setting a target for the reduction of unemployment from nearly 11 per cent to 5 per cent and creating 12 million jobs in 5 years. The employment guidelines finally adopted do not mention this target, but merely speak of increasing the number of unemployed who are offered training from the current average of 10 per cent towards at least 20 per cent (taking into account their starting position). The employment guidelines focus on measures to achieve greater employability, entrepreneurship, adaptability and equal opportunities (EU9712174n). These guidelines are to be translated into member state action plans by April 1998 and will therefore continue to occupy the employment policy debate for the foreseeable future.

As another element of the employment debate, the European Commission released a Green Paper on new forms of work organisation in April 1997, with the purpose of stimulating European debate on how competitiveness and employment opportunities can be improved through new forms of work organisation based on the model of a high skill, high trust and high quality economy (EU9707134f).

The EU-level debate on employment and the European social dimension has changed significantly in its form and content over the past 15 years. During the late 1980s and early 1990s, the Commission, under the leadership of Jacques Delors, favoured a more legislative, interventionist approach, which culminated in the adoption of the (albeit not legally binding) Charter of Fundamental Social Rights for Workers, or in short 'Social Charter' and its Action Programme. The emphasis was on the creation of a high skill, high employment security economy, with minimum rights where set at the European level. While the achievement of this aim remains a panacea in European Commission pronouncements, the approach has changed significantly since the implementation of the Maastricht Treaty and the December 1994 Essen Summit. Emphasis has shifted from legislative attempts initiated by the Commission, to the new arrangement of consultation and possible negotiation between the social partners as set out in the Maastricht social protocol, and has shifted away from an emphasis on the regulation of minimum standards to one of 'negotiated flexibility'. The case for partial deregulation of the labour market alongside the wider introduction of new forms of employment and work organisation is being increasingly accepted as the means of improving competitiveness. Additionally, the new forms of employment and work organisation are claimed to meet the demand among employees for a greater flexibility in working time arrangements. At the same time there is a growing emphasis on the co-operation between management and employees at all levels of decision making.

While the emphasis on an integrated approach, including education, training, social security, taxation, macro-economic and structural policies, as well as policies on the information society and worker involvement was widely welcomed, many issues so far remain unexplored, including the uneasy balance between security and flexibility. This therefore ensures that this debate surrounding new forms of work organisation will continue to shape the policy debate in 1998.

As has already become apparent in the analysis of collective bargaining at the national level, employment creation was a prominent issue throughout the EU with both national governments and social partner groups eager to tackle the problem. At local level many collective agreements also favoured the negotiation of employment security in return for other concessions.

Austria

Employment growth continued in 1997, as did a reduction in unemployment. Efforts to reinstate the long-term unemployed continued with the main focus being on the older, the less educated and women. This was combined with new social security regulations (AT9711144F) to aid the increasing numbers of lower paid (AT9705115N).

Working time flexibility was a prominent issue (AT9702102F, AT9801156F). Despite progress in this area being restricted to a few industries, this was achieved in significant sectors such as construction and metalworking. Working time flexibility and a drive towards a 35-hour working week are likely to remain topical throughout 1998.

Belgium

Other than measures mentioned in the section on collective bargaining, federal employment policies have three aims; firstly, to reduce labour costs by aligning them with those of its three main trading partners, France, the Netherlands and Germany, through pay restraint and a reduction of social contributions. Secondly, to achieve a redistribution of labour through a better integration of job seekers in the labour market; an improved response to workers' aspirations, allowing them to choose their working time; and a more flexible organisation of work. Finally, measures to integrate target groups were aimed primarily at young people and the long-term unemployed.

Denmark

Throughout 1997, government and the social partners have discussed the issue of how to reduce the marginalisation from the labour market, and to improve the employment opportunities for individuals with a reduced ability to work. The objective of the government is the creation of some 40,000 'flex-jobs' by the year 2005. Flex-jobs are intended to offer people with a disability, illness or reduced ability to work, jobs on special terms. Employers receive a wage contribution between one-third and two-thirds of the minimum wage, depending upon the employee's ability to work.

While the social partners support the idea, they do not agree on replacing the tradition of voluntary agreements with legislative provision, as proposed by the government.

The scene for dealing with new forms of work organisation and working time was set by provisions made in the early 1990s for them to be dealt with by collective bargaining. This continued in 1997 especially in the banking sector, in which the parties agreed to introduce the possibility of Saturday opening.

In the 1997 budget, a 40 per cent penalty tax on overtime payments was introduced in the civil service in order to reduce the level of overtime work. As a result, overtime payments have declined by 40 per cent over the first three-quarters of 1997. Some see this as an indication that institutions have reorganised work and improved planning in order to avoid the penalty tax on overtime payment, while others argue that overtime work merely may have taken another form i.e. time off in lieu, unpaid overtime work and permanent pay supplements.

In 1997, an analysis of the prevalence of home-based telework carried out for the Ministry of Research and Information Technology showed that within the next decade the number of persons conducting home-based telework is expected to increase from the present level of 9,000 to potentially 250 000 persons. At the 1997 collective bargaining round the social partners within the state bargaining area took the first steps toward regulating home-based telework in collective agreements.

Finland

The employment situation in Finland improved significantly during 1997, particularly for younger and highly educated workers. Long-term unemployment remained prevalent among older workers and low skilled individuals. New legislation was introduced to improve job security for individuals on fixed-term contracts, thus making such forms of employment more attractive. In line with the 1998 Commission Employment Guidelines, the Finnish government is preparing a special plan to ensure unemployed younger workers have access to job integration schemes, before they have been unemployed for more than 6 months.

Further education and training services will also be provided and the services of the public employment services improved for younger workers. The government has also made a commitment to keep the proportion of long-term unemployed, as a percentage of total unemployment, lower than 5 per cent. Job seeking plans will be developed for the long-term unemployed and a special programme to assist the retention and re-employment of older workers will be implemented. Special employment assistance measures will also be developed for women and disabled individuals. Policy on working time and work organisation will be developed further in consultation with the social partners and initiatives in this area are already under way.

France

Continued growth in GDP created 130 000 new jobs in 1997. Employment growth was mainly created in the service sector, as employment in manufacturing and construction continued to fall.

Undoubtedly the most significant event in 1997, at a political and social level, was the unexpected change of government in France and the return of the Left to power. The Socialists and their allies based their entire election campaign on an employment platform, believing that increased growth alone would not be sufficient to reduce unemployment. The government put in place initiatives such as a 4 per cent increase in the minimum wage, and a law creating 350 000 new jobs in the public and associated sectors has been passed. Discussions are also taking place on the formulation of legislation to introduce a 35-hour week, however, progress has so far been limited.

The government is concentrating on certain sectors and individual companies in an effort to get negotiations restarted over a 35-hour week. Indeed, many companies, inspired by the Loi Robien, have initiated full-scale experiments in reducing the working week; 1500 new agreements, affecting 166,066 workers, have been signed. When these collective agreements were signed, the companies involved stated that they had been able to create new jobs or save positions totalling 11 per cent of existing ones. This issue, which dominated the final quarter of 1997, is likely to remain at the forefront of social debate in 1998.

Germany

The social partners and the federal as well as the state (Länder) governments discussed the issue of preserving and creating employment. The most important initiatives of the German Government in 1997, were:

(i) The 'Partial Retirement Law' (Altersteilzeitgesetz) which supports the gradual transition of older employees to retirement under certain conditions. In

1997, there were a number of sectoral and company level agreements concluded on the basis of the new law (DE9710133F).

(ii)   The 'Labour Law Act on the Promotion of Employment' (Arbeitsrechtliches Beschäftigungsförderungsgesetz) which came to effect on 1 October 1996 and includes an easing of redundancy provisions, the reduction of the statutory level of continued payment of remuneration in case of illness from 100 per cent to 80 per cent of the previous income, and improves the possibilities for fixed-term labour contracts. In 1997, there were many collective agreements concluded on the basis of the new law, especially regarding the continued payment of remuneration, the majority of which ensured the continued payment of 100 per cent of the previous income (DE9710131F).

(iii) the 'Employment Promotion Act' (Arbeitsförderungsgesetz) which came to effect on 1 April 1997 and includes the promotion of employment for problem groups, support for the foundation of new firms, and restrictions on job-creation schemes.

(iv)   the 'Act on Temporary Employment Business' (Arbeitnehmer-überlassungsgesetz, AÜG) which came to effect on 1 April 1997 and includes the relaxation of the legal regulation of work at temporary work agencies (DE9710138F).

The whole of eastern Germany (DE9706117F) and Bavaria are covered by regional employment alliances. Company level agreements mostly intend to avoid redundancies (REF).

As regards working time organisation, the BMAS reports a further flexibilisation through the increased use of working time accounts and annual working hours. However, many traditional systems were complemented with elements of flexibility by collective or works agreements.

In 1997, there were numerous collective and works agreements concluded on the issue of working time flexibility, e.g. at Siemens (DE9710136N) but there was also an increase in the number of cases of working time which violated collective agreements. As in other European countries, the debate on working time variations as a means of increasing employment is gaining ground (DE9704208F, DE9709127F).

Greece

The spectacular rise in unemployment in recent years sparked intense dialogue between the social partners concerning the need to find immediate, effective solutions (GR9702101). Examples of good practice are the product of negotiation between the social partners at the national level, including proposals submitted to the Luxembourg summit (GR9711142N).

On the practical level there are very few co-ordinated actions or measures aimed at boosting employment at local levels. While a Pact of Confidence was agreed between social partners (GR9711138F), local initiatives have proved more difficult to reach (GR9703109N).

The government would like to see greater labour market flexibility, but views regarding the means by which structural changes in the labour market will be carried out are extremely divergent. Apart from special cases, such as the banking sector (GR9711137F), it is quite clear that the social partners are having difficulty agreeing how to reduce working time without a reduction in pay (GR9704110F and GR9712145F). This is also the case with regard to the new forms of work and working time organisation both at the national level (GR9708122F, GR9708123N, GR9708124N and GR9707120F), branch level (GR9712144F), and company level (see GR9706116F).

Ireland

The Irish government prioritised changes to taxation in order to encourage employment growth. In addition, the government also introduced a range of active labour market policies which seek to tackle unemployment directly—for example through general and skills training, employment subsidies, direct employment schemes, and so-called area-based partnerships. Irish expenditure on active labour market policies (as percentage of GDP) is one of the highest amongst the OECD countries.

An innovative, localised approach to tackling long-term unemployment and social exclusion was introduced in the early 1990s as part of the national agreement, *Programme for Economic and Social Progress (PESP)*. These measures to tackle unemployment have involved a great deal of input from the social partners.

Many commentators have argued that the best way to secure a strong national competitive advantage is to try and develop a high-wage, high-skill, highly innovative economy with adequate social protection. This was built into the P2000 framework, which attempts to recognise the different competitive pressures facing industries.

Ireland has also introduced new legislation on new forms of work and working time organisation in order to comply with European initiatives.

Italy

Employment creation became one of the priorities of collective bargaining, especially in the southern regions which are characterised by high unemployment. The social partners pursued this objective through the use of territorial pacts, area contracts and gradual alignment agreements (IT9704203F, IT9706207F). The trade unions' commitment to foster employment creation led to the unitary agreement reached by CGIL, CISL and UIL which identifies the means available at local level to sustain employment: work-entry policies, training, bargaining on working time and wage levels (IT9801219F).

Together with the introduction of temporary work, law 196/97 addressed fixed-term employment and it included a set of incentives for part-time work and for the redefinition of working time schedules. Law 196/97 also introduced new rules to re-launch apprenticeship and to sustain work/training contracts, training and continuing training.

As part of a continued deregulation of the labour market, law 196/97 also introduced temporary work in Italy. The law defined both the cases in which it is possible to resort to temporary work, and the requirements that temporary work agencies have to meet if they intend to carry out labour intermediation activities (IT9707308F).

Furthermore, as far as innovative forms of work are concerned, new experiments on telework started (IT9712218F). At sectoral level, the commerce industry-wide agreement introduced a specific chapter on telework (IT9707118N).

In November 1997, the social partners signed an agreement for the implementation of the European Union Directive 93/104 on working time (IT9711140N). This led to substantial increases in bargaining on working hours, including an endeavour to improve the reconciliation of work and family life (IT9710215F).

The industry-wide agreement for the chemicals included some proposals for an innovative working time management (IT9710313F), in which trade unions proposed a different system to manage overtime and the introduction of work-entry hours.

Luxembourg

The reduction of unemployment was given a boost by the European Jobs Summit organised under the aegis of the Luxembourg Presidency (Lu9712134f). Unemployment is low but rising, yet Luxembourg is one of the few countries where the number of jobs has increased (Lu9707112n and Lu1020en comparative) despite the fact that the system of allocating unemployed workers is not working as well as hoped.

A tripartite employment conference is planned for February 1998 (Lu9801138n). Talks are to focus on encouraging social partners to take more responsibility in the field, especially by focusing on young people and the long-term unemployed. It hopes to do so by additional training and cash incentives for employers who recruit unemployed workers registered with the Employment Administration.

It is not at all clear inside Luxembourg itself that a reduction in working hours would necessarily lead to jobs being created for registered unemployed workers.

Nonetheless, one thing is quite clear: any reduction in working hours can only be achieved through a negotiated agreement within the tripartite structure, and greater flexibility will necessarily have to be conceded in exchange.

Talks on voluntary part-time work concluded with a law of 26 February 1993, which granted considerable guarantees to employees working in part time and temporary employment.

The Netherlands

Employment in the Netherlands is growing rapidly, with women, the young and long-term unemployed benefiting from these developments.

In accordance with agreements reached at the Luxembourg Special Employ-ment Summit, the Dutch government has drafted a national action plan to implement the Employment Guidelines for 1998. This plan emphasises the con-cept of 'employability'. A recent example of EU-inspired policy is the Employ-ment Pact concluded by three Dutch Provinces (Noord-Brabant, Limburg and Flevoland) on 20 February 1998. Dutch job creation policy operates on two fronts. The first concerns direct job creation for target groups while the second concentrates on wage subsidies.

In 1996, the Dutch government launched proposals for a new law on 'flexi-bility and security'. These proposals led to legislative reform which is at present going through parliament. The initiative aims to enhance labour market flexi-bility, while giving atypical employees more rights.

In practice, trade unions and employers are already involved in new forms of work in return for employment security. Temporary and part-time work continues to grow and proposals to regulate for such types of work are underway.

Norway

Norway has seen a rapid growth in employment over the past few years, lead-ing to a fall in unemployment for those with the most significant entry problems (immigrants and youth). The number of persons participating in employment schemes has been significantly reduced, so that at the end of 1997 employment schemes encompassed 0.9 per cent of the labour force.

Young people below the age of 20 years have a right to either schooling or a placement in an employment scheme, while youth below the age of 25 years are given priority in the employment schemes.

Proposals to increase labour market flexibility by softening statutory provisions have so far not received sufficient political support in the Norwegian Parliament (NO1018EN, NO1044EN, NO1051EN).

The employer organisations would like greater flexibility with regard to types of employment (permanent/temporary/leased) and working hours, mainly in order to utilise labour more efficiently and to reduce overtime costs. The 1997 LO

Congress (Norwegian Confederation of Trade Unions, Landsorganisasjonen i Norge) also opened for discussing more flexible working hour arrangements. LO emphasise that these types of arrangements must be regulated through collective agreements (NO1010EN).

Portugal

Employment creation is regarded as a crucial issue by the social partners. The approval of a joint declaration on the part of the government and the unions and employers' federations—a rare occurrence in Portugal—which was presented to the European Council on Employment serves to highlight the point.

With respect to Community action in this domain, it should also be noted that three regional networks have developed whose aims are to promote job creation initiatives, which are incorporated into the so-called Territorial Pact on Employment.

The debate over new forms of work organisation has concentrated on part-time work, with the government having discussed draft legislation on the matter with the social partners.

With the exception of changes in organisation of working hours, increased flexibility in the labour market has been at the expense of a growth in less stable forms of employment.

Although a reduction in the working week has been linked to the introduction of more flexible forms of organisation and time management, the social partners have so far not taken advantage of opportunities for putting new solutions into practice in this area through means of collective bargaining.

Spain

The number of those in employment has increased by about 371,000 in comparison with 1996. Nevertheless, fewer jobs were created than in the previous year despite greater economic growth. Employment policy was marked by the Multi-Sector Agreement for Employment Stability (AIEE), signed in April 1997 by the employers' associations CEOE and CEPYME and the trade unions CCOO and UGT (9702203f, 97032205n, 9706211f).

One of the fundamental objectives of this agreement was to encourage stable employment and to reduce temporary employment. Nevertheless, the temporary employment rate has remained at 33 per cent, the highest in the European Union and job creation has had a smaller effect on unemployment than in previous years.

Recent years have also seen a significant increase in part-time employment, which has been encouraged through measures aimed at two groups of unemployed persons: women and persons under 24 years of age (9703203F).

During 1997 the trade unions have been pressing for the reduction of the working week to 35 hours, a proposal that has met with a response from employers' associations and the government.

The banking and retail sectors have witnessed greater working time flexibility. In 1997 the opening of offices in the afternoons was negotiated in the banking sector in exchange for creating new jobs in these offices.

Sweden

On several occasions in 1997, leading members of the cabinet urged the employers to meet the unions' desire for a reduction of weekly working time. The government has even threatened to legislate, should the employers not show willingness to negotiate on this subject. In general these demands are however not motivated by a wish to reduce unemployment. The idea that a reduction of working time would lead to more jobs has not prevailed in Sweden. It is primarily perceived as a means of furthering workers' well-being and indirectly also a means of furthering equality between the sexes, as it makes it easier for both men and women to combine gainful employment and parenthood.

Instead measures generally promoting productivity, growth and competitiveness of companies are seen as the main instruments for employment creation.

UK

The Labour government has declared the fight against unemployment as one of its top priorities. At home they have committed themselves to getting 250 000 young and long-term unemployed people back to work in their 'welfare to work' deal, which has largely received a positive reception from social partners. In Europe, Labour are also keen to make employment a priority as part of their EU presidency, through boosting flexibility, employability and competitiveness (UK1036).

The Welfare to Work programme is essentially three schemes aimed at unemployment among youth, long-term adults, and lone parents (UK1043). The new initiatives have received support from the CBI and the TUC and many new companies have signed up to take part in the New Deal (UK1068/1075).

Changes in work organisation have also been linked with employment issues. In particular, some firms have introduced employment security agreements which are usually aimed at committing the permanent full-time employees to the process of change in exchange for job security (UK1064). Many of the agreements are signed on the basis that they can use temporary or contract labour flexibly. These agreements are intrinsically linked to the pay round and are not valid in law. Paradoxically, they are also highly associated with job losses. Of all the EU member countries the working time directive is likely to have the greatest impact in the UK due to the historical legacy of 'non-regulation' of working time and the fact that in the 1980s the government dismantled what little legislation there was to protect women and children (UK1003).

EMPLOYEE INFORMATION AND CONSULTATION

The announcement in February 1997 by French car maker Renault, of the closure of its plant in the Belgian Prime Minister's constituency of Vilvoorde, generated an unprecedented storm of protest from the labour movement and the political establishment of the European Union (EU9703108f). It raised questions over the ability of European legislation to prevent multinational companies from enforcing economically motivated decisions on the locale of production without prior workforce consultation. In the light of the approaching deadline for EMU, the Commission was keen that European integration should not become associated with job losses and quickly condemned the decision by Renault as being in breach of the spirit of European legislation on employee information and consultation and collective redundancies. It gave unprecedented vocal support to a legal challenge of the actions of the company. French and Belgian courts subsequently condemned Renault's actions. When called upon to strengthen existing legislation and to impose heavier fines on those breaching EU law, Commissioner Flynn argued that existing legislation was sufficient. However, he argued that consultations were to be speeded up with the social partners on measures to complement existing legislation which should govern information and consultation at the national level (EU9704118f).

Another area of information and consultation which has long been on the agenda of the European Union is that of employee involvement in the proposed 'European Company'. Proposals for a European Company Statute have been on the policy-making agenda of the European Commission for 25 years and the Commission has repeatedly stressed the importance of legislation enabling the incorporation of companies at EU level, in order to improve the competitiveness of European companies. In 1996 a high level expert group on worker involvement was set up with the aim of breaking the deadlock in this debate. Proposals for employee representation in these structures have long been blocked in the Council, particularly because of concerns from countries with advanced information and employee participation systems, because of the fear that such legislation could be used to circumvent national legislation in this area. Similarly, objections were voiced from countries which currently have no provision for the appointment of worker representatives in information and consultation mechanisms. The Davignon Group reported on 14 May and recommended that priority should be given to free negotiation between the parties directly concerned, as to the system of employee information and consultation that was to be applied. Only if the parties should fail to reach agreement, a set of minimum reference rules should come into application. The procedures proposed were therefore similar to those contained in the EWC Directive, but it was suggested that reference rules should be stronger than those applied in the EWC Directive (EU9705128n). The cultural and legal differences in national information and consultation will continue to make European regulation in this area difficult, the voluntary approach taken by the EWC Directive, with minimum statutory provisions being implemented at member state level, is now becoming established as a solution and the experience of the existing European Works Councils is particularly instructive in order to assess the impact of such legislation.

With the UK inclusion into European social legislation concluded under the Maastricht social protocol, all countries have now either adopted the EWC directive, or are in the process of framing implementing legislation. According to a recent study carried out for the European Foundation for the Improvement of Living and Working Conditions, 386 companies headquartered in 25 countries have concluded agreements establishing EWCs under Article 13 of the 1994 directive (Table 1; Marginson *et al.*, 1998). Another 60 companies are thought to have introduced EWCs under Article 6 of the Directive, since the ratification of implementing legislation in the member state.

The study found that despite a strong tendency to opt for information and consultation arrangements similar to those prevailing in the country in which the undertaking is headquartered, this is by no means true of all agreements. A significant number of agreements concluded in companies where employee-only representative bodies are the norm, have opted for joint structures in their EWC

TABLE 1
Country of Origin

Country	%	Number	Country	%	Number
Austria	2	7	Netherlands	5	18
Belgium	4	17	Norway	1	7
Denmark	2	6	Portugal	–	–
Finland	4	14	Spain	1	3
France	11	42	Sweden	6	22
Germany	23	89	*EEA 17*	*63*	*244*
Greece	–	–			
Iceland	–	–	Switzerland	5	19
Ireland	1	3	UK	15	58
Italy	4	14	Japan	4	14
Liechtenstein	–	–	USA	15	59
Luxembourg	1	2	Rest of the World	1	5

Source: Marginson *et al.*, 1998.
Base: All agreements, $N = 386$
Note: percentages total to more than 100 per cent and numbers add to 395 because in nine cases, organisations are headquartered in more than one country.

(EU9803191f). It remains unclear whether this implies a trend towards a watering down of national provisions, or whether these constitute deliberate moves to safeguard stronger national agreements which already exist in these companies. The impact of European legislation on national information and consultation systems thus remains unclear.

THE ROLE OF THE SOCIAL PARTNERS

Another feature of policy making at the European Union level has been the increasing importance accorded to the dialogue and autonomous consultation and negotiation between the social partner organisations at sectoral and intersectoral level. This role was boosted by Articles 3 and 4 of the Maastricht agreement on Social Policy which extends the provisions of Article 118b considerably by imposing an obligation to consult management and labour before presenting a proposal in the social field. The social partners can decide, after a two stage consultation process, to open autonomous negotiations with the aim of concluding a European framework agreement, which can then either be implemented through a Council Directive or in accordance with national structures. The latter process had previously led to the implementation of a directive on parental leave. In May 1997, ETUC, CEEP and UNICE concluded a framework agreement on part-time work, after many months of difficult negotiations. The conclusion of this agreement, which has now been translated into a Directive and is to be implemented by the member states within two years, was a considerable success, bearing in mind that previous legislative initiatives which had been under discussion for some 15 years had failed. It has to be viewed in the light of the imminent conclusion of the intergovernmental conference and the Amsterdam Summit, as well as the somewhat dented estimation of the European social partner organisations after they had failed, post-Renault, to reach an agreement on a code of conduct for companies faced with the need to restructure.

ETUC, UNICE and CEEP also issued joint contributions in relation to the Confidence Pact for Employment and in regard of the Luxembourg employment summit. Having thus demonstrated their willingness to co-operate on such issues, it was decided that they should be involved in bi-annual meetings with the Council troika in order to discuss employment issues (EU9711168f). More recently, the decision has been taken to move on to intersectoral negotiations on the working conditions of workers on fixed-term contracts, a subject previously excluded from negotiations at the request of UNICE. Nevertheless, two rounds of consultation on the issue of national information and consultation of employees has failed to produce consensus for the establishment of autonomous negotiations between ETUC and UNICE and the formulation of a draft Directive in this area now appears the most likely course of action (EU9803192n).

At the sectoral level, the social dialogue process has also concluded an unprecedented number of joint statements and opinions in recent years. The year 1997 saw the conclusion of the first ever sectoral recommendation framework agreement on the improvement of paid employment in agriculture (EU9709145f), as well as the first agreement on a working time in the maritime transport sector (EU980282f), which is now to be translated into a Council Directive. There was also significant progress in the dialogue in other sectors, particularly on the issues of employment, equal opportunities and training (EU9710153f and EU9705126n).

Nevertheless, this process continues to be fraught with difficulty because of the perceived inadequate representativeness of certain social partner organisations and the desire by a number of bodies currently excluded from consultations (particularly under the Maastricht social protocol) to attain a greater voice and involvement in these processes. In order to ascertain the desired paths for the future development of the European social dialogue, the European Commission has issued a consultation document, to which all organisations have responded. A second consultation document is now imminent and is set to have an important impact on the nature and focus of the social dialogue process and the involvement of different actors.

While the role of the social partners at the European level was significantly boosted, at the member state level, many trade union organisations have been faced with continuing membership loss. Many have responded with union mergers in order to retain their bargaining strength. Nevertheless, tripartite arrangements have largely remained intact, or were indeed revived, in the case of the UK.

EMU

It is almost certain that 11 countries will qualify for EMU. Denmark, Sweden and the UK will not join the first wave and Greece is the only country which may not qualify. Even so they are being encouraged to join sooner rather than later.

There has been little research or thought into the actual industrial relations consequences of EMU, instead most have concentrated on issues such as inflation, budget deficits, employment effects and wage policy. Some countries, however, have begun to realise this fact and to attempt to prepare the way for some issues. For example Belgium, Luxembourg and Portugal have all put in place national framework agreements for future collective bargaining. In the case of Belgium and Luxembourg this was because the social partners themselves could not come to an agreement. The German trade unions fearing pressure on their system of collective bargaining through intensifying international competition called for a 'Europeanisation' of collective bargaining through the extension of European social minimum standards and a stronger co-ordination of collective bargaining policy at European level. In 1997, for example, IG Metall started to establish transnational bargaining networks and invited foreign trade union colleagues to participate in German collective bargaining (DE9707223N).

1998?

As the introduction made clear the big issues of 1997 are likely to remain dominant throughout 1998. In many countries with national, regional and sectoral collective bargaining, negotiations over new agreements are due in 1998 and are likely to include clauses for flexibility of work and working time, employment security and job creation. As the deadline for EMU approaches ever closer most economies are likely to be exerting a dual pressure of creating more flexible labour markets whilst holding down wage demands in order to keep down inflation.

REFERENCES

Marginson, P., Gilman, M, Jacobi, O. & Krieger, H. (1998) *Negotiating European Works Councils: An analysis of agreements under article 13*. Interim report.
EIRO records:

Record No.	Month	Title
AT9705111F	5	Troubled relations in key tourism industry
AT9705112F	5	Salary grades in industry
AT9705115N	5	Minor employment to gain social security coverage
AT9706117F	6	Civil service strikes
AT9706120N	6	Provincial agreements in tourism
AT9707124N	7	Another year without strikes
AT9709130F	9	New round of metalworking pay bargaining opens
AT9709132N	9	Industrial action threatened on the railways
AT9710138N	10	Pay round off to a good start
AT9711144F	11	Pension reform nears completion
BE9702101F	2	Apparent breakdown of Belgian central bargaining
BE9705106N	5	Experimental reduction of working time at Interbrew
BE9706205F	6	New sectoral collective agreements cover 1.4 million workers
BE9707111N	7	Hours reductions and flexibility in insurance
BE9707214N	7	Focus on employment creation
BE9710220N	10	Jobs should be top priority, say Flemish employers
BE9711123F	11	Debate on overall reduction of working time in Belgium

Bookshelf

Edited by Ed Clark and Anna Soulsby

In each Review, we have the capacity to include some nine or ten critical reviews of recent books, journals and monographs that contribute to our understanding of broadly industrial relations issues in the European context. On this first occasion—thanks to the joint efforts of publishers and reviewers, for whose promptness in meeting tight deadlines we are extremely grateful—we have been able to assemble an excellent example of what we are aiming for.

In any new publication, it is important that publishers, reviewers and readers have a clear idea of the scope of the review section. In the tradition of the *Industrial Relations Journal*, we define our subject matter fairly broadly, but at the same time are adamant about maintaining a clear European focus. We would like to operate with the following guidelines:

1. The books should focus on issues, themes and developments of broad industrial relations relevance, or on matters that have clear implications for industrial relations. By industrial relations, we include all aspects of trade unions, management, employee–management relations and industrial conflict from the shop floor to the multinational corporation; work, workers and the working environment; changes in the management, structure and size of industrial organisations and their consequences; workers' participation, industrial democracy and workers' control; discrimination in the workplace; the origins, experience and implications of unemployment; the impact of technological change on the workplace; legal and social institutions relating to the above issues; the nature and impact of developments in the management of human resources, its ideology and its practices.

2. We would review only books which have a clearly *European* focus, that is, which are not solely based in the United Kingdom (such books will continue to be reviewed in the regular *Industrial Relations Journal*). This would include single-nation studies from non-UK European countries; comparative studies of European societies, institutions and workplaces (where the comparators might include the UK or non-European countries); studies of multinational corporations operating across Europe; and so on. We are particularly interested in reviewing books that examine the emergence of IR-related patterns within the post-communist transition economies.

Ed Clark is Principal Lecturer and Anna Soulsby Senior Lecturer in Human Resource Management at the Nottingham Trent University Business School.

221

3. While *Bookshelf* will naturally treat academic reports as its bread and butter, the editors are also keen to review books that approach the above subjects in a less formal way—especially those that are written by practitioners or are more practitioner-oriented. We would even welcome journalistic or fictional accounts where they enlighten aspects of the European IR scene.

4. The books should have been published within the two years leading up to the appearance of *EAIRR*. For example, in the case of the present edition, we have been interested in books published in 1997 and 1998.

We would like to thank those publishers which responded promptly to our call for books, in particular to John Wiley & Sons, Oxford University Press and Clarendon Press. Books which did not meet the above criteria have been passed on to the *Industrial Relations Journal* for consideration in their regular review features. Where readers, especially from the continent of Europe, would like to review books that meet the above criteria, they should contact us.

BOOKS RECEIVED BUT NOT REVIEWED

Anderson, N. and Herriot, P. (eds) *International Handbook of Selection and Assessment*, Chichester, John Wiley, 1997.

Antonides, G., *et al.* (eds) *Advances in Economic Psychology*, Chichester, John Wiley, 1997.

Cooper, C. and Robertson, I. (eds) *International Review of Industrial and Organizational Psychology*, Chichester, John Wiley, 1998.

Cooper, D. *Improving Safety Culture: A Practical Guide*, Chichester, John Wiley, 1998.

Fredman, S. *Women and the Law*, Oxford, Clarendon Press, 1997.

McColgan, A. *Just Wages for Women*, Oxford, Oxford University Press, 1997.

Schabracq, M., *et al.* (eds) *Handbook of Work and Health Psychology*, Chichester, John Wiley, 1996.

West, M. (ed) *Handbook of Work Group Psychology*, Chichester, John Wiley, 1996.

European Union—European Industrial Relations? Global challenges, national developments and transnational dynamics
Wolfgang E. Lecher and Hans-Wolfgang Platzer (eds)
Routledge, 1998, 312 pp., £50.00

The stated intention of this book is to offer an assessment of the prospects for, and limits to, the development of a system of transnational industrial relations within the European Union in the light of major political and economic changes throughout Europe. This book is thus the first collection of articles in English which focuses solely on the development of an authentic European system of industrial relations. Lecher and Platzer have fruitfully brought together over 20 voices on the subject, including both academic specialists and practitioners.

Anyone dealing with European industrial relations faces two basic problems: first, one has to come to grips with the complexity of the subject matter, which stretches not only horizontally across national systems of industrial relations, but which also includes a vertical dimension encompassing the various levels of employment regulation at the multi-sectoral, sectoral and company level. Second, one has to take into consideration that seemingly specific terms such as 'industrial relations' or 'collective bargaining' are charged with different connotations and meanings depending on the respective national tradition.

Lecher and Platzer cope with these problems by pursuing an 'integrated comparative approach' which is based on a broad definition of the term 'European Industrial Relations' as embracing 'all forms of cross-border or supranational relationship between the social partners at the various levels at which they may exist, together with the interplay of national and EU institutions and the social partners in formulating and implementing employment and social policy' (p. xii). This inclusive approach allows for a lively and comprehensive debate among practitioners and academics on the nature and future prospects of a European system of industrial relations. However, because this broad definition enables the different authors to deal with the issue from their specific national and/or organisational perspective, it still allows room for quite narrow definitions of industrial relations, which in turn inform the various assessments of the future of European industrial relations.

The book is divided into four parts. The contributions in Part I combine the above-mentioned horizontal and vertical dimensions in presenting theoretical reflections on the actors' willingness and organisational capability to get involved in a system of industrial relations at European level. Part II contains political and strategic assessments by the key actors at national and European multi-industry and sectoral level, thereby providing an empirical background for the analytical contributions in Part I. The national accounts are made up of contributions from practitioners from two very different industrial relations systems: the UK and Germany. Part III narrows the focus considerably to the company level by addressing the specific role of European works councils (EWCs) in the development of transnational industrial relations. The fourth and final part of the book puts the discussion about European industrial relations into a global context by contrasting it with industrial relations developments in North America and Japan.

Although they rely on different analytical points of reference for their assessment, all the authors in Part I take a sceptical point of view with regard to the development of European industrial relations at sectoral and multi-industry level. At the same time, however, they see greater potential for the development of transnational industrial relations at the company level. Buda, for example, reviews the history of the Social Dialogue and the role and the interests of the relevant actors therein, and concludes that the European company level offers the best prospects for a move towards European labour relations. The situation at sectoral and multi-industry level is, according to Buda, characterised by the employers' associations' unwillingness to enter into a dialogue at the European level (or only in the face of legal initiatives from the Commission) and the trade unions' lack of power to force the employer side into arrangements at this level due to diverging interests of national trade union organisations and the absence of a legal framework providing for a European right to associate and to take industrial action. This assessment is corroborated by several practitioners' contributions in Part II. Representatives from both national trade unions and employers' associations emphasise that collective bargaining at the European level is very unlikely to take place in the near future. Blank, for example, from the German IG Metall, points out that due to the national diversity of industrial relations systems and corresponding interests of the relevant actors, collective bargaining, as the core element of each industrial relations system, 'for the foreseeable future will remain a national matter' (p. 165). As a corollary of this, it is difficult for the national trade unions to transfer bargaining powers to the European level organisations. This line of argument is also taken up and further elaborated in the analytical contribution by Armingeon, who emphasises that industrial relations institutions have a great ability to resist change, so that the continuation of national diversity makes it 'highly improbable that national systems of industrial relations will converge so much in the next one or two decades that a European-level system of employee interest representation will become possible' (p. 79).

The second point made by Buda that the trade unions lack power at the European level due to the absence of an appropriate legal framework is confirmed by the article by Gerstenberger-Sztana and Thierron representing the European Metalworkers' Federation; they explicitly state that the negotiation of European collective agreements is only a very long-term objective, because too many 'crucial framework conditions for the successful negotiation of collective agreements still have to be created' (p. 183). Representatives of the European trade union organisation at the multi-industry level, the ETUC, are slightly more optimistic. Although Buschak and Kallenbach stress that for the ETUC 'social dialogue is a discussion forum for the social partners' (p. 176) which serves to exchange views, they still point to the possibility of concluding framework agreements (such as the one on parental leave and the provision on part-time work). Writing from the viewpoint of UNICE, the European level peak organisation on the employer side, Hornung-Draus stresses that the Maastricht agreement on social policy 'does not create the legal basis for "classic" collective agreements in the sense of the autonomous regulation of employment by the social partners' (p. 202). The British employers' associations have been especially vocal in defending this position. Reid and Burgess in their articles point out that negotiations at European level would run counter to the process of decentralisation and flexibilisation taking place at national level. Since employers' associations in the UK are in most cases no longer involved in industry bargaining, they don't believe that a European level organisation should determine terms and conditions for UK companies. However, at the same time Hornung-Draus emphasises that the social dialogue procedure even in its pre-Maastricht form has led to the formulation of joint opinions on 'tricky subjects' (p. 198), which can be taken as a positive sign concerning the development of a European system of industrial relations, if one follows the broader concept of industrial relations as it was set out by the editors.

These arguments illustrate a methodological trend which is evident throughout the book. On the one hand the broad definition of the term 'industrial relations' leaves room for a controversial discussion of the development of a European industrial relations system, but on the other the different assessments are based on very different interpretations of the concept of industrial relations. In general, the broader the understanding of industrial relations, the more optimistic the authors are in their assessment. This can best be exemplified by comparing the two analytical contributions by Keller and Platzer. Taking the highly institution-alised German system of industrial relations as a point of reference, Keller equates the existence of industrial relations with free collective bargaining which is, in relative terms, a very narrow definition of the term. Against this background he draws a pessimistic conclusion, because even though negotiations at cross-industry level have taken place in the context of the Social Dialogue and have led to framework agreements, this procedure is still 'far from being identical to free collective bargaining . . . which includes the possibility of industrial action from either side' (p. 56). Platzer, by contrast, adopts a broader concept of indus-trial relations, which takes greater account of the political-institutional dynamics of the EU system. Against this background he sees signs of 'a discrete but none-theless dynamic process of transnationalisation . . . in the sphere of European-level organisations' (p. 104), which he had defined as one basic requirement for the development of transnational industrial relations (p. 99).

Regardless of the authors' assessment of the developments at the sectoral and the multi-industry level, all of them agree that European Works Councils (EWCs) at the European company level play a crucial role in the development of a Euro-pean industrial relations system, because at this level it is possible to circumvent the obstacles which continue to hamper progress at sectoral and multi-industry level. At that level, EWCs represent an institutionalised starting point for the exchange of information between management and employee representatives which can lead to negotiations. Even Keller reckons that 'it is quite conceivable that the managements of multinational undertakings could, in the not too distant future, decide that they should begin to act in the field of employment regulation . . . and enter into direct negotiations with their EWCs on problems specific to their organisations' (p. 59).

This importance was anticipated by the editors in devoting an entire section to examining the most significant strands of research on EWCs. Rehfeldt reviews the experience of the early French voluntary initiatives, Marginson investigates the actors' rationales for choosing between different options to negotiate an EWC agreement and Lecher examines problems which might crop up in the integration of EWCs into the national systems of interest representation in the four countries where most of the companies which have to introduce them are located: France, the UK, Italy and Germany.

Overall, this book represents a valuable and detailed source of information for practitioners and academics about previous and future developments of a Europeanisation of industrial relations. Compared to its first version which was published in 1994 as a 'Handbook for Employees' in German this English volume is extensively revised and the analytical component considerably strengthened. In combining contributions from practitioners and academics this volume can not only function as a reference book but also make an important contribution to the theoretical debate about the development of a European system of industrial relations.

Torsten Müller
Warwick Business School

Changing Industrial Relations in Europe. Second edition
Anthony Ferner and Richard Hyman (eds)
Blackwell, Oxford, 1998, 550 pp., £65.00 & £24.99

Industrial relations have not disappeared from the societies of Europe. Indeed their importance has seemingly increased in these last years of the century (and of the millennium). Those who predicted, if not the demise of industrial relations, at least their drastic scaling down, may be disappointed, but certainly not those who have always believed that they are an intrinsic feature of pluralist democracies. A dwindling of industrial relations may mean that democracy itself becomes eroded—which is a significant premise for a review of this book, aimed at industrial relations scholars and practitioners but also useful for political scientists and economists interested in the way in which Europe continues to regulate conflicts of interest, address labour relations issues, and pursue European unity, of which monetary union is only a beginning.

Well done, one may say, to the editors of this collected work, Anthony Ferner and Richard Hyman. The book is not a comparative analysis in the proper sense of the term (nor was this the authors' intention). It instead provides an analytically-grounded guide to the various national situations in Europe (the 15 countries of the European Union plus Norway and Switzerland) written by national experts, many of whom, moreover, are well-accustomed to conducting comparative research on more specific aspects of industrial relations. Traditional in its approach but sound and reliable, this book is perhaps the best of its type currently available.

In their short but brilliant introduction, the editors first explain the features of this second edition of the book (principally, the closer attention paid to current problems of change in national systems of industrial relations). They then raise a crucial question which has cut across all the most important studies on European industrial relations conducted in the past 20 years: is it convergence or is it divergence that provides the key to interpretation of European experiences? Although not unequivocal, the editors' answer is somewhat surprising: there is substantial evidence of convergence—amongst other things because the most pessimistic hypotheses of a decline in the regulatory capacity of industrial relations have not been borne out. A confirmation of these hypotheses would have triggered the most striking divergences, but this has not happened. The method of industrial relations has withstood, by and large, the pressure towards internationalisation, the search for flexibility, and the difficulties besetting the welfare states. The traditional institutional paths have undergone major changes (the German case is emblematic), but they have resisted. It is this resistance, in my view, that emits significant signals of convergence, the most conspicuous of which has been the recent revival of centrally concerted agreements. In certain respects, this second edition of the book revises the most drastic forecasts made in its first edition: a revision evidenced, on the admission of the contributors themselves, by the changes made to the subtitles to some national essays. Although European industrial relations are changing, the institutional paths have been able to steer, or to contain, such change.

The features of this change are depicted by the national reports, which not only describe the institutional framework and dynamics of each country's indus- trial relations system, but also outline its collective actors (trade unions and employers' associations). The pattern of change and continuity—as well as the revision of the more drastic hypotheses—emerges from the start with the essay on Britain, certainly the country which has seen the most radical challenge raised against the regulatory method of industrial relations. On reading this essay— written by a team of leading British industrial relations scholars (from P. Edwards to D. Winchester in alphabetical order), all of them belonging to the 'Warwick school'—one realises at once that the watershed of 1979 was not as crucial as has long been believed. There is no denying the changes that it brought, yet the continuities are substantial, not least because the advent of competing methods of regulation (principally human resource management) was slow and haphazard, and not explicitly intended to replace the trade unions; and also because pre- 1979 British industrial relations were much less coherent and institutionalised than is often thought: 'It was thus not a matter of a shift from a fully institutional- ised system to an equally clear deregulated one' (p. 1). Of course, regulation via the market increased (also as a result of privatisation), but it did not give rise to the full individualisation of employment relationships. It may be that the deser- tion of collective bargaining (driven by declining employment in sectors with strong trade-union traditions) will continue, but there may equally be marked counter-tendencies as well, ranging from those produced by the impact of EU directives, through those brought about by some (not all) of the Labour government's changes of attitude and by realisation of the drawbacks to all-out marketisation. In short, even the most divergent of cases signals its possible shift closer to the 'European model'.

Also the *Nordic Model*, once the apparent stronghold of industrial relations and of the collective actors, displays several novel features. But here too, the conditionings and the orientations of the institutional path still exert their influence. The essay on Sweden (by A. Kjellberg) returns to the origins of the 'historic compromise' in the 1930s, but then immediately examines the erosion of the historical model of industrial relations founded on self-regulation by the social partners brought about by state intervention and pressure towards decentralisation. Substantial changes have taken place internally to the Swedish unions and, as in the British case, they have stemmed from the declining power of the traditional private-sector federations. Yet the trend towards decentralised bargaining, set in motion in order to curb the solidarist wages policy of the Swedish unions, does not seem to have overturned the traditional model. Tripartite bargaining with the more active involvement of the state—also in response to the increased number of bargaining actors and of levels of industrial conflict—seems to be the most likely pattern for the future. Whatever the case may be the author stresses that, compared with the 1930s 'a new Swedish model will probably comprise a different mix of self-regulation and state regulation' (p. 97).

While the *Nordic Model* has been radically shaken in Sweden, its original features have been more substantially maintained in the other Scandinavian countries. This is especially evident in the Norwegian case as described and interpreted in the fine essay by J. E. Dolvik and T. A. Stikke. In Norway, the institutional resources of the co-operative model of industrial relations have displayed unexpected vitality in coping with the pressures of internationalisation. The authors' conclusions are very clear: 'In the Norwegian case, it seems that the capacity of the corporatist bargaining system to contain wage-price inflation has served as a functional alternative to more restrictive economic policies and labour market deregulation' (p. 37). Denmark may be taken as representing an intermediate case between Sweden and Norway in the maintenance of the *Nordic Model*. Decentralised bargaining has reached Denmark as well, but it has been closely controlled and institutionalised by the centre. There is nothing to rule out, though, that state intervention will not increase, as witness the events surrounding the general strike of spring 1998. Industrial relations in Finland, where bargaining centralisation has slackened, but not disappeared, adhere more closely to the traditional model.

Perhaps the greatest surprise is provided by the German case, the core of the 'European model', described with great critical skill in the essay by O. Jacobi, B. Keller and W. Müller-Jentsch. It is a surprise explicitly evidenced by the change made to the chapter's subtitle, from the 'Co-determining the future' of the first edition to the more neutral 'Facing new challenges' of the second. The future of the German model now seems more uncertain, although the forces of destabilisation should not be exaggerated: 'in the new century it is likely to be more decentralised, more fragmented, less legalised, less cohesive, and more internally differentiated' (p. 233). The stability of industrial relations, a vital factor in Germany's economic success, can no longer be taken for granted, the authors conclude. And yet, despite these uncertainties, the fundamental principle of the German system—the dual structure of interest representation—still seems able to furnish efficient criteria of regulation with which to hinder the deterioration of industrial relations.

Another change of subtitle is symptomatic of the Dutch case, which has achieved unusual celebrity in European political and trade-union affairs during the last two years, mainly through the efforts of its outstanding commentator, Jelle Visser, who is also the author of this essay. The first subtitle to the chapter was 'The end of an era and the end of a system': an end obviously declared too hastily, so that Visser has amended it in the second edition to 'The return of responsive corporatism', thereby acknowledging that his analysis requires adjustment, and that some partial errors of perspective had been committed. Corporatist collaboration has not collapsed with the dwindling of the unions' power and representativeness. Quite the reverse. The essential principles are still 'concertation with consensus' and 'jobs before income'. The traditional ideological-cultural pillars of Dutch society (Catholicism, Protestantism and socialism) have paradoxically continued to act as a source of social cohesion. The formula for the Dutch success is not clear, although Visser's analysis takes account of the most interesting details, only rarely verging on *ad hoc* explanation. In any event, Holland too displays substantial signals of the regulatory capacity of industrial relations.

France, as the great 'odd man out' in European industrial relations, is brilliantly treated by J. Goetschy in a chapter which emphasises the marked continuity of the French experience: 'industrial conflict and legal intervention, rather than collective bargaining, have been the traditional modes of "rule making" in the sphere of employment relations' (p. 357). Within this institutional framework, Goetschy tells us, collective bargaining may even increase in intensity (as has happened in the last two decades) but without augmenting the power of the unions or the capacity to regulate conflict (as shown by the wave of strikes in December 1995). The exceptional nature of the French case persists. Even Spain, when compared with France, shows signs of moving into the mainstream of the 'European model', with its endeavour to transfer some regulatory tasks from the state to the industrial relations actors (see the April 1997 bilateral agreement on the labour market).

Perhaps the best news regarding the regulatory capacity of industrial relations comes from Italy, as well described by I. Regalia and M. Regini. The weakness of the Italian system of industrial relations has always been its 'low level of institutionalisation, in the sense of lacking formalised and stable rules governing relations between the actors' (p. 494). This shortcoming was eliminated by the trilateral agreement of July 1993. This latter was a mix between an accord on incomes policy and a Scandinavian-style basic agreement which, after the 'hot autumn' of 1969, marked the second great turning-point in Italian industrial relations, providing an unexpected resource during Italy's political transition and its difficult progress towards membership of the European monetary union.

These and other lessons can be drawn from this fine and extremely useful book. At least three insights emerge from the essays as a whole. The first is the resistance of institutional paths of national industrial relations systems. The second is the appearance of weak, but nonetheless highly significant, signs of convergence among national systems: one begins to discern the 'wood' of the European model, and not only the 'trees' of the individual national cases. The third insight, which heartens not a few scholars and practitioners, is the renewed regulatory capacity of industrial relations; and the signs of convergence, indeed, are due principally to this capacity. I conclude with an observation and an invitation. The observation concerns a certain theoretical weakness in industrial relations studies which is confirmed by this nonetheless praiseworthy collection of essays. It is a weakness which precludes accurate forecasting (always difficult in the social sciences), which leads to over- or under-estimation of change, and which sometimes gives rise to excessively *ad hoc* explanations. It is a weakness in industrial relations studies that should be remedied. The invitation is to the editors of this book, Ferner and Hyman: why not, on the basis of this book, make the theoretical effort? Perhaps the time is ripe.

Gian Primo Cella
University of Milan

Comparative Industrial and Employment Relations
Joris Van Ruysseveldt, Rien Huiskamp and Jacques van Hoof (eds)
Sage/Open University of the Netherlands, 1995, 356 pp., £40.00 & £16.99

Industrial Relations in Europe
Joris van Ruysseveldt and Jelle Visser (eds)
Sage/Open University of the Netherlands, 1996, 424 pp., £45.00 & £17.99

Writers and teachers in the field of comparative industrial relations face the perennial dilemma of whether to present and analyse material thematically (exemplified by Ron Bean's text, or Christel Lane's UK–Franco–German comparison), or by means of a country-by-country series of profiles (such as the

Bamber and Lansbury book). The former approach is more dynamic, more able to tackle developing processes and can more easily deal with the increasing range of transnational phenomena and developments. Against this, the advantage of the national profile approach is to give the reader or student a holistic image of the unique configurations engendered by different historical and cultural experiences—the societal effect—in individual countries; however the inevitable tendency to talk in terms of 'systems', even if only as a conceptual shorthand, can result in a static and descriptive view of employment relations.

In recent years, the solution has been to bring out twin volumes (such as the Ferner and Hyman books), one dealing with thematic or 'processual' issues and the other with more institutionally based analyses of different countries' systems. The two texts reviewed here (together with a companion work on comparative HRM) are the Dutch Open University's response to this challenge, the Comparative book (hereafter referred to as CIER) being the 'thematic' work, and the European book (IRE) a detailed look at some of the major systems within the continent.

Both have a great deal to commend them, but both have slight weaknesses. CIER is hampered from the outset by the ambiguity of its title; in terms of its content it is, in reality, preoccupied with contemporary European developments even, as the editors admit, being focused primarily on the 'larger' European countries. Some of the contributors copy the Lane format of a three-way comparison between Britain, France and Germany, while others at times get a bit nervous about the need to be comparative and make occasional passing references to North America or Japan. It would have clarified things for author and reader alike if the remit had been *explicitly* European, and then had the range of European material of the companion volume.

That having been said, the overall approach of both books is very welcome, stressing as it does the importance of a sociological approach to understanding industrial relations based on a clear understanding of the nature of the employment relationship. This is spelled out clearly and admirably in van Ruysseveldt's introductory chapter to CIER. This distances itself both from old-style institutional IR, in which the only subject for study was collective bargaining, and also from the new academic 'HRM industry' in which management is the sole actor, and reminds us of a few home truths about power, authority and the employment bargain. Similarly I found Visser's overview introduction to IRE a mini tour de force which I would make compulsory reading for all students of industrial relations. The stress on the importance of history comes out very clearly in the same author's knowledgeable discourse on the nature of trade unions, which goes way beyond the usual bland chronology of trade union histories.

CIER is divided into thematic sections covering the labour market actors, change and transition in bargaining and participation, wages time and qualifications, and technological and organisational change. All the chapters contain useful insights and some good comparative analysis, although the quality of contribution ranges from the competent to the excellent. I particularly liked the very good chapter by Marsden on wages, de Lange's thoughtful discussion of time, and Dankbaar's comparative analysis of the European auto industry. I found the two chapters by Arndt Sorge somewhat disappointing as, in both cases, the author's usual analytical clarity was marred by dated material. This was particularly the case in discussions of Britain, where we find mention of AEU and TASS, the closed shop, and the somewhat startling statement that in the UK 'union membership has not undergone any drastic change'. There is also a translation glitch which results in us being informed that, after the French Revolution, the Jacobites (rather than the Jacobins) forbade co-operative association: reading this in Scotland may give latent supporters of the Stuart cause a thrill, but students of the 1793 Reign of Terror may find this hard to follow.

IRE, as the 'national system' volume has no subdivisions but, following Visser's introduction, chapters by contributing authors on Britain, France, Germany, Sweden, Belgium and the Netherlands, Italy, Spain, and Eastern Europe, concluding with a round-up chapter by Colin Crouch (which displays a continuing concern with neo-corporatism not reflected in much of the preceding analyses). This is of course the sort of book that is destined to be overtaken by events but, at present, the material is very up-to-date in terms of the developments of the 1990s, and brings contemporary conceptual and theoretical approaches to bear on analysing and understanding these trends; the statistical tables in the appendix will be a useful source material for lecturers. Also, as an added bonus for British readers, the multi-lingual skills of our Dutch friends provide us with data drawn from French, Dutch and German research, in translation for the first time.

Taking the two volumes as a whole it cannot always be said that the aims of the editors shine through every contribution. There is still an occasional tendency towards a rather institutional approach, but this is probably unavoidable in comparative work which has to make the reader aware of unfamiliar territory. There are some important omissions from the IRE national chapters; for example, apart from a brief discussion in the French chapter, there is not much reference to the importance of capital ownership patterns (crucial in the case of Sweden, for example, given the dominance of family-based groupings such as the Wallenbergs). Also, we get no real impression of the sheer scale and vehemence of the international employers' offensive of the 1980s and 1990s.

These are however minor quibbles. Both books are extremely clearly written and explained and this reader found a host of new ideas and perspectives on areas I thought I was familiar with. These titles will be featuring on my list of strongly recommended reading, and not just for comparative and international courses.

Chris Baldry
University of Stirling

Labour Markets in Europe: Issues of Harmonization and Regulation
John T. Addison and W. Stanley Siebert (eds)
The Dryden Press, London, 1997, 304 pp., £18.95

The various contributions to this volume examine different aspects of state intervention in labour market affairs to provide support or protection for workers within the framework of the European Community. Most are written with overt or implicit approval of a standard neoclassical model of labour markets but there are some contributors, notably Deakin and Marsden, who are more favourably inclined towards intervention to protect workers. Different sides of the debate over intervention and regulation are well represented with a mixture of conceptual and analytical papers and studies of aspects of regulation looked at from the perspective of a single country.

Addison and Siebert, after a concise introduction which summarises the papers well, provide in chapter 2 a detailed examination of the development of labour market regulation in the Community. They begin at the beginning and spell out the developments of intervention from the early 1970s underlining the importance of interventions prior to the Social Charter, bringing out well the long history of social policy and ascribing major responsibility for its regular appearance in EC discussions and policy-making to Directorate General V concluding that 'this activist directorate has outmanoeuvred and outlived its principal antagonists' but that 'DGV's justification for intervention has never been clearly set out, and that its analysis of impact effects has been cursory'. Whether or not one shares their views of the role of DGV (and even if they are correct Machiavelli came from a member state) most would appreciate that they give a very good description of the development of policy and interventionist measures, bringing together and summarising a great deal of information. They give essential information on the content of Council Decisions, Directives and Regulations as well as succinct details of non-binding measures. Appendices to their chapter reproduce the relevant text of EC Treaties, the Charter on Fundamental Social Rights of Workers and Agreement on Policy. Excellent teaching material.

In chapter 3 Addison, Barrett and Siebert seek to remedy one of the defects they ascribe to DGV by analysing the justifications for labour market regulation with an assessment of the possible impact of certain measures. While they present arguments both for and against intervention they do so from a strong neoclassical view of how labour markets do and should work. The main justification for intervention is therefore given to market failure mainly resulting from asymmetrical information. Market forces determine the overall total of the compensation package but the market allows trade-offs, for example between higher wages and greater risk of injury. It therefore seems to follow that if labour market regulation imposes certain costs, most obviously by a minimum wage or a requirement that all employment shall be fairly remunerated, there must either be a reduction in some other component of the total remuneration/labour cost package or employment will be reduced. Their overall view of the labour market differs a little from some classical writers in that the underlying assumptions here are that employers determine terms and conditions of employment, presumably adjusting wages when labour supply problems dictate, and workers choose which of the offers from competing employers they prefer. This version removes any need for a collective voice for workers or trade union, or for state intervention to protect them. Workers shop around until they find the package they like best. Whether the package could be improved by intervention and why this approach would lead to higher employment and preferred benefits for all is not really pursued.

The analysis is rigorous and thorough given the conceptual starting point, but less neoclassically minded economists might choose to use other justifications for labour market interventions as are later introduced by Marsden. Others might choose a more dynamic model which gives more importance to changes in labour productivity arising from changes in terms and conditions of employment either by following some form of more recent efficiency wage arguments or by assessing the effects that compulsory health and safety measures might have in improving labour productivity. Similarly, minimum wage or other wage regulation imposition can lead to increases in marginal productivity either as workers change their effort input or as employers reorganise production. However, if you want a neoclassical treatment of social policy or labour market regulation this is as good as it gets.

In chapter 6 David Marsden considers the social dimension as a basis for the single market. His starting premise is that in many Western European countries postwar prosperity has been built on co-operative industrial relations. He then considers the proposition that a Single European Market (SEM) and internationalisation may destabilise worker–employer relations and so undermine economic growth. An important element in his analysis is that productivity is not fixed or given but subject to constant change and that changes in productivity exert strong influence on the level and rate of change of wages. Co-operation depends on trust and mutual expectations of reciprocal treatment and needs wider institutional support. Marsden distinguishes between 'process' which is important because of the need to understand the motivations of each party, and 'substance' which can prevent process from degenerating into cheap talk. He concludes that social dialogue is one of the most important elements in the SEM's social dimensions and this is important for productivity and economic growth. While discussions in European Works Councils or between the social partners in Brussels are unlikely to have much effect on productivity their indirect effects are considered important in giving support to co-operative workplace relations. This argument is way across towards the other end of the spectrum of economists' approach to that of chapter 3 and the editors have done well in giving a wide

ranging and opposing choice of approach. Marsden has written a powerful case
in favour of the importance of institutions and worker/employer relations in
determining crucial economic relationships.

Simon Deakin in chapter 5 presents a clear well structured exposition of the
importance of law and legal processes in the emergence of social policy. The
central and crucial role of the European Court of Justice is well explained as is
the need for fundamental changes in Community law if social protection is to
be given greater priority. He is somewhat sceptical of the importance or impact
of Maastricht in tackling the real problems of social protection and stresses the
importance of developing a clearer and stronger rationale for social protection,
not only to underwrite the economic case for intervention but to avoid criticism
that it is little more than disguised protectionism in an economic sense. He provides a very good summary of the roles of various bodies within the Community
legislative process to match that of the development of intervention given in
chapter 2. The second part of his chapter presents the case for transnational
labour standards. Deakin sees the need for the extension of legal provisions. This
should be to provide a floor of labour rights which rather than seek the imposition
of uniformity or parity of labour costs encourage social convergence. These are
seen as having a crucial role to play in ensuring that market integration and
growth of international trade proceed in an orderly and progressive fashion. Labour standards are also seen as guarantors of economic participation and development. To him the question is not whether intervention is good or bad, should or
should not be permitted, but what are the most effective necessary means of
intervention required to ensure orderly and constructive progress towards the
agreed objectives contained in the creation of an economic community and single
market. He provides a first-rate analysis and statement of the case for legal intervention. Another excellent teaching document summarising legal developments
for non-lawyers.

Karl-Heinz Paqué in chapter 4 argues that the provisions for social protection
existing in a country are important determinants of that country's competitive
position. From this he argues that for the Community to seek to intervene in
these but not in the other determinants of a country's competitive position—such
things as its endowments of raw materials or stock of human capital—is in fact
to distort the existing relative competitive positions of countries. He further
argues that the social systems which develop in a country are market determined
in that those that survive pass a market test, and those that fail to pass the test
are removed or abolished. This can be used to explain the changes in social
rules and labour market interventions by the previous Conservative government.
Increasing international competition in product markets applied market tests and
previous legislation giving trade union protection was abolished as no longer
satisfying new market conditions. He therefore concludes that countries should
be left to develop their own systems rather than be forced into harmonisation.

He goes on to examine and reject harmonisation as a moral precondition for economic integration and then turns to its political justification. He believes that there is less justification on political than on economic grounds. He raises interesting questions about the nature of the determinants of competitiveness from both economic and moral/political positions.

Most of the remaining chapters concentrate on individual countries. In chapter 7 Soltwedel examines the position of German corporatism in the developing social policy of the EC. In particular he stresses the difficulties arising from conflicts between ECJ decisions and existing German labour law. These are interesting arguments, which, while of relatively little direct application to the UK, nonetheless contain the seeds of potential conflict with UK laws and the EC. Hitherto many UK supporters of greater intervention and social protection have welcomed ECJ decisions, but this may not always be so. Soltwedel raises some challenging questions.

Argandoña in chapter 8 discusses the position in Spain which has a very regulated labour market. The case is developed that such detailed intervention causes the very high unemployment Spain experiences. He also brings out well the way in which labour market practices adapt to changing conditions and legal opportunities citing the wide use of fixed-term contracts as a response to the difficulty and cost of terminating regular employees. He too raises the issue of corporatism but in a different context to Soltwedel and with somewhat different conclusions.

An interesting comparison with the North American Free Trade Agreement is given by Mirka and Ruhm in chapter 9. The differences between the two trade arrangements are brought out and the considerable differences in social policies and attitudes explained.

The final chapter by Siebert is a short but very useful overview of European labour markets giving information on various labour market features in European countries. It is a very handy dozen page briefing and ought to have been put at the front of the book. It certainly should be read first.

Overall this is a useful contribution for students of the development of a European labour market and the possible consequences of EC intervention. Some of the chapters rest more easily together than some of the others so the book is likely to appeal to two different groups of readers, those more concerned with the arguments in favour and against integration and social protection, and those more interested in country case studies. Each group will probably be a bit frustrated at the space given to the other. At the same time both groups should be pressing their librarians to make sure they get copies.

Derek Robinson
Oxford University Institute of Economics & Statistics

**Trade associations in Britain and Germany: responding to
Internationalisation in the EU**
R.J. Bennet (ed.)
An Anglo-German Foundation Report, 1997, 117pp., £12.00

Corporate restructuring in Britain and Germany
G. Owen and A. Richter (eds)
An Anglo-German Foundation Report, 1997, 60pp., £12.00

The first report is an edited collection of some 20 papers, most of which were
presented at a seminar in Düsseldorf on 2–3 December 1996. Three chapters and
the introduction were added later to provide an overview of key trends and provide a more complete picture. The papers assess the role of the trade association
(TA) in Britain and Germany and focus on four themes. First, the relationship
between TAs and their members; second, the changes in the two national systems
and how these relate to globalisation of trade and its objectives of governments;
third, how European Commission, European Parliament and other EU institutions
are influencing change; and finally, how individual TAs are responding to the
pressures on them.

Robert Bennett begins the report with an overview and introduction to the key
themes in the report: first, the issue of new challenges, second, internationalisation, third, new relations of TAs with members, fourth, national reorientation,
and finally European institutional demands. In his second paper he provides a
comparison of German and British TAs. He concludes that despite the historic
differences between German and British TAs, the range of services, membership
density, size of membership emphasis on subscriptions and focus of activities are
similar. He suggests that financial pressures may reduce the traditional strength of
German TAs resulting in the German system coming closer to the British system.
Christel Lane focuses on the inter-firm relationships in Britain and Germany, in
particular buyer–supplier relationships. Lane emphasises the importance of social
contexts and institutions in determining these relationships. She suggests that
German TAs, because of a number of nationally specific features, are more likely
to promote close and co-operative supplier relations than their British counterparts. Marcus Bierich provides a short overview of the activities and challenges
faced by the German automobile employers association (*Veband der Automobil-
industrie—VDA*) and the possibility of future mergers.

Sian Bowen focuses on the importance of representation in the EU and, in
particular, 'information advantage'. Bowen suggests that there is an increasingly
competitive market for access to policy makers in the EU. In some sectors large
transnational organisations may challenge or outstrip TAs in their ability to lobby
EU institutions effectively and thus TAs will not provide the only route to gain

influence. However, in other sectors where company size and government regulation are different, TAs are likely to remain influential. Klaus Bräunig discusses the challenges and activities facing the Federal Association for German Industry (*Bundesverband der Deutschen Industrie—BDI*) while Hajo Weber provides an analysis of German TAs focusing on their structure and future prospects. Mark Boléat follows this with an examination of the trends and challenges facing British TAs and this is complemented by Marcus Berry's overview of British government objectives and details of the Department of Trade and Industry's best practice guide for Trade Associations. John MacGregor provides a personal view of the effectiveness of British TAs in the EU when dealing with international trade, and points up a number of areas in which he feels there is room for improvement. Albrecht Mulfinger examines the role of TAs in the lobbying process in the EU from the perspective of the European Commission. Similarly David White also looks at the role of TAs from the perspective of the European Commission but focusing largely on the practical aspects of this relationship. Richard Eberlie provides the viewpoint of UNICE the European Employers Federation. He argues that TAs need to have a more proactive communications policy. This is followed by an examination of the role of European level trade associations by Patrick Knox-Peebles, considering the work of ORGALIME which represents the electrical mechanical, electronic and metalworking industries. Andrew Moore provides an overview of the supporting activities available to British TAs from the British Business Bureau whilst Peter Agar, writing from the perspective of the Confederation of British Industry, sets out how he believes British TAs need to act in order to gain influence over EU policy-makers. Gordon Gaddes then puts forward the views of the Federation of British Electrotechnical and Allied Manufacturers' Associations (BEAMA) and this is followed by an overview of the activities of one of its German TA counterparts, the *Verein Deutscher Maschinen- und Anlagebau* (VDMA), by Burkhart von Rauch. The last two papers offer an overview of British and German TAs but this time in the service sector. Jörg von Fürstenwerth provides an analysis of the German Association of Insurers (*Gesamtverband der Deutschen Versicherungswirtschaft—GDV*) and Martin Hall analyses the (British) Finance and Leasing Association. Both emphasise the need for further co-operation especially in lobbying Europe.

Overall the contributions vary considerably in terms of their length and content. Some papers appear to represent position statements or information for readers, while others are more objective pieces of analysis based on research projects. This is also reflected in the positions which the writers hold: some are active TA members, some government or EU representatives and others academics. The result is a mixture of academic analysis and up-to-date reporting of contemporary and practical concerns. As such this report should be a useful reference point for both academics and practitioners who are interested in the role, perceptions and activities of German and British TAs in Europe.

The second report is based on a one-day conference held at the Centre for Economic Performance at the London School of Economics in May 1997, and consists of four papers and a short introduction written by Sir Geoffrey Owen, the director of the business policy programme at the LSE. The report examines the impact of increasing international competition and more demanding capital markets on the corporate structures of British and German firms. Ansgar Richter, also of the Centre for Economic Performance, begins the report with his analysis of the trends in corporate restructuring based on his survey of 120 large German and British companies. His survey covers the ten-year period from 1986 to 1996 and focuses largely on the trends in diversification and specialisation. He suggests that, while many companies have restructured, this process has gone much further in Britain than in Germany. In Britain he states, 'a fundamental rethinking of the traditional model of the multi-business company seems to be underway'. In Germany on the other hand the trend is less clear. Some companies are refocusing but others are moving in the opposite direction with a number of companies arguing that well managed conglomerates can create synergies which outweigh the disadvantages of multi-business 'blindness'.

In a complementary study Stephen Davies and David Petts, of the University of East Anglia, examine the issues of refocusing and Europeanisation in leading German and British companies. Their sample of companies comes from a data-base called the 'EU market share matrix' which includes some 140 of the largest German and British manufacturing companies operating in a number of industries across the EU. Their study is a quantitative statistical and econometric analysis which focuses on: growth and exit; changes in diversification and multinational-ity; relationship of diversification and multi-nationality to firm size; and the extent to which firms are refocusing their activities. Their conclusions broadly support the findings of Richter's study that there is more evidence of British firms returning to the core while German firms appear to be increasing their diversifi-cation. They also suggest that for British firms increased multinationality has been a substitute for diversification, whereas no such effect was found for Ger-man firms. The authors stress the fact that the findings are restricted to manufac-turing operations within the EU and may not be representative of non-manufac-turing operations and activity outside the EU

Günter Müeller-Stewens and Michael Schaefer of the University of St. Gallen in Switzerland examine the German market for corporate control. Although the authors admit that Germany does not as yet have the same kind of Merger and Acquisition culture compared to the USA or Britain, they suggest that significant developments have taken place in Germany's market for corporate control in the last two decades. They suggest that recent moves to deregulate the German fin-ancial markets, together with the activities of German investment banks, are beginning to push the German system in an Anglo-American direction. They point to three factors that are likely to shape future activities. First, the German

Mittelstand (medium-sized companies) are increasingly facing problems of ownership succession and that this is likely to lead to an increase in buy-outs, new investors, or sell-offs. Second, the increasing importance of services offered around the main product are likely to lead to more acquisitions of smaller service firms. Finally, increasing industry deregulation is likely to create more merger and acquisition activity. The final paper, by Richard Young of Goldman Sachs International, considers the issue of corporate restructuring in Europe from an investors point of view. He suggests that there has been a lack of progress in restructuring in Germany. However, he argues that the scope for German firms to raise their return on equity through restructuring is considerable and that the pressure on them to do so is likely to increase. He sees the integration of the emerging markets such as Eastern Europe into the global economy and the increasing importance of technological innovation in production and distribution as key trends driving restructuring pressures.

The report is rather short and would perhaps have been strengthened by the addition of some studies based on qualitative analysis. For example some examination of corporate executives' motives and decision-making processes would have complemented the existing studies. Nevertheless, the report provides some interesting and useful insights into the corporate activities of British and German firms and trends in German markets.

Tony Royle
The Nottingham Trent University

Fianna Fáil and Irish Labour: 1926 to the Present
Kieran Allen
Pluto Press, London, 1997, 232 pp., £13.99

Since first taking office in 1932, Fianna Fáil have been in government for 46 of the subsequent 62 years, a political dominance which has ensured that the party has left an indelible imprint on both Irish political culture and the state itself. In charting the evolution of Fianna Fáil, Allen refutes the party's ideological claim to be the party of national and social unity, arguing rather that their historic twin objectives have been the establishment of an indigenous capitalist elite and securing the legitimacy and sovereignty of the 26-county Irish Republic.

The author stipulates that his primary concern is to present a Marxist analysis of the '*special*' relationship that this centre-right (centre) party has fostered with the trade union movement in seeking to achieve primary political goals. It is the author's contention that this *special* relationship has effectively stymied the development of an independent labour movement and facilitated Fianna Fáil's establishment of political hegemony over the working classes. This hegemony is exemplified both by the capacity of this party consistently to capture 40 per cent of the working class vote and by the perennial electoral debility of left class-based parties.

In the first four chapters which cover the period 1926–1958, Allen argues that this party-labour relationship was premised on the articulation of a populist agenda and the development of informal and highly personalised linkages with sections of the labour movement's leadership. Thus during the 1930s the party made informal overtures to major unions such as the ITGWU and actively sought to exacerbate nationalist-inspired tensions between Irish-and British-based unions as a means of forging closer ties with the former. The 1941 Trade Union Act went even further for not only was it prejudiced against British Unions but moreover it aimed, though ultimately failed, to facilitate greater state regulation of industrial action by encouraging the rationalisation of what was a highly fragmented trade union movement.

Fianna Fáil's historic rejection of protectionism in 1958 and its pursuit of export-led industrial development based on foreign investment however necessitated a reconfiguration of relationship with organised labour on a more formal and institutional basis, which is explored in the subsequent chapters. The incumbent Taoiseach Lemass, in an attempt both to incorporate the interests of labour into the party agenda and to galvanise support amongst key economic actors for this industrial strategy, embraced social partnership and the 1960s witnessed the emergence of a plethora of bipartite and tripartite consultative bodies and committees. The emergence of peak-level concertation however occurred in tandem with an escalation in industrial conflict and strife culminating in the Maintenance Men's Strike of 1969 which represented a militant challenge not only to employers but also to the authority of ICTU. A growing concern over industrial relations developments thus facilitated, under considerable pressure from the Fianna Fáil government, the bipartite negotiation of the 1970 National Wage Agreement which established centralised pay determination.

There were to be five further agreements and indeed by the mid-1970s the government, now composed of Fine Gael and Labour, were indirectly involved in the negotiations offering budgetary concessions for wage restraint. These neo-corporatist arrangements were taken a stage further by Fianna Fáil in 1979 and 1980 with the negotiation of two National Understandings in which collective bargaining over pay and conditions was informally integrated within the broader economic and social policy domain.

The failure to negotiate a third national understanding heralded a return to decentralised collective bargaining and for the trade union movement this period was one of increased political, economic and social marginalisation. Fianna Fáil's electoral victory in 1987 was to ensure a 'return to normal' as Charles Haughey skilfully negotiated the re-establishment of Social Partnership in the guise of the Programme for National Recovery (PNR). This however was not to provide the basis for a reconstitution of the historic relationship as the institutionalisation of the social partnership within the party political landscape has ensured that it is no longer considered the sole property of Fianna Fáil.

The author's extensive use of archival material presents a thorough insight into Fianna Fáil's approach to political mobilisation and in particular how it has sought to incorporate organised labour through the promulgation of the politics of national interest. Allen's thesis reaffirms the importance of Fianna Fáil's determination to prevent the politicisation of social conflict and the failure of the Labour party to act as a persuader for class alignment, in helping explain the relative absence of class-based politics in Ireland.

Where this book is weak however is that it offers no real insight into the political, cultural and economic factors which have shaped and conditioned organised labour's perspective on social partnership arrangements. Allen's instant and scant dismissal of social partnership as a strategy for the subjugation of working class militancy which only serves the needs of capitalism and a cadre of bureaucratic trade union officials ensures that he does consider the potential political and material gains offered to trade unions by institutionalised political exchange. Certainly the author appears unwilling even to discuss the persuasive argument that, by engaging in such arrangements, Irish trade unions have displayed a collective commitment, however fragile, to the pursuit of social democratic policies in the interests of workers (Roche, 1997).

This limited perspective is compounded by the largely unexplained belief in the revolutionary potential of virtually all industrial conflict despite the fact that such action was at times motivated by purely sectionalist interests and, as in the case of the Maintenance Men's strike, could actually engender division within the labour movement.

The highly polemic nature of this book is particularly evident in the cursory treatment of the decade of social partnership since 1987. Aside from discounting the 1987 agreement as a mechanism for securing trade union support for radical fiscal correction, the subsequent three year national agreements which have contributed to the emergence of a relatively stable system of peak-level tripartite political exchange barely warrant a mention. This is a major flaw as the Irish social partnership has exerted a considerable influence over economic, political and industrial relations developments in the past decade. Moreover a central theme of the book is that social partnership is a barrier to the emergence of a working class political alternative yet Allen stridently asserts in the final pages that the potential now exists for Marxists to combine working class industrial militancy with a socialist political agenda. These points aside however Allen has made a laudable if at times overly polemic contribution to the historical debates concerning Fianna Fáil's relationship with the trade union movement.

Damian Thomas
University College Dublin

European Employment and Industrial Relations Glossaries
Tiziano Treu and Michael Terry (General Editors)
Sweet & Maxwell and Office for Official Publications of the European
Communities, Vols 1–10, 1991–1996, 214–396pp., £21.95 per volume

This major publishing initiative of the European Foundation is now two-thirds
along the way towards full coverage of the present EU membership. The first
three glossaries appeared in 1991 (UK, Italy and Spain); the next five between
1992 and 1994 (Belgium, France, Germany, Greece and Ireland); the most recent
two in 1996 (Portugal and the Netherlands); and with the remaining five
(Denmark, Luxembourg, Sweden, Austria and Finland) now in the editing pipe-
line. In due course it is also likely to include the first wave of new member
states from central Europe. Each country has, or will have, its own national
volume, published in its own language, and incorporating extra entries and
material peculiar to its own laws and national traditions. Additionally, each is,
or will be, part of an English language series with the text of the glossary entries
in English but with headings in the national language and indexed in both languages. This English language set of volumes is reviewed here.

The glossary entries are the greater part of each volume. Each is written to
appeal to a non-specialist national readership as well as those seeking, for whatever reason, greater understanding of the employment and industrial relations
systems of countries other than their own. For example, a British reader wishing
to know more about the French minimum wage system would find six sub-
headings in the English index under 'Minimum wage (Guaranteed)'. The main
entry, of about 150 words, concisely describes the origins, nature, functions and
method of implementation of the SMIC ('salaire minimum interprofessionel de
croissance') (pp. 196–7).

As well as the glossary entries (the German volume has the most at 813) each
volume includes an introduction to the history and special features of the country's
system, again written for non-specialist readers in a jargon-free, accessible style.
Also there is a collection of tables of relevant data and a bibliography. Each
volume is also (and importantly) available in electronic form.

Not surprisingly, this ambitious project covering 15 countries with employment
and industrial relations systems characterised more by diversity than similarity is
the work of many hands and brains. The general editors sub-contracted the editing
of the volumes to national specialists although they did find time to edit their own
national glossaries—for the UK (with Linda Dickens) and Italy—themselves. The
national volume editors also brought in editorial committees and special contributors
to lighten and strengthen their labours. But the outcome is still impressive. So far,
the length of the English language edition runs to 2753 pages and will easily exceed
4000 when all the present EU membership is included. This is not counting the
15 national language volumes published in the member states, referred to earlier.

Is it all worth it? Furthermore, will such a giant vessel founder under its own weight, and cost? On cost, the 15-volume set at today's prices will require an investment of almost £330! The answer to the second question—assuming a wholly commercial venture—is likely to be already known in the publishers' offices. However, any commercial risk is essentially underwritten by the financial support of the EU through the European Foundation. This is as it should be: important additions to the stock of useful knowledge are entitled to public subsidy. Such matters are not, however, the main concern of reviewers. The main concern is answering the first question, and the answer must be 'yes'—although with some qualifications.

On the scale of the project it is, in fact, more limited (and by design) than it seems. Although the diversity and complexity of the systems of 15 countries merits 'encyclopaedic' treatment the general editors wisely opted for a 'glossary' treatment which they define as '. . . an annotated guide to key issues and concepts' (p. xviii). Hence the series is less than an encyclopaedia but more than a dictionary for the use of translators and interpreters, even though it is likely to be close at hand for such professionals. A dictionary would not, however, meet the wider purpose of the European Foundation as an '. . . important aid to international understanding in the complex field of employment and industrial relations' (p. xiii). Additionally, an encyclopaedia would be even more vulnerable than the glossaries to becoming dated (and therefore inaccurate) over a long period of gestation.

A further, self-imposed limitation is the exclusion of detailed treatments of national employment and industrial relations legislation leaving such refinements to be followed up by the reader through the bibliographies. Here the rationale is again understandable although experience suggests that users of such works of reference would welcome such detail in the volume at hand. In most cases that should be possible to incorporate, and concisely, within the pages of an appendix. Such an addition could be considered in future, revised editions.

Each volume in the series can, of course, be used independently of the others, following readers' specific country interests. The series can also be used comparatively given the general editors' design of a core of common terms and institutional arrangements and practices ('integration') across all the volumes, such as the 'social dialogue' instruments of collective bargaining and collective agreements. The comparative value of the series is also evident in its inclusion of common basic trade union and employment rights and working conditions and practices, and the role of virtually universal bodies such as works councils. But the volumes also reflect, in many entries, the still tenacious hold and substantial influence of national systems ('differentiation') despite the pressures towards convergence of the single market and EU legislation.

This is undoubtedly a worthwhile series bringing together authoritative, national language, comparative glossaries within the lingua franca of English. It has much to offer both academic and practitioner users, as the general editors rightly claim. Its main weakness lies in its publication, in parts, over a long period of time which will, in due course, amount to ten years. Fortunately, this weakness can be greatly limited by the availability of the glossaries in electronic form. Indeed, this could potentially either replace the printed format or make piecemeal, or new, completely revised editions, a relatively easy proposition. There is also a strong case for an additional glossary on the EU itself, including the increasingly important developments in EU law. The EU now has its own identity beyond those of its member states, including in employment and industrial relations affairs. An additional glossary would usefully reflect this.

Brian Towers
The Nottingham Trent University

Negotiating the new Germany: Can Social Partnership survive?
Lowell Turner (ed.)
ILR Press/ Cornell University Press, 1997, $ 35.50/14.50

The book is a collection of essays from British, American and German authors, edited by Lowell Turner. It is based on original contributions at a conference held at Cornell University in 1994. After an introduction from the editor, the book consists of two parts. The first part deals with the consequences of the reunification and the transfer to the east of West German law and the institutions of industrial relations and social partnership. The role of training and training institutions, labour market policy and employment as well as the special situation of the unions are in the centre of five essays from Peter Auer, Richard Locke and Wade Jacoby, Mathias Knuth, Michael Fichtner and Lowell Turner.

The second part of the book is devoted to more general aspects of crises in and reform of the German system of political economy. Christopher Allen, Stephen Silvia, Gary Herrigel, Kirsten Wever and Douglas Webber discuss a number of problems, such as the limits of German manufacturing flexibility, new trends in Labour-Management-relations, political responses to growing labour market segmentation and the implications of deregulation. The underlying question is how the German system based on a developed social regulation (the importance of law, corporatist structures, collective bargaining, co-determination at the enterprise level etc.) can adapt to the changes in the world economy, and, at the same time, meet the challenges of European integration as well as German reunification. Last but not least, Lowell Turner offers a concluding comment about the 'uncertain outcomes of conflict and negotiations' in industrial relations of the new unified Germany.

Despite a few rather pessimistic contributions about the survival of the German model of social partnership, the authors 'agree that reform and adaptation are possible, starting from the existing institutions, given appropriate actor strategies aimed at both institutional reform and innovative policy' (p. 255). They sharply disagree with conservative and liberal analysts who 'see the social market economy as an expensive and outdated relic of a welfare-state past' (p. 256). The authors see the system under great pressure but 'relatively intact'. At the same time, they underline the openness of the developments in progress. Much depends on the flexibility of the contemporary German institutions and their capability for reform and adaptive change. Here, the positions of the authors are very different. Fichtner, for example, emphasises the East–West tensions within the labour unions which result from the rigid transfer of Western institutions that fails to take into account the cultural background of the actors and the specific situation in the East. Herrigel points out that the rigidities of Western work organisation cause many problems in relation to the challenges of lean production in German industry. Silvia shows that the development in German labour markets seems to be moving in the direction of polarisation, as in the United States, with erosive consequences for the partnership model. Other authors (e.g. Auer, Turner, Webber) show with examples from the 1990s that negotiated problem-solving is still a suitable approach to the problems caused by reunification, despite all the dilemmas and failures stemming from the institutional transfer to the East. In general, these authors evaluate the transfer of the Western institutions to East Germany in a positive way.

With respect to system changes, Wever highlights the fact that signs of more flexible bargaining can be found, especially in the new *Länder*. She underlines that this could be seen as a 'renegotiating' of the German model. So far, collective bargaining seems to be strengthening the enterprise level (*Verbetrieblichung* in the German debate) and this includes negotiations at the 'point of production' (Herrigel, Wever).

One conclusion drawn by the editor could be seen as an adequate description of the development in contemporary German industrial relations: 'The dual system (. . .) is evolving into a flexible "triple system", . . . that includes greatly expanded employee participation in daily ongoing work place decision making' (p. 257).

The book is very interesting, even for insiders. This is especially due to the competent analyses from different perspectives including the views from 'outside-in'. The inner German debate is mostly focused on very few topics and often dominated by personal resentments. The only perspective that I have missed is a 'true' East German one, and more information about the developments at the enterprise and shop floor level would be enlightening. Moreover, since the analysis is located in the changes of the early nineties, further research and discussion in this field are obviously needed to consider the post-privatisation developments in East Germany.

Rainhart Lang
Technological University of Chemnitz

Index